UNMANAGEABLE: A MEMOIR

<<<<<<<>>>>>>

UNMANAGEABLE: A MEMOIR
Copyright © 2019 by Lela Fox. All Rights Reserved.

Cover designed by Queen Graphics, Fiverr,
Photography by Deposit Photos
Contributing Editors: Teri Eicher and Noah Lloyd

Unmanageable: A Memoir is a 95-percent-true story of four trying years of the author's life. Some incidents are used factiously or may be products of the author's imagination. Names of people and places have been changed. Any resemblance to actual events, locales, businesses, organizations, or persons, living or dead, is entirely coincidental.

Lela Fox
Visit the author's website at www.LelaFox.com

Printed in the United States of America
First printing June 2019
A-FEX Publishing
ISBN 9781072838036

<<<<<<<>>>>>>>

UNMANAGEABLE

Drunken Wisdom

<<<<<<<>>>>>>>

Book Four of the Series
The Life & Times of a Curious Drunk

LELA FOX

DEDICATION

I dedicate this book to my oldest sister Jennifer.

She has supported my sobriety, especially in refusing to be supportive through the worst years of my drinking.

As loyal as a dog, unwavering, steadfast in her moral code, and relentless in facing her own physical challenges. I'd admire Jennifer even if I wasn't related.

Big sister, I love you. You once said something I replay in my head on bad days. So I'll repeat it here: I'm proud of *you*, too.

TABLE OF CONTENTS

<<<<<<<<>>>>>>>

DRUNKEN WISDOM

Good decisions come from experience.
Experience comes from bad decisions.

−WILL ROGERS

LELA VS. LELA
PROLOGUE

My life was crumbling faster than I could run from the rubble. It was 1997 in Rockville, Tennessee: a big-enough, progressive-enough Southern city where I'd lived for 21 of my 38 years. I used to be quite famous in Rockville. "Queen Copywriter," adorned with a boatload of advertising awards, and the accompanying fame and fortune.

To top it off, I married the handsome "King Art Director" and we led an enviable life. Miller McKeown and I shared two six-figure incomes, the respect of the advertising community, nationwide recognition for our creative work, and applause for our philanthropic endeavors.

But now I was drunk, living alone in our basement. One level of the house and a hundred-thousand miles separated Miller McKeown and me. Deeming divorce a bad thing for my thirteen-year-old son Bo, we pretended to be happily married every-other-week when custody was mine.

Tension was thick. Surely Bo felt it, too, but it seemed he was too busy playing baseball and being a pleasant and kickass kid to notice the tension. Or that's what I choose to believe.

While I was never Mother of the Year, stepfather Miller was a hero to Bo... teaching him sports, the value of teamwork, and the best place to pee in our somewhat-private backyard. I still don't understand why men do that.

But Miller's loyalties lay with Bo, not with me. Though he adored my son and raised him as his own, it was sobering to learn the sonofabitch thought I was the baggage, not the prize. When I realized this, the marriage fell apart, and I collapsed like the Wicked Witch under water. The pain of it was a dagger in my heart.

My advertising career was gone – thrown away. I quit because being creative on demand interfered with my drinking. Besides, I didn't like how clients treated me; as if I was just a regular vendor! They didn't seem to understand I was the one responsible for their success. So I quit. I showed *them*, by God. I sure did.

For "work," I founded a hand-crafted jewelry company and spent a fortune promoting it. The problem: Moonlight Jewelry was based on a bald-headed lie. See, I didn't design and cast the dangly charms as I promoted; I bought them from an obscure vendor in South Africa, Quest Castings. And my growing debt to Quest loomed.

As I drank vodka-laced coffee, my "employee" ran the doomed business. Her name was Lola (right – Lela and Lola) and she was my greatest enabler.

Lola became my best friend, most others dropping away as my disease progressed. Maybe she wasn't the most brilliant gem in the ring... or maybe she ignored it, but the fact was glaring: too little money was coming in. Too little to pay for inventory, payroll, travel expenses, or a damn pack of chewing gum.

I thought nobody knew the ugly half of my life or that I was already dying inside. But somebody else *did* know, and things became worse. Bo's dad, my ex-asshole Andy, had started questioning me about being drunk at Little League games. I told Andy to fuck off; he didn't seem to appreciate that.

In my basement, with its private entrance, I entertained dates in my bedroom even as Miller slept above. Sex was healing to me, I thought, and I reveled in it. But as I came to find out later, I was the only one who thought my attitude about sex was normal. I didn't know my "need" for it was an attempt to even the score with my rapists. Right, a plural of the word. Who would think leftover feelings from a rape at age sixteen would flavor my choices in my late thirties?

But the second rape, I still believed, was my fault. My fault because I was born to be a slut, it seemed. But at least I had something to offer. Lela Fox didn't show up at parties empty-handed.

I had the freedom to do anything I wanted and an unlimited supply of drinks and drugs, an unlimited supply of "fill in the blank."

But all the self-medicating in the world couldn't stave off my unhappiness.

The core of my misery sprang from my old friend and constant companion, Shame. Yes, with a capital S. I'd wallowed in it, feeling "less than" for 25 years, obsessively replaying the night it began.

It was the first time I got drunk. Age 13. Drunk in a gravel alley where two albino sisters left me with the full six-pack. On the fourth beer, I felt the hideous ogre of instant addiction suck my soul into its gut.

I heard the slurp.

And I knew from that point forward what my vocation would be: I would drink every possible drop of alcohol for the rest of my life. And I *did* achieve my goal, with a minimal break for pregnancy and breastfeeding. At the time, when I was in my early twenties, I was able to quit for a good-enough reason.

But no more.

Loneliness wasn't the problem; it was grief. Grief for the death of the former me. The former badass Chick in Charge. The former Serene Irene. The former confident success, the woman my parents applauded. I missed being able to make my Daddy smile. And I missed the former me who didn't compare herself to others and feel the Shame of living a lie.

True love had eluded me. People mistreated me. Both husbands had turned into monsters after a few years of marriage. I knew something was wrong with me, knew it was probably my fault, but I couldn't put a finger on what I'd done.

I tried but there was no way to run from my mind or the inner voice who hated me. *Oh, shut up, Lela. You're too smart to listen to your own bullshit and lame excuses. You know exactly what you did. And you're still doing it.*

Sober, I'd come to despise myself. I could hear people whispering behind my back. And I could hear my daddy's voice over my shoulder, urging me to "straighten up and fly right." Though I said nothing, I knew I was a fuck-up, a disappointment to my parents and two sisters. In fact, my friendship with my oldest sister Jennifer, who also lived in Rockville... our chummy relationship ended a few years ago. She said something like, "I can't stand to see you destroy yourself."

I didn't exactly know what she meant at the time, but it hurt my heart. So I told her to go to hell.

Even my hero-sister Karen, the one who loved me so much you could see the vibrations of her feelings in the air, now looked at me with eyes full of pity.

She cried when she thought of me, she said. And that was before this new fiasco.

After nine months of living in the basement apartment, Miller McKeown, the Upstairs Asshole, kicked me out. His words reverberated in my head: "You're an idiot, a drunk, and a cheat! I want a divorce." Screaming the phrase into the mirror and chanting it repeatedly as I packed to move, I found a rhythm to the words and hummed the tune absent-mindedly.

There was a tried-and-true solution to the repeating stabs of emotional pain: an extra-large vodka-tonic in my favorite bright-pink plastic cup. Though my mixology started earlier in the day now, I knew a real alcoholic drank early in the morning, too, so I thought I was safe. I thought waiting for a splash of vodka in my *second* cup of coffee meant I was safe.

But the same voice that told me I was fine also told me otherwise, detailing the dirtiness of my life and hopelessness of my future. I knew was killing myself, digging a hole that had no bottom.

HOW I GOT HERE
LIFETIME NUMBER 5

The way I see it, I've had nine Lifetimes in my 59 years, each Lifetime markedly different from the one before it.

Lifetime Number One, my happy childhood, ended in the alley with my first beer... when instant addiction stole my soul. Prior to that trauma, I enjoyed a loving and joyful childhood... not a subject for a book unless you want to read about Rebecca of Sunnybrook Farm.

Lifetime Number Two became the book *Powerless,* covering my teen years and the beginnings of dysfunction that thrived between my own two ears.

Lifetime Number Three became *Denial,* the slow-motion train wreck of my college years and first marriage. Husband Andy couldn't hang with my Bi-Polar spikes and moved on before I came up for air. What had been binge drinking became a daily habit, igniting the slow boil of alcoholism.

The next book, *Chaos,* is about Lifetime Number Four. That's when I chose a second husband to save me from myself. While loving my son, he tired of my nagging and sloppy drunkenness. When he asked for a divorce, my best-of-both-worlds Lifetime Number Four exploded.

Each new Lifetime created a shift of priorities and goals, a major change in circumstances. And in each Lifetime, there was no shortage of drama. Or trauma.

Unmanageable deals with Lifetime Number Five, which mercifully lasted a mere two years. Most people, non-alcoholics usually, wonder why I would rehash all the bullshit of Lifetime Number Five. If you drank as I did, you probably know I have no choice. To be peacefully sober as I am now, twenty years almost, I've had to embrace my past as part of my present. The good, the bad, the funny, and the sad... all a part of what makes my current Lifetime Number Nine serene.

If my Higher Power, who I choose to call "Dude," accepts me as I am, then who am I to hide my past? Was I not a child of Dude in *all* Lifetimes? Had to be. Otherwise, I wouldn't have survived.

Each time my life took what I thought was an unfair turn, I would say, "This Lifetime is surely not the final one! This isn't the way it's supposed to end!"

I was right. It wasn't the end. It was the beginning, nine different times.

<<<<<<<<>>>>>>

THE GREEN HOUSE

CHAPTER 1

The day after I moved in, the toilet overflowed, spilling shitty water all over the bathroom. I called the landlord, and she sent a plumber to the house immediately.

After he fixed the toilet, I walked the plumber to his truck. He stopped in the driveway and looked up. "What in the world were they thinking?" he said, referring to the color of the house. It was a basic split-foyer but with green wood siding. Not just "green" but G-R-E-E-N, a color somewhere between lime and chartreuse. "Who would choose that color *on purpose?*" he asked, perplexed.

I could only shrug. "Maybe that's why the rent is so low."

"Well, the neighborhood is nice... your landlord is nice. Surely this is a mistake." He stepped to the left for another angle, now looking into the eaves. "But the paint job is fresh, brand new. Go figure."

Yep, the color turned heads, maybe a few stomachs, but the screaming-green house was a rare find. Ninety percent of the rental houses in West Rockville exceeded my budget, but this was one of the nicer ones. I was lucky.

Three bedrooms, a fenced backyard for Murphy the fat Sheltie, a two-car garage, new carpet, and neat as a pin. All for $500 per month. The landlords even mowed the yard as part of the deal.

<<<<<<<>>>>>>

"I love this room, Mom! So big! But please tell me we'll get rid of this bunk bed soon. Don't you think I've outgrown it by now?"

"Fourteen is not too old for a bunk bed, Bo. And good news, kiddo: the small sofa fits on the far side of your room, under the window. Your sleepover friends can crash there."

Continuing my tour guide narration, I stepped to the door of the next upstairs room. "This is what's *supposed* to be the Master bedroom but it will be my studio. Your G-Daddy will help me put it together with long countertops like the old one."

Bo blew a huff of a sigh, rolling his eyes. "Yeah, your dad is used to helping you move, right? One more time..." his voice trailed off.

"Bo, stop it! Don't be a smart-mouth to your mother."

"Just stating the truth, Mom."

I ignored his snarky teenage attitude and took a few more steps down the hall. "And this is my bedroom."

"The smallest room, Mom? Why?"

"There are more important things than my little place to sleep."

I saw Bo's face twist as he realized I had sacrificed my space so he could have more. "But... my room is *part-time* for me. Mom, *you* should have the biggest one."

"No, buddy. You're the biggest and the best around here!" Bo eyed me sideways, doubting my sincerity, I suppose. But when I could do something nice, I did it... maybe trying to make up for being a drunk and crappy mother. I didn't exactly display the Mother of the Year trophy on a foyer shelf.

Two days after I moved into the green house, my parents came to Rockville for a long weekend, spending two nights with my oldest sister Jennifer and her kids. In those days, I tiptoed around Jennifer, sipping wine instead of gulping. Underneath, I seethed, resenting her for forcing me to pretend.

Though my oldest sister and I used to be good buddies, partying together with our common friends, she'd confronted me four times over the last few years, accusing me of having "an alcohol problem." Fuck her. "I'm fine," I had said, but she just rolled her eyes.

On Saturday, Daddy and I went back to "Miller's house" in Skylark. My soon-to-be-ex greeted us with the warmth of an ice cube. Fuck him. Daddy and I worked in the basement, removing the same countertop he'd installed in the studio three years ago. Then I helped load everything in his truck, the *old* truck. "How did you talk Mom into riding in 'Old Joe,' Daddy?"

Scratching the shiny part of his mostly bald head, he chuckled. "She fussed the whole time, Lela... said she'd never-ever do it again." Daddy imitated Mom's high-pitched voice. "Eeew, Rick! The door panel is diiiiirty! Oh, Rick! My aching baaack!" I laughed at his impersonation of her. Back to himself, he shared his true feelings. "She's a love, but she sure can raise a ruckus."

"Did she throw a Benningham fit?" It was a family joke referring to Mom's side of the family, a parody of their calm and steady nerves, their notoriously even tempers. Daddy laughed by slapping his knee and honking through his ample nose. The melody of Daddy's horselaugh had been the same since I was a child. Heartfelt, it happened often.

The next morning, he came to attach the countertop around the perimeter of the huge upstairs bedroom at the screaming-green house.

Daddy also cut three pieces of plywood to cover the floor so three rolling chairs could move easily. He ended the day in one of his silly moods and we had a rolling-chair race across the floor. I would've won if he hadn't cheated... which made the loss even more hilarious.

As we always did, Daddy and I focused on having fun no matter the importance of the task at hand. My father was childlike and easy to laugh, never short of jokes and pranks. Simply put, I adored him. Always had.

As the last part of his mission, Daddy added shelves above two workstations. The corner area, the largest by far, was for Lola, my long-time assistant. I imagined her sitting there, Cherokee-Indian DNA coursing through her veins, throwing chunks of long, black hair over her shoulder... yes, she would work well in the space. "If she doesn't like it, Daddy, I'll fix it. My goal is to make Lola happy, no matter what. Without her, I'm lost."

Though I wouldn't admit it, Lola was the one who ran the business while I drank and made bad decisions. She worked part-time during the week but the schedule was flexible.

Lola knew what to do, no supervision required. She'd said things like, "The bracelet display needs attention. Can I work extra hours to do it?" I didn't ask what she wanted to do or how much it would cost, I simply agreed.

Or she'd say, "We need to restock the consignment booth at Skylark Crafts. I'll do inventory tomorrow." Again, I'd just nod and thank her for taking charge.

Without Lola, there would have been no Moonlight Jewelry.

And now with more room but less sense, I would add another assistant. The yet-to-be-hired second helper would work at the smaller workstation Daddy had defined with a counter and shelves above. "Lola, we just need hands... a factory worker, a mindless servant." She agreed. I ended with the stark reality. "But you tell her what to do because you keep tabs on the inventory, right?"

"Right. I'll take care of it, Lela. Just run an ad... maybe in the same newspaper where you advertised for me."

"I'll do it as soon as I'm settled."

"Uh... maybe do it before that."

"Why?"

"Because 'being settled' never really happens around here." Lola's sheepish smile didn't *seem* like an accusation, but it was. In my addled state of mind, I was oblivious to Lola's hints. Well, oblivious to most everything by that time. She never told me she knew I was incapable, never shamed me about it, just took control of more and more business tasks as my abilities ebbed.

When her boyfriend suggested the problem might be my excessive drinking, she insisted it wasn't. "It's her Bi-Polar medicine," she insisted. And she was more than half right.

When my former psychiatrist questioned my lies about "moderate" alcohol consumption, I fired him and started seeing another doctor. The new doc was an overweight gray-haired Dr. Cook who must have been in cahoots with every drug rep in the Southeast.

He prescribed seven different anti-depressants and mood stabilizers, plus Adderall for focus, and a massive dose of something to help me sleep. I usually woke up drunk and disoriented... and sorting out all those pills was one helluva feat. It seems I was always out of one prescription, so I'd skip it then double up when I got the refill. I could never get it straight.

Lola offered to take charge of my medication but I adamantly refused. Pissed, I shouted at her, "What do you think I am, Lola? An idiot? Incapable of taking care of myself?" I was livid... so livid I didn't realize her lack of response was a big, fat "yes" in disguise.

Raised to be a Southern sweetheart of a woman, Lola was a giver, and she considered it her job to be my caretaker. She took care of the business

as if it was her own.

As she witnessed me shrinking deeper into the Land of Lost Alcoholics, she doubled her efforts in trying to protect me. A loyal employee, a good friend, and my greatest enabler. Thanks to Lola, I reached my bottom slowly... painfully... like a suicide bomb with a mile-long fuse.

INAGURAL FIRE
CHAPTER 2

The night after Daddy and I put the studio together, I realized that ugly green house represented my freedom, my "new start." I could change direction, renew a dedication to quality. The word "quality" repeated in my mind over and over though I didn't quite know what it meant.

I repeated the word as I lit the first fire in my stone fireplace. A stack of split logs came with the house, a leftover from the previous tenant, I assumed. The wood was a little wet, but it lit and made the house smell like a wondrous forest. I sat on my new sofa and watched the logs crackle and pop. Alone, my thoughts turned to the serious side. *Have I done the right thing by moving out? Am I really up for starting all over again? Do I really drink too much, like he said? Do I even understand what ruined the marriage?*

Maybe I didn't *want* to understand why the marriage was over because I thought all fingers of blame pointed at Miller. He'd screwed me over. Lying to me about wanting a family, lying about his addiction and money problems, stealing the woman I thought I loved, lying about his hopes and dreams, the essence of his entire being! *You didn't see those things coming, Lela. But after you found the truth, you continued the marriage. You forgave him and blamed yourself. But it's not your fault! You got screwed!*

Even at the start, I knew Miller loved Bo more than he loved me. I had told Karen, even, but I ignored it and the pain it caused. No, I *chose* to ignore it. *Another bad decision, Lela. Drunken wisdom.*

Wanting only to be a father to Bo, Miller McKeown stomped all over my heart, seemingly on purpose. I couldn't help but blame myself. After all, I drank a lot. And I ignored the red flags, staying the course and staying hopeful that he would grow to love *me*, too. I just kept drinking and fucking up and forgiving shit; I didn't leave him until he forced me to go.

Yep, Miller was a hard-boiled heartless ass, born and raised that way.

The divorce wasn't yet final and wouldn't be for a while. My lawyer, a female up-and-comer nicknamed "Rabid Dog Annie," had drafted a separation agreement and a list of things Miller would pay on my behalf. For "temporary support," we asked him to pay my rent, car payment, auto insurance, phone bill, and $500 in cash per month for "household support." That arrangement would change with the final divorce settlement to become permanent alimony if I played my cards right.

The legal demand for temporary support was a pie-in-the-sky opening offer by Rabid Dog Annie, the point used to begin negotiations. Yet Miller accepted it without bargaining. His attorney, nothing more than an unreliable and lazy friend, had advised him to sign it. *What a dumbass! Goes to show how stupid Miller McKeown is... I'll ride this one out for as long as I can.* My attorney agreed.

For the final decree, I would ask for alimony in the same amount, but Annie said the judge would limit the length of payments to two years or so, she said. But for now, it was open-ended, as if he was "giving" me the money. Even a legal newbie like me understood he should move forward as fast as possible.

The profit I made from Moonlight Jewelry barely covered utilities and groceries. I used the cash I received at craft shows to pay for incidentals like prescriptions, shampoo, vodka, and makeup, and a piece of clothing here and there. I wasn't rich by any means, but I lived well and with no worries... and no thoughts of the future.

My "financial management rule" stood: I paid myself first each month, whittling it down to set aside a whopping $20 for my savings account. Twenty bucks. By the time I got to the bank, that's all that was left. Still, I thought I'd planned everything beautifully, and patted myself on the back for my financial responsibility. *Smart Lela, you're gonna go far, kid, doing the right thing. Just remember... "Quality." That's your mantra, your promise to the world.* I still didn't understand what the word "quality" meant in relation to my life at the time, but it sounded good.

"Quality," I said, and threw another log on the fire. I fixed a drink, placed it on my newly polished coffee table, and dashed out the backdoor for another seasoned log. Just as I added to the *"quality"* fire, I saw the beetles. They ran full-speed-ahead, darting from the heat as each log began to char. Hundreds of beetles... racing across and down the stone hearth and onto my beige carpet like a flock of birds in a two-foot-wide parade. Their steps in unison, it was a crowded and creepy beetle stampede.

I freaked, gasping so deep that I choked. Like a rocket, I drove to the Mini-Mart and bought every bottle of bug killer they had, eight cans if I remember right. When I returned, there were no beetles in sight so I tiptoed to the fireplace with the first can of bug spray in-hand.

No. Aerosol cans and fire. No. I remembered the camping weekend with the church Youth Group. "Ka-boom would make it worse, Lela," I spoke out loud. "You need water. Quality water."

My heart pounded, threatening to make me sober as I worked. The third bucketful was the one that flooded the firebox, sending black gritty water onto the new beige carpet. Now crying, I found a few old towels and tried to blot up the stain. That's when I felt two beetles crawling up the back of my leg – *under* my jeans.

Yep, scared sober. Dammit.

I mixed a drink and double-timed it upstairs to my bedroom, closing the door behind me. The first week in the new house... I hope this catastrophe isn't an omen, a sign of more bad things to come. And I hope beetles can't climb the steps.

I fell asleep wondering if the soon-to-come bug man would comment on the oh-so G-R-E-E-N of the house.

INHERENTLY STUPID
CHAPTER 3

Tuesdays and Thursdays were still reserved for Cowboy Logan, and our dating had expanded to include a few Wednesdays and weekends, too. I hated that he was married and nagged him about it, but my whining was drowned in vodka, forgotten with cocaine, and covered with Stetson hats.

We ate at expensive restaurants, then high-tailed it to Mel's gigantic house on the horse farm for a few chugs of his moonshine and a soak in the hot tub. Always partying, always crossing the border to impropriety – except for Lola; she made sure we didn't hurt ourselves.

That September, the four of us drove to Texas to pick up Mel's newly pregnant horse, spending the weekend as tourists, remembering the Alamo and sniffing the Fort Worth Stockyards. Somewhere along the way, we went to a rodeo where I fell down in the stands and was trampled by the crazy mob. "Here, drink this!" Logan directed, passing me a pint of vodka. "Like the Germans used to do."

"The Germans?" I asked.

"Whatever! The Vikings? Somebody. Like the cowboys use whiskey."

I took a swig, rubbing my left ankle, the one somebody had stomped flat. Straight vodka was never my shtick, but I took four generous gulps that afternoon, my appointment with Dr. Smirnoff.

Logan pulled me into his lap and poured vodka over the cuts on my legs and elbows. "Antiseptic. But this one might need stitches."

"Did the Vikings get stitches?"

He didn't reply; his eye-roll said all. I continued, "Then pour more vodka. Just don't waste too much."

"This one's gonna leave a scar."

"Texas souvenir. Give me that bottle!"

<<<<<<<<>>>>>>>

Lola and I were inseparable friends by this time and she had moved to the perfect party house, what we called "The Cliff Hanger." It was a cabin-like, three-room house balanced on the side of a mountain, yet it sat in the center of west Rockville. Heart-shaped leaves of ivy surrounded the house and wrapped the trunks of the oak trees that guarded the front entrance.

"More Madonna!" I screamed. Lola wouldn't let me operate the stereo anymore... not since I fell into the cabinet and crashed the shelves. As she changed the CD, I begged her, "Dance with me!" She refused; I considered that an emergency. "Anybody! Help! I need a dance partner!"

I had ten choices: eight drunk women about my age and two drunk guys a few years older. We made up the Saddlebag Gang, and Lola's Cliff Hanger was our headquarters.

The Saddlebag Gang rules matched the ones from our three years of girl's beach trips: no boyfriends allowed. Baron and Blitz didn't count; they were just friends, part of the gang. Besides, they were the ones who hauled in the kegs and tapped them so proficiently. The kegs were permanent fixtures, as was the puzzle box full of weed, kept under the sofa.

Friday nights, Girl's Night Out, brought the same name tags we had worn on beach trips in years prior: *"Hello My Name Is"*... we had a never-ending supply. We each had our favorite; I was usually Tess Tosterone. Others were Jenny Tailya, Connie Lingus, Sandy Slits, Dixie Normus, Lola's favorite, Lisa Greement. The guys remained "Knot Here" and "Visitor" and served as our security team until they, too, got drunk and unable to pay attention.

Then, on Saturdays after our Girl's Night Out, we took turns telling each other what dumb stuff happened and what stupid thing each of us had done. Usually, memories from the night before came in three varieties: vague, embarrassing, and ridiculous.

<<<<<<<<>>>>>>

I made sure to plan entertainment for most of my nights because I was afraid to be alone... afraid of myself and any remaining beetles. I dodged the fear and feelings of self-hate by relying on a lot of vodka and a bit of creativity.

"This is a flirty little dress!" I said to myself, "And some kick-ass high heels. Oh-la-la! Anybody would believe this is a date outfit." Lipstick on, I drove the five miles to my favorite neighborhood bar, the Titanic Bar and Grille. It was a respectable place, popular with folks in their 30s and they'd done a great job with the theme. Huge graphic murals of black-and-white glaciers wrapped the walls, the bar was "the captain's bridge," complete with an oversize ship's wheel, and accents of riveted steel peppered the place.

The bartender, Jamie, knew me well and had my vodka-tonic on the bar before I sat down on a stool. He said in a loud voice, "Are you meeting another one who stood you up?"

"Hush, Jamie! Are you trying to give it away already?"

I sat alone, looking at my watch every few minutes and eyeing the groups of men who had stopped by for happy hour. I flashed them innocent, shy-girl smiles... then I'd look at my watch again. As planned, one of the guys would ask to buy me a drink. "No, I'm waiting for my date... but I think I've been stood up."

In the bellowing voice of a man determined to rescue a damsel in distress, the man would invariably puff out his chest and say, "Stood up? Now, who would stand up a pretty woman like you?"

Success!

Free drinks for the rest of the night and an opportunity to play the vixen. Using sex as power, playing men like toys. Sometimes I would take them home with me, but rarely. Instead, I would have them take me to play pool, to a club, or go on an all-night shopping spree. I was the consummate bad girl, and I was damn-good at it.

<<<<<<<<>>>>>>

Logan and I went to the Titanic with Lola and Mel one night after having too many drinks at a two-for-one happy hour down the street. Mel urged Logan to do his trademark thievery. "Get the spider plant this time, Logan," Mel said.

Cowboy Logan dug up the live plant from the flower box beside our booth. Holding it by the roots, he walked out of the Titanic as if nothing was amiss.

Logan was a kleptomaniac; I never figured out why because he had a shitload of money. That cold Thursday night, I said, "Great houseplant! You've outdone yourself! And it sure beats a coffee cup or another sugar bowl."

Instead of upsetting me, Logan's kleptomania made me laugh... especially that night because he gave me the plant. "I'll need a pot and a way to hang it, too, Logan. Can you steal that for me?"

"From where?" Then he stopped himself. "Hell no! I just do restaurants. I don't want to get in trouble, ding-dong."

<<<<<<<>>>>>>

If alone and bored on winter nights in my screaming-green house, I drank myself to oblivion and spent hours crying and feeling sorry for myself. Then I'd pick up the phone, searching for "help" that couldn't help me at all. I was just bored and lonely.

"Have her call me ASAP. I'm in crisis!" I left a message with my therapist's answering service around ten PM. When she called back, I was no longer upset... too drunk to hold a thought for more than sixty seconds. Through peals of laughter, I told her I had a column of snot that reached the floor, but otherwise, I was fine. She sent me a bill for $50 for that "appointment" and I never called her again outside of office hours.

With my therapist off the list of possibilities, I perused the yellow pages to find a friend. Never thinking I was taking time from somebody who honestly needed help, I entertained myself by calling crisis lines: The Suicide Crisis Line, Sexual Assault Crisis Line, Narcotics Anonymous, any "Help!" phone number listed. With a drink in hand and a well-thought-out story, I'm sure my act frustrated those who answered because I refused to be helped by their scripted words. I simply repeated my supposed pain and problems over and over.

Only one guy hung up on me.

I whined to the older man who answered the AA Hotline, "But drinking makes me feel better... helps me hate myself less."

He answered calmly. "As I said, there's a program to take away those bad feelings without having to drink... a program that will give you a new freedom and a new happiness."

"But I'm a private person! I can't talk about my problems in front of people!"

"You don't have to talk. Just listening will help."

"Listen to a degenerate alcoholic? Ha! Who in their right mind would take advice from a drunk?"

"A drunk who no longer drinks isn't a degenerate. In fact, you'll find them to be quite wise."

"That's such bullshit! I wouldn't give the motherfuckers the time of day."

"So do you want to get sober?"

"Sometimes."

"Is right now one of those times?"

"No."

"Are you drunk right now?"

"Yes."

"Then I don't have time for your bullshit." And he hung up.

Alcoholics didn't play, it seemed. He had seen through my verbal tapestry of bullshit, knowing I was toying with him.

After the crisis lines lost their appeal, I made other types of cries for help. While men are usually the ones who make booty calls, I was the caller. I worked my way down a list posted on my fridge. The only requests: show up in a hurry, armed with joints and beer.

My life had become unmanageable, and I knew I had to do something about it, sooner rather than later. But underneath my bravado, I also knew I was too far gone to do it on my own.

Maybe there's a way out that doesn't require so much effort on your part, Lela. POOF! You're sober! Yeah... that's the way to do it.

About two months after moving to the screaming-green house, I found myself drunk in the early evening, crying my eyes out and fed up with being lonely and stupid. I called the AA Hotline again, sharing my honest truth. The girl said, "The 5:30 meeting, 2317 West Park Boulevard. I'll meet you there."

I slipped into the meeting room late, cried every minute I was there, and slipped out before the closing prayer. The girl I was supposed to meet... I didn't even look for her.

My mind was busy on the way home. I don't know who I was talking to or who I was arguing with, but the steam of my anger billowed from the silver van.

I'm supposed to get sober based on THAT bullshit? Hell, no! Those fucking people are weird, talking about how magic happens from not drinking... butterflies coming out of their butt and crap. For me, going a few HOURS without a drink is like dying a slow death. So HAPPINESS without it? No way! It could never happen for me.

Tears began as I felt myself sink further into hopelessness, quickly followed by the bravado that said I was perfectly fucking-fine and didn't need help, especially from the weirdos in that room.

The guy saying he'd been sober for fifteen years – I call bullshit. It's impossible! And you lied in front of all those people, dude! You've cheated somewhere along the way and you're lying about it, so why would I trust anything you say?

A REAL alcoholic can't get sober, no matter what AA says. LISTEN TO ME!!! That stupid meeting was a farce! AA just isn't for me. In fact, the whole concept is inherently stupid.

AUNT LIL'S LETTER
CHAPTER 4

The first time I got drunk as a teen, I made a promise: "Never drink alone." I had broken that promise hundreds of times, too many to count. In my 20s, I changed the pledge: "No getting *drunk* alone." Again, promise broken hundreds of times. Now, in my late 30s, I pledged: "Never get drunk alone on purpose with a bad attitude."

It was a night I got drunk on purpose, alone, and with a shitty attitude about Lela Fox. I got sloppy to hurt and humiliate myself further, I suppose, and I didn't want to relieve the pain with the fun of another crisis line or booty call. So I sat... singing woe is me.

I contemplated my earlier phone conversation with Daddy, full of bad news from his sister, my Aunt Lil. Just yesterday, he had said, Lil's husband Troy clutched his chest and collapsed in the shaving cream aisle at a Texas Walmart. Dead. Heart attack. And his loving wife wasn't taking it so well.

Aunt Lil was the second-oldest sister of the Fox clan, a writer... the one who defended me as a child, telling Mom my made-up stories weren't meant to deceive but were created by an exceptionally creative mind.

Even better, Aunt Lil was the mother of my coolest cousin; I called him Dude... real name Lewis Balyum. Lewis/Dude could light a cigarette with a Zippo lighter and ten toes... a feat that amazed me as a teen. He was a poet who lived in France, financing his bohemian lifestyle by driving a taxi in D.C. each winter.

Yet he was a fixture at Fox family reunions, and when he visited us in Burgess when I was still living at home, he put me under some kind of magic spell. No shit. A spirit radiated from him, an ethereal peace-filled aura, and just standing next to him, I had absorbed it. Dude's free spirit touched me in a way I'd never been touched; I was in awe of him. But there was more. He was the only person ever impressed by my collection of compound words. As I aged, he always asked about my writing and seemed to take a special interest in me.

And Lewis was crazy about his mom, my Aunt Lil. She wore artisan turquoise-and-sterling jewelry and if you complimented a bracelet or whatever, she'd take it off and give it to you. So not a "shirt off her back" person, but a "necklace off her neck" chick. I was in love with the lady I called Aunt Lil – and a "lady" she was.

My heart broke for her as an unhappy widow, and for Lewis the Dude suddenly without a father. Daddy was heartbroken; he'd cried when sharing the news. I remember this specifically because his tears brought some of my own and I had watched a tear roll into my beer as we talked on the phone.

I stepped to the foyer chest, where I kept a stack of greeting cards ready to send: birthday cards, anniversary cards, and a now-needed sympathy card. As I grabbed one from the stash, I stopped short. *A card is too generic for Aunt Lil. I want to write her a letter.*

Already drunkish, I hauled a six-pack upstairs and sat down to write. If I remember, it started appropriately and grammatically correct. *You're a writer, Lela. Make her feel better. Tell her how much she means to you, how much hope you have in her healing. Talk about God if you have to.* I popped another beer and hit ENTER to start another paragraph. It was a long letter.

I edited the first part repeatedly. But the second half, well, I remember little. Correction: I don't remember any of it. I do remember I was still typing when I popped the sixth beer, crying, and was telling her about *my* life. Only God knows what I said or how I said it. I had broken my "don't get drunk alone on purpose when you're emotional" pledge big time.

The HP printer came alive, spitting out six single-spaced pages of a heartfelt letter. I was first surprised by the length; thought I should edit some out. *Nah... long letters are good letters. After all, Aunt Lil is a reader, a writer, and my words, no matter how many, will help her.* I got a stamp from my desk dispenser and attached it to an envelope with a barely legible address. Then I stumbled to the mailbox in the dark and put the letter out for the mailman.

I woke up still intoxicated. The mailman ran early in my neighborhood, much earlier than my waking hour. So my drunken ramblings were on their way to Texas, to a grieving widow who read the Miss Manners column daily... a classy lady with a lifelong career of kindness and morality. I felt a punch in my stomach and knew I had done wrong, despite my best intentions.

"Oh, God!" I rolled over in bed, curling into a fetal position. I mumbled to the empty room, "You've screwed up now, for sure. And now *Aunt Lil* knows how screwed up you are." My tears wet the sheets for twenty minutes before I found balance and raised on one elbow up to light a cigarette.

I talked to the ceiling. "And not just Aunt Lil – she'll tell Daddy, she'll tell Dude. And Aunt Val... probably Uncle Jolly, too... because *he* sure knows about alcoholics. The whole fam-damily will know you're a drunk, Lela." Tears poured from my eyes as my stomach turned sour with Shame.

The familiar pressure between my ears screamed a buzz as my jaw clenched. Cringing, I realized I hadn't just ruined my *own* reputation, but Daddy's, too. And Mom's. I felt like a complete piece of shit... so much hate for myself.

Simply put, my life changed that morning. It was the day I knew I had gone too far.

I thought about the semi-intervention of a Little League mom... the "major problem" she'd accused me of having. And I re-heard what Daddy had insinuated so many times, and what Jennifer said about destroying myself... a rash of memories of people trying to intercede.

Still crying, I took a double-shot of vodka in my coffee that day, never sobering up... trying to erase the mistake and the pain in my gut. *Tomorrow you can sober up, prove to the world that you're not an alcoholic. If you can make it all day, then you're safe. And when Daddy calls to report Aunt Lil's reaction, you can honestly say you don't have a problem with alcohol.*

Yeah, tomorrow... tomorrow I'll show them ALL, by God!

<<<<<<<>>>>>>

Daddy never *directly* said Aunt Lil called to tell him about the letter, but the timing couldn't have been a coincidence. He was all fired up but serious and calm, confronting me in the most straightforward way as of yet, but he still couldn't say the hard words, like "alcoholic" or "drunk." Maybe those words left a bad taste in his mouth.

I defended myself to the Nth degree and, even though Daddy cried as he begged me to straighten up, he knew he couldn't help me if I wasn't willing to help myself. So he gave up with a sigh, ending the conversation with assurances of how much he loved me, ending with his standard line, "I love you always and always, my favorite baby daughter."

An alcoholic usually has some type of wake-up call before the downfall begins in earnest. The morning after writing Aunt Lil's letter was my wake-up moment. Some can stop drinking at this early burp, but I wasn't quite finished.

Very soon, but a world away, there was nowhere to go but up. And, thank God, when I reached out for help, a hand was there. It looked familiar, along with ten limber toes and a Zippo lighter.

A BIT OF REALITY
CHAPTER 5

I didn't hire the second assistant for a while; several women applied, but I deemed them "not cool" or too snooty to fit our little upstairs playground. Eventually, I hired a roly-poly woman who lived in the neighborhood, Caroline Griffin. She would work a few hours in the mornings, four days a week. Each morning, her first two tasks were done without my supervision. 1.) Make coffee. 2.) Wake me up with a freshly brewed cup. The second day, when I asked her to splash a little vodka in the mug, she cried. I almost fired her on the spot, but later softened. After all, I cried when I added the vodka, too.

Caroline did the repetitive work, and she worked hard, never belittling me or plotting an intervention. A few months after she started, I booked a four-day show near St. Louis so we could stay at her parents' house, saving a hotel bill. I'm sure Caroline was happy to visit her family and get paid to do it, but I'm also sure I did a hundred things to embarrass her, a thousand things to make her puritan parents uncomfortable.

I don't know what I did but I'm sure it was bad because I brought a twelve-pack to add to their fridge each day, not noticing they didn't drink a drop. By that time, I had lost the ability to be socially appropriate.

Later that season, I scheduled a show near Charleston so we could stay with Lola's brother. It was the weekend I met a good-looking watercolor artist and at the show's closing hour, I rushed to drop Lola at her brother's, then backtracked to the artist's room at Motel Six. I envisioned us painting beautiful pictures together, but he was an orgasm-screamer and scared the hell out of me.

After we finished in bed, the front desk called. I heard the artist's response to the question: "Everything is fine. Why do you ask?" he said, later explaining that the people next door had called the front desk to report a murder happening in our room.

I screamed at him for being a screamer, then left before the police could show up.

<<<<<<<>>>>>>

I had one connection to reality. He was about six-foot-four, worked as a postman, and had feet like Sasquatch. My level-headed, non-alcoholic friend, Damon Toomey.

His charms were front and center; he didn't apologize for being everything a woman would want. Dark brown hair ranging between "coifed" and "natural" matched his sparkly brown eyes; the same smiling eyes that looked at me with genuine kindness. Damon was a pale man, avoiding the sun to escape the skin cancer that killed his sister; sun exposure worries were new, just beginning to cause concern for everyday folks.

Fit and trim by nature, he had a clever, dry sense of humor and found the funny side of everything around him, even the bad stuff. That amazed me... his gratitude and positive attitude raised me up, gave me hope.

And things were never boring when Damon was around; he joked and laughed and kept the crowd going with his antics. He was exactly the kind of guy a normal woman yearns for, and the type a normal woman's mom would applaud.

We had a friend-of-a-friend-of-a-friend connection, but it was odd that such a nice guy would like me and choose to hang out with me. We seemed polar opposites, though both a little goofy.

Damon accepted me and my quirks, only throwing small, subtle hints that I could do better if I didn't drink so much. I suspected he wanted a date but was holding back because of my drinking. He said as much, but I let it pass for as long as possible.

I listened, but I didn't hear. By then, my judgement was nothing but vapor and I acted like a naïve child. But with Damon in charge of our outings, I didn't have to know anything or be anything or do anything. I had license to be a fuck-up, to do my thing without worrying about repercussions. Damon took care of me. Though I felt Shame for taking advantage of that, I just tried to think we were scratching each other's back... but in reality, I didn't do any scratching.

Damon knew my diet was shit and always brought a few bags of groceries when he came to the green house. Nutritious, easy-to-fix food. Bless his heart, he was on the side of a woman who had no sides; it seems all vodka bottles are round.

Damon helped with my loneliness, though I'd never told him how lonely I was. Maybe he was lonely, too, or maybe he sensed mine, but Damon always had a plan for activities that didn't include drinking. With his direction, we frequented coffee shops in the Old City, held two-person tournaments at miniature golf, and went to movies, book stores, and Rockville's new and ultra-funky downtown art galleries.

His dog was fat like mine, a boxer named DooDad. Damon brought him to the green house for playdates with Murphy. Then we'd take long walks, following the trails at Hope Springs Park, but we had to stop a lot because the fat dogs needed a rest.

On the benches, Damon talked about his coworkers at the Post Office, about his loving family, and did his best to steer me toward a normal way of thinking. Most of the time I didn't get it or found it boring and let my mind wander.

Even though I appreciated what Damon was trying to do and respected him without question, he pissed me off. I felt confronted, though he said nothing confrontational. Maybe I felt "managed," like I was his fucking project. The reality he was forcing on me was scary, but Damon was my only connection to reality. The sonofabitch was trying to make me normal. Knowing that fact brought fear and my old friend Shame. The Shame of knowing I'd never be normal and never had been.

You're too far gone, Lela, and any chance you had was squandered years ago.

Damon and I were sitting on the sofa one random night when I felt his eyes on me. I looked up at his face. Yes, he was gazing at me. When I looked away, he touched my arm. In a calm and casual voice, he said, "Lela, you know I'm in love with you, don't you?"

I froze, silent. In that instant, my ears stopped up, blocking out the music and the entire universe. I held up my hands in a defensive move, but I couldn't speak. Though Damon paused, when he saw I wouldn't scream and run away, he kept talking. "I want to be with you. The two of us, and Bo, and the dogs. Actually, I want to take *care* of you, but you're... you're out of my reach."

I wanted to know why I was "out of his reach," as he said, but I shook my head left and right, trying to make him stop talking. He didn't stop. "Maybe you just can't see me and the depth of my feelings, Lela. Maybe you can't see reality anymore at all. But here I am. I am real."

Chewing on these comments, I kept my head down. Then Damon hugged my shoulders and tried to pull me inward to his chest. Nope; my body was stiff and unmoving. Still, my friend continued his confession or whatever it was. "Out of my reach because... dammit! It's not just that you drink too much... that goes without saying. It's deeper than that! You've got a problem, alcoholism I'm pretty sure, hon. And if the problem wasn't there, I'd scoop you up and treat you like a princess, build you a palace, love you so much you'd explode."

"Damon, don't," I interrupted.

He closed his eyes and nodded. "You're right, you're right." Then Damon put his head in his hands and sighed, speaking through the peepholes of his fingers. "Lela Fox, I've tried so hard to *not* say all this. You're not ready to hear it, I know. Forget I said anything." A pause, a sigh. He snapped his head up with a jerk, looking straight at me. "Wait! Hell no! *Remember* I said it. Remember it *forever*. One day, you'll be able to understand what I mean. One day you'll love me as much as I love you."

Without regard for his feelings, I spewed a response. "And in the meantime, can you just back the fuck off and quit this drama shit? I thought we were *friends,* dammit! And now here you go accusing me of being a drunk! Does that sound like a friend-thing? Hell, no!" I spit the words, raising my voice, then I saw the hurt in his eyes and wished I hadn't been so mean. But what choice did I have? I wanted my emotions to speak just as loud as my thoughts: *Don't be in love with me! Leave me alone in my drunken misery!*

With my mind on overdrive, the screams continued unheard. *Please... please... don't be a dickhead, Damon, and don't try to straighten me out! You're so much better than me! If you must find a girlfriend, find a REAL one... not me.*

In the silence, Damon's eyes had filled with tears. No surprise; his heartfelt emotions and willingness to show them was the main reason I loved the man so much. But I loved him as a *friend*, not a boyfriend. To reduce the tension, I changed my stance. "Sorry, Damon, I don't mean to be hateful. It's just... it's not the time for me. I'm a fucking mess and maybe I can't take care of myself, but I don't want anybody else to do it for me, not even you."

He sat back on the sofa, staring at the lights on the stereo as if they held the secret to the universe. He spoke carefully, "Keep the possibility of you and me, as a couple, in the back of your mind, okay? One day you'll sober up and we'll get together. Then we'll be–"

"Damon! Stop!" The scenario had made me feel worse about myself, made me see how hopeless my life had become. Sudden tears, erupting like a volcano... Damon reached to rub my back as I boo-hoo'ed like a two-year-old.

<<<<<<<>>>>>>

It was late. Since Damon's confession, we had gone to dinner at "The Crack," Cracker Barrel, and came back to play a game of Spades. I'd had just a few drinks before dinner and two more as we played cards. Standing to stretch, Damon said, "Well, I guess DooDad and I will head home. Are you ready for bed yourself?"

"I may stay up a little."

"Well, please don't go out. Do you have enough vodka?"

"I'm good. Thanks.

"Sleep sweet, Curly."

I got a lick from the dog and a kiss on the head from Damon. With his hand on the doorknob, he stopped. "Lela, I'm sorry if I upset you tonight, but it was time to tell you how I feel. Thanks for not kicking me out. I thought you might."

"It's cool, Damon. But now we've defined our boundaries a bit better, right? Thanks for all you do."

"For all I do? I just want to have fun with a funny lady."

"A *drunk* funny lady. A drunk-funny-lady-alcoholic-scum-of-the-earth."

"Quit putting yourself down. One day you'll stop that, too."

"When pigs fly maybe."

"When you sober up."

I had no response to that, doubting his prediction could ever come true. He shut the door behind him, and I burst into tears again, curling into a ball in the corner of the sofa.

Damon would reappear in my life at the least expected time… as if our destinies had been pre-planned. Had he been appointed my guardian angel? Maybe some kind of salvage team organizer for Lela Fox? Or a Navy Seal, an operative for the CIA, Milky Way captain? Whatever it was, our universes aligned many times at just the right moments and my life wouldn't have been the same without Damon Toomey.

Sorry… I'm getting ahead of the story.

BYE, BYE, BABY
CHAPTER 6

Andy and Ella had taken the lead in taking care of Bo, and just in time. Tending to his needs had become a Herculean task as I struggled to hide my "little problem." Bo was on a traveling baseball team by then, with some overnight trips hundreds of miles away. Andy and I split the responsibility for getting him to out-of-town games, but my weekends were humdingers; a real pain in the ass. And expensive!

I fit in like an alien with the normal families who also traveled with their baseball kids. Once, in Lexington, I mistakenly took my nighttime medicine in the morning and slept through the game and the celebration afterward. Bo had to catch a ride back to the hotel and create a story to cover my absence.

What I needed most was relief for the "I'm a shitty mother" Guilt, but I found none. I sat aside while Andy and Ella took the stage, outshining me in every way.

And I couldn't hide my failings from Andy; he knew how much I was drinking and shared his dissatisfaction with my lack of mothering skills at every opportunity. Ella was even snottier about it. Naturally, I began to hate them both. Not only were they right... I had no defense.

<<<<<<<>>>>>>

It was a sunny Thursday. I picked Bo up from school and we rushed home to change clothes and throw his bat bag in the van. "We'll just grab some burgers in the car, bud. We're running late."

As Bo took the field, I saw Andy. He waved and pointed to a pair of open seats in the bleachers, away from the crowd. I was instantly suspicious.

Why is he even here? This game was marked as my job on the calendar... and why does he want to sit with me? What's going on? And where's Ella and their roly-poly toddler?

I had brought a cooler of beer and a baseball-themed coozie but I wouldn't dare drink in front of Andy. We sat down, settling in for the usual two-hour game. He began with small talk. Three minutes into it, I spewed at him, "Andy, spit it out. You don't chit-chat, so something's wrong. Tell me. Now."

He looked at the ground, silent as I squirmed in my seat. Five seconds... ten. Then he looked at me, his nervous tic causing his lower lip and right eye to quiver. "Best to just spit it out, I guess," he said.

"Yes, Please."

"Lela, I've been transferred to Nashville. We're taking Bo."

There was a long moment of silence while I let that sink in. I didn't breathe; it was as if my lungs had collapsed. I repeated the two sentences in my head several times before reacting.

I felt my stomach whirl as the taste of bile filled my mouth. Breaking from the time-warp, I jumped up and shouted, *"The HELL you say!"* The sudden movement toppled my cooler. I didn't realize how loud I yelled until I heard the silence behind me. I turned to see an ocean of parents' eyes staring at me.

My hands were shaking as I looked back at my ex. "No, Andy, the custody agreement will not change! You can't take him away from Rockville. It's in the papers! A legal document!" The sound was like fingernails on a blackboard.

Andy's eyes were wide, his jaw clenched. He whispered, "First, sit down, Lela." I didn't respond through three similar requests, finally sitting when he raised his voice. "Sit! Let's talk. You're acting like an idiot."

With my blood pressure spiking, I had a hard time sitting, so I sat in increments. I'm sure I looked ridiculous, but I was too upset to care. "I'm not acting like an idiot, you idiot, I'm reacting as any mother would!"

A huff of a chuckle escaped Andy's pale lips, a huff of doubt, it seemed. "Listen, think about it. You're single and alone and can't keep him full-time yourself. And you travel for a living!" He paused, and I looked away. "But there's more. Lela, you're a drinker, probably an alcoholic. And speaking of legal, I could go to court and take full custody right now, because it's easy to prove you're an unfit mother."

"Unfit, my ass–" Andy talked through my interruption.

"Dangerously unfit, in fact. Bo is afraid of you... and ashamed of you. He's told me that more than once."

Tears had started as soon as Andy said "drinker." My heart hurt. But Shame caused *Anger* on that day. "How long have you practiced that little speech, Andy? You ass! Dammit, you can't *do* this to me!" More tears erupted, but I knew he could, indeed, do this to me. The thought of it gave me shivers.

"Lela... *think*. It's best for Bo to have two parents, a stable family, a brother, and no drinking or drugs. You're out of control, and I won't let you put Bo through your own hell. Not anymore." I tried to interrupt but realized I had nothing to say, no comeback that would stop him.

Andy continued. "And now there's no Miller McKeown to balance things out. It's over. A done deal. I've talked to a lawyer and the custody arrangement will be legally changed. You know it has to be this way. You *have* to know it! Look at you! Tell me what's in that cooler, for instance."

Hurt and scared, I was crying uncontrollably and snot ran from my nose; I didn't bother to wipe it. Stretching out the syllables with my sobs, I said, "Andy, I can't just let him go-o-o! I'm his m-mother! He *ne-e-e-eds* me!" I was making a scene but didn't care.

Andy grabbed my hand and pulled me to a standing position. "Let's go to the Jeep." As we walked toward the parking lot, I continued my appeals, repeating that a child needs his mother. He finally burst with a comment that sent a spike through my heart. "*Ella* is more of a mother to him than you! You can't take care of *yourself*, much less Bo, for God's sake!"

I stopped walking, feeling weak in the knees, and stood with my mouth agape. I felt myself crumbling, and as in a dream, I saw visions of a frail me whirling in the wind. Andy resumed some kind of conversation I didn't hear; it sounded like Charlie Brown's teacher's squawk.

I realized he wasn't going to shut up. *This is real. This nightmare is really happening.* My stomach burned and pumped like I was ready to vomit. *Unbelievable! NO! THIS ISN'T HAPPENING!*

Andy's voice became clear again, though my head throbbed and my eyeballs hurt. Without thinking, I wiped my nose on the sleeve of my t-shirt and "came to" at the end of Andy's squawk... "So don't make me do it the hard way, Lela." *If that's the last of the sentence, what the hell was the first part? Oh hell, I'm in trouble.*

"Don't fight it, Lela. It's going to happen. Bo's moving with us. In August. Get used to it." Andy stared at me with piercing eyes, his breath now ragged.

Why is he so angry? Am I really that bad? Is this the end of me or the beginning? What will I do without Bo? Does he hate me? He told his dad he's ASHAMED of me? Ashamed of his own mother! And AFRAID of me? Oh God, what have I done? I've ruined my son's life!

Andy waited for a response; at least I thought that was why he paused for so long, then he said something that still resonates in my mind. "I'm sorry, Lela. I've given you plenty of chances. You've failed every time."

Failed? Failed! FAILED! So not only does Bo hate me, his father hates me, too! They all hate me – maybe more than I hate myself. My tears began anew, leaning against Andy's Jeep for stability; I still felt like I would faint. Or puke. Or sink into the pavement, never to be seen again. *You big, fat fuck-up, Lela Fox. A lifelong fuck-up... that's what you are.*

The only defense was denial. *Run, Lela, run!*

In a snap, I asked, "Are you staying for the whole game?" Andy's brow creased; he cocked his head in confusion, maybe questioning the abrupt change in subject. He didn't answer fast enough to suit my timing, and I screamed. Loud. "Just answer!"

It took several seconds for him to nod yes. "Then I'm leaving. I can't stand here and act like nothing is wrong. Just take him to your house. *You* keep him tonight. I can't look the kid in the face. Maybe I'll call later to see how he did in the game."

I'd walked ten feet when Andy yelled at my back. "Don't call if you're drunk! And you probably will be."

"Fuck you!" I shouted over my shoulder. The sting of a target burning like a cow brand on my back propelled me forward. I stomped across the lot, entered my van, and slammed the driver's door.

Windows up, I grabbed the steering wheel and screamed. "Aiiieiiiiwii! FUUUUCK!" Once, twice, three times... each scream louder than the one before it.

I stayed in the parking lot in my crazy state for ten minutes before I remembered the beer cooler, now in the passenger floorboard. I chugged about half of one. *There, that's better.*

I found a napkin in the glove box and blew my nose, wiped the mascara from my cheeks and the drops of tears trickling from my jawbone. *Deep breath, Lela. Get your shit together.* My throat was sore from screaming. The rest of the cold beer soothed it and I drowned another, trying to drown the knife in my heart.

I cried for the full forty miles back to Rockville, and drank the full six-pack. When I got home, I switched to vodka, pouring a double. I guzzled the first drink and poured another. Andy was right. I was drunk within the hour and I wouldn't be able to talk to Bo tonight.

Confused and embarrassed, I wondered what I would say to Bo when we were next together. He would surely know the whole story. I felt Shame run up my spine and explode in my head. Shame. Always Shame.

I've heard it said but never thought it was possible: I cried myself to sleep, hoping to wake up a different person.

I realize now that losing custody of Bo was a key turning point in my life. In that moment, I lost hope, believing I'd never be a worthy person, never be an achiever or have victories over tough challenges. So what the hell... I let myself be weak and needy. Part of that weakness was feeling justified in drinking myself to oblivion any damn time I wanted.

I had failed my son, that much was true, but in losing him, I lost myself. And I lost any hope of moving forward with a happy life. Bo was the one and only good thing left for me and I had to let him go to improve his life. Then he was gone, and I was shattered.

Would it serve to change me? That remained to be seen.

BARNEY FIFE
CHAPTER 7

Trying to cut down on my drinking, I played a game; setting strict rules would save me, I thought. So instead of stocking up on beer, the rules said I could buy only one six-pack at a time and each six-pack had to come from a different store. The next day, I would start over with the same rules. I found it a clever ploy.

I followed the rule for nine days before realizing it wasn't cutting down on my consumption, only increasing my drive time... sending me further and further away from home. Still, I followed the rule, searching for anything to make me believe I had control of my drinking.

On the tenth "rule day," my drive sent me through the back roads. As if on auto-pilot, I stopped by my favorite pub, The Cellar Tavern. *I'll see my old buddy CJ, playing that damn trivia game, as always.* CJ was an old radio guy friend of mine who now free-lanced as a voice talent and audio engineer working from his home. CJ smoked filter-less cigarettes; he even had an antique ashtray in his studio... it said, "Property of West Rockville Hospital."

Sure enough, CJ was at the Tavern, drinking Coors on draft and setting new highs on the video trivia game.

I slid onto the second stool at his table. "Hey, hey, my big CJ!" I bellowed, "How's it hanging?"

He looked at me sideways through thick glasses, offering a simple "Hey." CJ wasn't known for social exuberance. His reply was so dismissive that I laughed.

I knew better than to take it personally. Besides, he was my favorite vendor from my advertising days and we were of like mind.

It was a crowded bar, the pool tables lively with a combo of college boys, rednecks, bikers, and fifty-somethings. My eyes wandered to the college-boy table in the corner. Booming voices, hearty toasts, and a dozen off-color comments about some girl named Donna. Obviously, she was screwing her way through the fraternity and I flashed back to my days as a Little Sister at Alpha Sigma... when I was the Donna.

I rushed to the bar, ordered a beer, and carried my own trivia game box to the table with CJ. I tried a few questions, but my eyes crossed trying to see the tiny words on the wall monitor. Within minutes, I gave up trying and chose random answers. "Hey CJ... let's have a toast when I'm correct, okay? Just something to keep it interesting."

"Sure." Again, his lack of enthusiasm cracked me up.

"You're as dull as your dishwater hair, CJ." His response: three huff-chuckles, never taking his eyes from the monitor. "How do you know all this shit, anyway?"

"Because it's on a short rotation. This is the third repeat."

I threw my head back to laugh. "Then why do you *play?*" More laughter. "Damn, CJ, I thought you were smarter than you looked, but I guess not. You big cheater."

CJ raised a blondish eyebrow but remained silent. I pushed the trivia game box away and took up people watching. *I'll show that damn CJ! I can ignore him just as much as he's ignoring me.*

The Cellar Tavern's drinkers entertained me through another six-or-so beers and I stayed until the bar closed at three o'clock. I kissed CJ when I left, but he returned it only half-heartedly. It pissed me off... a girl wants to be wanted, after all.

On the way home, my vision became fuzzy. I was suddenly so, so, so sleepy and pulled off the road onto a new, blackest-black asphalt street with distinct big-equipment tire prints. Orange tracks, pure Tennessee clay. The street was the entrance to a soon-to-be subdivision with marked lots but no houses. About a hundred feet from the entrance, I stopped and put the van in park. Then I passed out.

<<<<<<<>>>>>>

I awoke to a loud tapping on the driver's side window. A cop, and another behind him. "Ma'am, step out of the vehicle, please," he said. I tried to shake myself awake, but apparently, he thought I was shaking my head no, as in refusing to get out of the van. The reaction sent his tone to the stratosphere with stern, clipped words. "Out of the vehicle, ma'am. Now!" I obeyed, apologizing. I stumbled and nearly fell; my foot was asleep.

I had no clue how long I'd been asleep there. *Oh, shit!* I heard the whirr of the van's engine running. It took a minute to realize I was major-DUI-busted. The cop asked me to walk a straight line, touch my nose, count backward – the typical field sobriety test, but something I'd never had to do. Afterward, I looked closer at the second cop... he wasn't a cop at all! Just a short and squatty security guard like the kind who roamed the mall. Busted by a fucking Barney Fife. As it turned out, he had tried to wake me but couldn't, eventually calling the cops.

The cuffs snapped around my wrists and the cop pushed my head down as I entered the back seat of his squad car. *Just like they do on TV.* At the jail, they put me in a small cell for almost an hour before leading me downstairs for fingerprints and mug shots. Then to a holding room with square concrete benches. Those hard benches lined the walls of the square room and the center benches rose like caskets in four rows.

The room reeked of sleazy rednecks, underworld good-for-nothings, as Daddy would say. And they were all drunk. But what did I know... some could have been murderers. Or drug lords, rapists, prostitutes, dog abusers... all I knew is they didn't look like me. The respectable, well-dressed, smart and sensible me.

I kept to myself and tried to get comfortable on the concrete bench, looking down my nose at the mass of people stupid enough to end up in jail.

My one phone call was to Cowboy Logan. *He will bail me out; he'll know what to do.* The schoolhouse clock on the wall ticked loudly as I waited. And waited. And waited.

Two hours later, a butchy-looking woman in a skin-tight uniform entered the holding room and barked like a seal. Feeling like a common criminal, I followed her to the cashier window to retrieve my belongings. I was free to go.

The sun was up; it was hot. A few paces from the jail's exit door, Logan huffed on a cigarette as if the stick was life itself. He stood out from the navy-suit downtown lawyers, dressed in casual-Friday khakis and a Stetson hat... looking handsome.

He saw me and laughed. Cackled, in fact. I thought nothing about that day was funny. Nothing at all. I felt my knees weaken as tears came to my eyes. "Don't laugh at me, Buttwipe."

"Aww, you poor baby," he said, but he spoke through laughter. Then sweet Logan pulled me into his chest and wrapped his long, soft arms around me tightly, even though he continued to laugh. I ignored his bucking chest and sobbed on his shirt, staining it with last night's makeup.

"Oh, my cowboy, my savior. Thank you so much for coming. I'm so messed up, so crazy-upset. I knew you would be my knight in shining armor." More mumbles of gratitude, more sobbing. I felt despondent and doomed, happy Logan had come, horrified by my situation, guilty for what I'd done, pissed that I'd been caught, scared they'd throw me *under* the jail... in that order and three times around the cycle.

After fifteen minutes of crying, I said, "What should I do first?"

"First, quit crying and grab that coffee I brought. It's yours."

"Bless you! I need coffee more than anything."

"That's not what you said the other night." Logan's eyebrow shot up and immediately came down to accommodate a wink.

"Stop it! I'm in serious trouble! And you wouldn't believe the kind of people in there!"

"No worries. I've got it handled."

As I had hoped, Logan took over. He drove to an ATM so I could get the cash I'd need to get my van. The waiting area at what we jokingly called the "dog pound" was wall to wall with people... another group of good-for-nothings, including one acne-face guy I recognized from the holding cell just a few hours prior. I waited in the Green Line for twenty minutes, only to find I was in the wrong line. The window at the Blue Line was popular, obviously, with about thirty people waiting in a crooked snake.

"Lela Fox?" the fat black cashier asked. The papers she demanded were in the glove box of my van; Logan walked with me across the 200-yard lot to gather them. We held hands walking back to the block building... now to wait in the Red Line. Frustration!

Finally, we sat, waiting on the lot man to bring the van to the exit area. "Jeez, Logan, why the rigamarole? This is the most disorganized bunch of shit I've ever seen–"

"You're the low man on this totem pole, sweetness. Get used to it because the courts will be exactly the same." Logan looked away, but the burn of his brown eyes stayed. He was right.

A long rush of air came from deep in my lungs. *Courts. What if I get my license taken away? Oh, I'm in deep shit.* Along with the sinking feeling in the pit of my stomach, I was bleary-eyed with a hangover and tired as hell.

"Shit, Logan! I feel like such a loser. I don't deserve this!"

"Or maybe you do."

"Shut up! Don't make me feel worse." I commiserated with a series of mumbles to which Logan didn't reply. My emotions ran the gamut of regret to indignation. Then I realized the responsibilities of the rest of the day remained. This was just a bump in time. "Oh, no!" I said too loud. Heads turned.

I turned to finish the thought with a Logan-only whisper. "Caroline will be at my house in twenty minutes, ready to work."

"I guess she won't have to wake you today."

True statement. "Which only reminds me how much I need a shot of vodka in this coffee."

"Maybe it should be a sober day," Logan suggested with a sideways chuckle.

"Why? There's no reason to–"

Interrupting our hush-hush conversation, a man with a slice of pasty-white belly bulging beneath his soiled mechanic's shirt stepped inside. "Fox!" he called in a slow, back-country accent.

Logan followed me out of that horrific place, then helped me into the waiting van. As I re-adjusted the driver's seat, he planted a kiss on my cheek through the still-open door. "See you tomorrow. I should know more by then. I've put in a call to a lawyer, a good friend of Mel's, and I think he can get you out of this with no problem."

"No shit? Out of it altogether? How?"

"Just leave that to me. See you tomorrow, Curly Britches. Never fear, the Fix-It-Man is here!"

"My dad says that, too!"

He ignored the comment. "I'll tell you one thing, girl: you're lucky it was Barney Fife who found you first. That's the ticket out. Security guards don't make much money, always hungry for a little on the side."

My eyes bulged out of their sockets. "You're going to *bribe* him? My God! That's illegal!"

Logan laughed. "Illegal? You're worried about *illegal?* Think about it, Lela... who just got out of jail?"

Oh. Right. "Well you don't have to be so–"

Logan patted my thigh a few times. "Calm down, baby. I'll take care of it and I'll cover the lawyer's retainer. If something goes whacko, I'll get Mel to intervene. He has connections with judges and shit... that's Plan B."

A broken-down Chevy pulled behind me, alarmingly close to my bumper. Logan spoke fast. "You gotta go. And I hope Caroline found something to do. Time is money, ya know." He closed the driver's side door and blew me a kiss like a girl.

I drove back to West Rockville in a daze. *Damn! DUI. Lola will have to drive us to the shows, drive me everywhere. This is gonna suck cheese. And what if I have to spend time in jail? I am so screwed! Mom and Dad will find out! And Andy! You dumbass Lela Fox.*

It was 10:30 AM when I arrived at the green house and as I feared, Caroline's car was in the driveway. *Good girl, Caroline. But now go home.* She met me at the door, blubbering about how worried she had been... had bad I looked. Blah, blah, blah. I interrupted her incessant high-pitched words to yell, "Chill the hell out! I'm going to bed. Go home. Don't worry... I'll pay you for the whole day."

She continued the chatter as I turned my back and trudged up the steps. A few minutes later, I heard her loud grumbling muffler as she backed out of the driveway.

<<<<<<<<>>>>>>

Three days later, I met with the lawyer Logan had hired. Charles Mossman. A name way too close to Charles Manson, I thought, but his looks were the polar opposite of his infamous sound-alike. Three-piece suit, cufflinks, a mirrorlike shine on expensive shoes... an attorney straight from Central Casting. He, too, assured me I'd get out of the DUI with no problems. "Security guards rarely make it to the courtroom," he said.

"You mean you break their knees?" I asked, whispering.

Charles laughed a hoot, then another hoot. "You think this is the Mafia?"

"Well... I don't know about these things... I'm just a simple girl who–"

"Then I'll just keep it simple for you. If this security guy doesn't show up to testify, even if the cop shows, your case will be dismissed. And that's the goal. That's what you pay me for."

"But how can you be so sure he'll be a no-show?"

The lawyer pulled at his cufflinks, straightening them just so. "Money talks, Ms. Fox. They're coming down hard on DUI cases these days, the whole country and definitely the platform of our new fuckhead mayor. They're calling it an epidemic."

"I guess it *is* an epidemic. And dangerous as hell. A drunk driver could kill somebody!"

His brow knotted as I finished the sentence. "Drama, drama, Ms. Fox." He cleared his throat and shuffled papers on his desk.

"Are we finished here?"

"Until next time. I see you've filled out the contact information we need. I'll be in touch."

"Can you say when?"

"Before your court date. That will suffice."

I stuttered a few "but, but" sentences; he wouldn't commit to any specifics. Finally, I stood and shook his hand. "Thank you, Charles Mossman. Do whatever you can because I can't afford to have this on my record."

"In the meantime, keep your nose clean. No more drinking and driving. Another arrest would cloud the waters."

"Understood."

I stepped into the elevator feeling like a low-class loser. All that money from Logan... all the deceit getting ready to happen... and I wasn't even that fucked-up at the time! I mean... I pulled over because I was sleepy! What's the big deal?

The two weeks between the arrest and the court date were a blur; I was flat-out scared and doubtful of my fitness as a person, a friend, a girlfriend, a business owner. Hell, I couldn't even be a decent drunk.

I didn't honor the one-six-pack-at-a-time rule anymore, blaming the DUI on that stupid idea. However, realization hit. I grasped the concept that the cause my problem wasn't stockpiling beer. No, it was the beer in my belly. So I did what I'd done before and switched back to vodka. I bought the biggest bottle the liquor store had and stocked up on tonic water and grapefruit juice. Now settled in, I sat back to bide my time.

I felt the slow erosion of depression drag my soul down, down, down. *Fucking Bi-Polar bullshit. How can I be depressed with all the medicine I'm taking?* Each day I thought of calling the obese psychiatrist and asking for more meds, or fewer meds, or a fucking machine gun.

The lower I fell, the more I slept. Soon it became Lola's job to wake me at one o'clock instead of Caroline's job at ten. I was a no-show at a series of events, including a family gathering at Jennifer's, missing a chance to see my parents... which *never* happened. And despite Lola's urging, I blew off a weekend art show in Columbia, South Carolina. Booked months ago, paid for, and destined to be a profitable weekend... my depression was bigger than any logical reasoning.

"Fuck it" became my motto. I don't remember laying drunk during those weeks... I think I was too depressed to drink that much.

<<<<<<<>>>>>>

Logan met me at the entrance to the courtroom though I didn't ask and didn't expect him to be there. I'd never been in a court other than my two visits at divorce court and I was, literally, shaking with fear. Logan held my hand and purred assurances, also telling me what was happening with the judge, the bailiff, and the mechanics of what happens in a criminal courtroom.

"So how do you know all this, country boy?"

"I've had my share of courtroom appearances."

"DUI?"

"Twice."

"And you still have your license?"

"They were years apart. And it didn't used to be such a big deal... almost expected from a McMann County redneck kid. But they still don't yank your license with just one charge, Lela. And you won't get charged anyway, so you have no worries at all." The pats on my thigh emphasized each syllable of the last sentence.

"How can you be so sure I won't be charged?"

Logan chuckled. One quick one, a pause, then a series of chuckles building to a silent belly laugh. That's when the lady in the purple dress walked in.

She took a seat beside me, scooting in close... so close that a waft of her perfume encompassed me. She wore an air of confidence that smelled as expensive as her perfume as she pulled a clipboard from her designer bag. The movement flashed a glint on her red, oversized *Mothers Against Drunk Driving* lapel pin.

Shit.

A typed form topped her clipboard, and I saw my name, first on the list of twenty-or-so names. I turned to Logan to tell him what I'd seen, but he put a finger to his lips and shook his head no. *Oh. Quiet around MADD. I understand that.* My frazzled nerves took off like a rocket.

The judge entered the courtroom and everybody stood. That much I knew would happen. I watched eight DUI cases and thought I understood what would happen with mine. The unnerving part was the MADD lady ruffling papers as each case paraded in front of the judge, huffing a sigh when the case was dismissed. Then she'd scribble notes on the police reports stapled on the back of what looked like a profile sheet of the accused. Very organized, very official-looking.

When they called my case, I heard her papers shuffling, and that's where my memory fails me. I'm sure she circled the name of the notably absent Barney Fife.

Sure enough, the case was dismissed. I was free, off the hook. As I walked back to the bench where Logan sat, my knees gave out, the air in the courtroom seemed to disappear, leaving none for my lungs. "I don't feel so good, Logan," I said, "I think I'm going to faint."

He grabbed my purse from the bench and pushed me out of the courtroom. The rest of the day remains a blur. In fact, several days... maybe months were a blur.

After the court date, I remained depressed, but not so much that I rejected my lovely bottle of Popov Vodka. I was lost in the bottle and close to reaching my bottom; the term "bottom" had stuck in my mind, hearing it in the *one* AA meeting I attended.

I thought "reaching my bottom" may be what was happening and I

thought the answer was to fight it… to "pull myself up by the bootstraps," as Daddy would have said. Or as I say now, "fetch myself up sharply."

The first eight months in the green house were miserable for me, the classic going-down of an alcoholic at the end of the disease.

I could feel myself falling into a hellish hole, and on rare mornings when I woke up sober, I swore off alcohol and trickery. But once I started drinking, with just one little drink in me, all hopes of improvement flew out the window.

Something had to give. Something had to happen. And in the eighth month of the green-house lease, something did happen.

SMALL PRINT
CHAPTER 8

I slept late one steamy Saturday morning in July, not hearing the plop of the *Rockville News-Courier* hitting the front porch. Stumbling downstairs, I brewed a pot of coffee and, as I waited, spread the newspaper on the coffee table.

Reading the news was an every-morning routine, a way to catch up without having to watch the idiot anchors on TV.

Being a word freak from birth, I could feed the need, first with the crossword puzzle then the word scramble. Today I sighed, unable to solve either.

I often imagined the assholes-nerds who designed such puzzles, overpaid evil snobs, hell-bent on embarrassing even the most educated. They probably had a quota of "easy ones," and hated those days, making fun amongst themselves in the lunch room. Another sigh.

I was fighting it but worried that the weeks-long depression caused by the court system was the beginning of a major depressive episode.

Prior to that trauma, my mood had been consistent for six months, a miracle considering the circumstances. But lately I'd been low and going lower, unable to fight it off despite the latest pharmaceutical cocktail.

Why worry? Like you're going to change it? Like you can control your brain chemicals? I turned on the music and settled in with a bowl of Captain Crunch. Killing time, I scanned the classified ads to see if there was anything interesting for sale, cheap. Not much unless you needed farm equipment. I looked at dogs for sale, lost and found, and several more.

Eventually, my eye roved to the employment ads and my mind churned. *What if I got a REAL job? Steady money. But can I do it?* I paused to think. *Hell, no! Who would want a real job?*

"No advertising jobs listed, anyway. And nobody wants a washed-up writer," I said to the dog, who wagged his tail in response, "Now people think they can do it themselves."

Basic photo-editing and page-layout software had just become available for the common man and it changed the advertising business completely, especially for smaller clients with needs bigger than their budgets.

I folded the classified section back to its original shape, leaving only a few categories visible. First up were the Legal Notices... lawyers with info about dead people, searching for their heirs, wives hoping to find missing husbands, stuff like that.

Next came the personals: men seeking women, men seeking men. Curious, I read a few of the ads. *What if I could find a nice guy and start all over? Somebody who doesn't know my past, who wouldn't call me a bitch, a loser, a drunk. Someone who wouldn't know how fucked up I am.*

With the next-to-last spoonful of Captain Crunch, a dollop of milk overflowed my spoon and plopped on an ad near the top.

(Under Men Seeking Women)

Charming romantic, 40 yrs old, 5'8" & fit. Educated. Seeking funny, happy woman for conversation, fine dining, 80s music, holding hands, snuggling at fireplace. Must love dogs. Stuart W. #3279

Interesting... The ideal forty years old, just two years older than me. Is 5'8" short or tall? Educated is good, and it says "fit" so... not fat. A "charming romantic" sounds wonderful! And "must love dogs" makes it perfect!

I read the ad again. *Really, Lela? Would you dare do this?*

Buzzing thoughts were loud in my head. I never imagined I'd be the type to answer a personal ad, but I knew there weren't a lot of places to meet nice men.

They're not at the bars where I hang out, that's for sure. And where else would they be? Church? Hell, no! The art museum? Fuck it! Your friends didn't know any single men or you'd already be dating. There's nobody new to meet. I flipped past the Personals section, to Houses for Rent, but my mind kept going back to what I'd read.

Lela, your mother would flip out if you found a boyfriend in the newspaper! Drop it. Then I skipped to the Want to Buy section to see if I had anything somebody else wanted. Another sigh. I couldn't concentrate and flipped the page backward. *He doesn't sound like a psycho or anything...*

The number at the end of the ad was like an extension number. To answer the ad, you called the main number and entered those four digits. Then you'd hear a recorded message from the person who placed the ad. *Hmm. What could it hurt? I don't have to leave a message or talk to him. So I could just listen... see what he sounds like.*

I called. The message repeated the words in his ad and offered nothing new, except to say he was from Florida. It was a nice, happy-sounding voice. He laughed a few times but it may have been from nerves. I guessed it took balls to place a personal ad; I couldn't have done it. But could I answer this ad? *Dare I do it?*

The message ended and a long beep played. I heard the click of the voice recorder turning on but I chickened out and hung up without leaving a message.

<<<<<<<><>>>>>>

That afternoon, at Mel Durren's pool with Lola, Debbie Doo-Doo, and a new girl called Bowden, I mentioned the ad. Lola wouldn't even let me finish the sentence. "No, no, no! No!" There were murmurs of agreement from the others as she looked me straight in the eye. "Lela, don't do it. Promise me. You never know who you'll meet... a mass murderer, pervert... who knows?"

I responded immediately. "Well, we'd meet at a public place! I'm not *that* stupid!" I felt attacked and went on the offensive. Just then, Baron and Blitz came back out to the pool; they had gone inside to fix a drink and bring snacks. Lola told them what I had said, but exaggerated, saying I already had a date. So, again, I chose offense.

"Hey, I didn't say I was *going*, for God's sake! I'm not stupid! Just looking for opinions."

Blitz, ever my protector, spoke without hesitation. "Right, you're not stupid, Lela. Only stupid people answer personal ads." I opened my mouth to argue, but he kept talking. "Besides, you've got *us*, so how could you be lonely? It's a dumb idea, Lela Fox. Your dumbest idea yet... and there have been plenty to choose from."

The rest of the group, my closest friends, agreed with Blitz. Shouts of "I'll take you on a date," and "Who needs a damn man, anyway?" and "I'd be scared to death!" echoed around the pool. I looked at my friends. None smiled.

My lips squeezed thin. "Y'all can kiss my ass," I shot back.

<<<<<<<>>>>>>

I got home around five o'clock, drunk and sunburned. I had forgotten about my dog, leaving him hungry for the day. "So sorry, Murphy! Poor little doggy! Mommy's a bad girl!" I doubled up on his food, overfilling the bowl. Murphy ate the kibble, looking at me between bites. I screamed at the dog, "Quit shaming me! Don't give me that evil-eye look!" I wasn't more delusional than normal; I sincerely believed Murphy judged me and my drinking. He had seen it all.

Deciding my day was over, I plopped on the sofa and turned on the TV, sun-zapped. Sometime during *Wheel of Fortune*, Murphy joined me in a nice, long nap. The sun was going down when I awoke. Only one lamp was on: the one that shined on the newspaper classified ads. I had circled the ad from "Must love dogs" in a red Sharpie and it glowed in the lamplight.

The time was 8:50 PM, and the night was young.

A YELLOW ROSE
CHAPTER 9

The magnifying side of my makeup mirror let me see each individual eyelash. The new mascara I bought that day coated each one, one at a time, in a perfect flow of "Blackest Black." I had killer eyelashes; ask any woman I'd ever known. Enviable eyes, they said. Blue-green and "lit from behind." After coating each bottom lash in the same OCD manner, my face was on. Mascara was the only eye makeup I wore. No sparkly shadow or eyeliner for me. Too girly.

I wanted to look my best that night; I had a date. On the phone the night before, I had talked to Stuart "Must Love Dogs" Weinstein for almost two hours! We would meet at the Sassy Steer at seven o'clock sharp; he'd be carrying a single yellow rose, he said. In fact, I remember his exact words: "A yellow rose is a symbol of true friendship... a friendship we are sure to have." We had fun on the phone; he seemed like a great guy with a sense of humor that matched mine, leaning to the corny side.

I got as much scoop as I could, trying to discover his worthiness as a boyfriend, and he had talked about his life with ease. He was in the transmission business, he said, had owned his own repair shop in Fort Lauderdale, but after six years of raking in the dough, he explained, he got burned out. "I walked away from it... left the key in the lock. Lost it all," another exact quote. There seemed to be more to the story than he admitted... something about an ex-wife trying to get his money.

He had also shared his childhood memories, most the opposite of my working-class family remembrances. He grew up in Westchester County, New York... and that spoke volumes. Westchester County is the home of high-rollers, some of the wealthiest zip codes in America. I knew that trivia because one of my ex-husband's cronies had been a golf pro in Yonkers.

As Stuart told more of his story, he shared his loneliness. He'd moved to Tennessee after a divorce from his crazy wife of six years, leaving his almost-five-year-old son in Florida. My heart broke as he described his pain.

Then, the ending quote: "I don't know a soul in Rockville and I hope you can show me around." The giggle afterward had intrigued me. It wasn't the least bit manly... more of a girl-giggle. *How could a guy who giggles be a bad guy?*

About his looks, he said he'd started turning gray in his early 30s. "More salt than pepper now," he said. Stuart admitted to a little beer belly, but said he worked out "on occasion," and, I quote, "You won't be embarrassed to be seen with me." It sounded honest enough.

I hadn't called Lola to tell her I was going out; nobody knew I had answered the ad, half because I was leery, and half because my friends had been so against it. I didn't want to hear their paranoia crap. Stuart seemed to be like any normal guy looking for a girlfriend.

<<<<<<<>>>>>>

I wore a blue-and-white top, on the skimpy side, and my favorite white jeans, which were too tight, I admit. I walked into the bar at Sassy Steer and spotted him with ease. Yellow rose. Gray hair... *there's no pepper at all, dude! But it's nice hair and a nice look.* He wore a navy sports coat and a striped button-down shirt with brown dress pants. With one foot on the bottom rung of the bar stool, I noticed his brown loafers; they looked new and expensive.

Overall, a sexy and nice-looking guy. "Must Love Dogs" looks A-OK fine! Fear number one checked off the list.

He caught my eye and smiled, raising his glass in a toast. Then he stuck the yellow rose behind his ear, raised his eyebrows, and crossed his arms as if doing a Romanian dance or something. It was truly funny, and I laughed. Stuart motioned me toward him.

People had crowded in the bar, and it took some maneuvering to get to the table on the far side. He stood to greet me, took my hand, and kissed it while staring at me through thick black eyelashes. Kissing my hand made me think of my hot Ecuadorian lover and the first time I met Logan. *Why is it that men kiss my hand? Do they think it's an original act... something to melt my heart on the spot? I'll admit – it's memorable, but it seems like Must Love Dogs could do better.*

Just to be contrary, I reached for *his* hand and smeared a big smack-a-roo on his knuckles. "Whoa!" was all he said, looking sheepish. *Good! I need to keep him guessing. Be your silly self, Lela! Bring out the confident woman in you, the one that cracks people up, the Lela that loves herself and others. But remember... don't get drunk and don't sleep with him. Remember the chant you sang on the way here. Don't get drunk, no matter what.*

Stuart passed the long-stem rose to my hand; the smell was faint but sweet. "Hello, Ms. Lela Fox. I assume you've figured out that I'm Stuart." His face was scrubbed and shiny with blue-gray eyes sparkling over dark-pink lips, lips upturned in a genuine smile. The smile coupled with a nervous laugh that sounded like the girl-giggle I heard last night. *Manners, roses, a sport coat, a kiss on the hand... and a giggle. Let your guard down, girl. You're not out with a serial killer.*

Stuart motioned for me to sit. "What to drink, dear?" I was in a wine mood and told him the house Chardonnay would be great. "Oh, but no!" he said, "No house wine for *my* date. Let's get a table." He stood and took my hand, marching in front of me and directly to the hostess stand. I supposed he had talked to her beforehand because she called him by name.

"Follow me, Mr. Weinstein," she said. Stuart put his hand in the small of my back to usher me forward ahead of him. A touch in that spot always sent shivers down my spine. It felt like a sign of gentleness and respect; I felt instantly adored.

"Is this the table you wanted, Mr. Weinstein?" the hostess asked.

"The exact one. Thank you." In one fluid motion, he pulled out his wallet and slipped her a ten. I had never seen anybody tip the hostess at a regular restaurant, for God's sake, but he had done it. Admittedly, it was a nice place... and the best table in the place, but the action appalled me.

"Stuart! A tip for a *hostess? Here?* This isn't The Four Seasons!"

"She's been saving this table for us... a half-hour now. It's away from the pack, in a cozy corner. I wanted it to be perfect for you." A waiter appeared almost instantly. Stuart reached for his wallet again and held out a twenty-dollar bill. "You won't turn this table tonight, you see? Don't rush us, but don't worry... I'll make it worth your while." The waiter stared at the money without speaking, not understanding, perhaps, then he snatched the bill. Stuart held on briefly and looked him in the eye. "Bring your wine list, please, and another Crown and Coke."

Again, I was shocked. His behavior was so out of the norm for East Tennesseans; it's considered uncouth to "buy" service workers beyond an accepted after-the-fact tip to servers. *So he's rich, and trying to impress you... and he's a Yankee who doesn't know Southern rules. It doesn't make him a bad guy, just... odd. And you like odd, right?* I tried to shake off my discomfort but envisioned my sister Karen's face in this circumstance. She would hate him instantly. Her disdain for rich people, and of Yankees in particular, ran to the extreme. And she couldn't stand people who tried to use money to impress people.

Maybe he *was* an asshole-hotshot-Yankee, but he got what he wanted: the best table and no obligation to hurry. He saw my face, half-impressed and half-confused, and said, "What? We need the time and place to get to know each other, and here we are." I laid the yellow rose on the table as he held the chair for me to sit.

Stuart sat across from me and held the rose upright, the stem resting on our white tablecloth. "Madame! The rose speaks!" The fragrant smell wafted toward me. Stuart's cadence sounded like he was making a speech to a British queen. "The yellow rose of friendship has been shared... Lela Fox and Stuart Weinstein, at the royal Sassy Steer, at the beginning of a long and happy bond!" I blushed. *He's funny. I like him.*

We both had steak and shrimp. I drank the entire bottle of wine, a very nice French Chardonnay, and he drank several more rounds himself. We were just the right amount of tipsy to talk uninhibited and tease each other a bit.

He asked about my former advertising career and seemed intrigued by the inner-workings of my traveling-display jewelry business. It was easy to talk to him because he seemed honestly interested.

After the meal, we shared a huge slice of cheesecake and sipped hot coffee. I leaned back, stuffed and happy. "That was excellent, Stuart. Thank you." He insisted that "next time" we would go somewhere more in line with his gourmet taste. He hadn't studied the offerings in Rockville, he said. I mentioned several places that Cowboy Logan and I had frequented, but he mentioned a guidebook I didn't recognize and said he would look there. *A guidebook to Rockville?*

"Stuart, I've lived in Rockville for 21 years... you don't need a *guidebook*, for Christ's sake!"

"Excuse me, for *whose* sake?"

My brow knotted, confused. Then it hit me. *Weinstein. He's Jewish.* "Har har. You'll find only a mere sprinkling of Jewish people in Rockville; with only four synagogues on this side of town. See, now you'll have to contend with the polar opposite. This is the buckle of the Bible Belt, Mr. Sir. Overrun with Southern Baptists, the hypocritical mother-fuckers."

"I'm not active in the synagogue anyway, but I used to be. The family thing, right? My father was a Cantor." He saw my confused looked and instantly explained. "The leader of the singing, to simplify."

"Okay..."

"Went to Hebrew school, had the Bar Mitzvah, all that. But now I don't go to services at all...haven't since I was in my early twenties, but my fucking ex-wife was so Jewish it pissed me off. She had a thing for the Rabbi, I think."

"Whaaat?"

"You think that doesn't happen?"

"Well... I don't–"

"Why are we talking about religion? Not a subject to discuss on a first date! Not politics, either." Stuart said, draining his drink.

"You're right. My guess is you're almost always right." It never hurts to stroke a first date's ego, right? "So let me ask you... no bullshit, okay?" I played him, pretending the question would be deep and ultimately personal. He nodded with wide eyes. "Do you play pool?" I asked.

He laughed. "That's *one* way to change the subject."

"I'm straight-forward like that."

"I like it. I absolutely like it! And of *course* I play pool, as they call it in the South. It's billiards, I'll have you know, and I'm an ace player."

"Billiards my ass. It's called 'pool' in these parts, buddy." I threw my head back to laugh, and the room took a little spin; I almost lost my balance sitting in the damn chair. "Whoa there!" I said as the dizziness ebbed.

"Are you okay?"

"Yeah, just a little drunk. You?"

"Perfectly so."

Stuart threw a handful of twenties on the table and swerved around the table to pull out my chair. "So chivalry isn't dead?" I remembered asking some other guy the same thing, some random guy maybe, but this time, I decided I'd put much weight on his answer. It would determine his intentions and potential, determine if the gentleman act was phony or sincere.

He answered after a hoot of a laugh. "A pretty lady, hilariously funny and shit-faced drunk, deserves the Queen Treatment all the way. I am at your service, Madame."

<<<<<<<>>>>>>

He said he'd drive, and I was too drunk to object... too drunk to risk another DUI, so I agreed. The pool hall I liked best was about ten miles away and we went straight down Valley Pike, red lights and all, because I wanted bright lights and lots of people around. The paranoia of a "blind date" had returned, though he said nothing or did nothing to spark the need for it.

His car was a snazzy Lexus with all the bells and whistles, sleek, glossy black and brand-spanking-new. I pushed a variety of buttons just to see what they did and Stuart stammered through a comment that confused me. "There you go again, pushing all my buttons, Lela."

"Ha ha! That's a good one, Stuart!"

"No, babe. You're pushing more buttons than you know."

"But you're a gentleman, right? You're not going to assault me in the pool hall?"

"I wouldn't assault you anywhere, not here and not there, not in a box, not with a fox, not in a house or with a mouse, not in the rain or on a train, I would not assault you, gentleman I am."

I laughed as he finished. "So how do you know all the words?"

"I was the bedtime reader to my son." Then he clenched his jaw, staring straight ahead in silence.

"Sorry, man."

Ten seconds later, he said, "That's another topic to avoid, like religion and politics, I guess. At least for me. I miss my son terribly."

"Do you ever get to see him?"

"I'm a thousand-plus miles away... and his bitch of a mother makes me walk a tightwire in return for a damn afternoon in the park."

"Can she *do* that? I mean legally?"

"She's found a way. You were lucky for all those years sharing Bo. That's a story that makes me smile."

"But I've lost him now. These past ten days have been the longest of my life."

"They'll get longer."

"Thanks for the encouragement."

Stuart laughed and said, "aww" at the same time. "I'm sorry. I didn't mean it like that, babe."

It was my turn to be silent. The light turned green, and I directed him to the left. "Down the big hill and behind the building."

"Dark back here."

"You won't assault me in the dark, either, right?"

His laugh was genuine. "Not here, not there, not anywhere. Stuart patted my thigh and turned toward me immediately after putting the Lexus in park. "Hey... look at me. You're safe with me, okay? I will honor your wishes, but only hope your wishes include fucking my lights out. Because see... I think we're meant to be."

My silent stare lasted several seconds before I huffed a chuckle. "We'll see, won't we?"

"Just thanks for giving me the chance."

EIGHT BALL
CHAPTER 10

"No scotch, no vodka. Beer on tap only," the pool hall bartender barked in a gruff, long-time smoker's voice. I laughed when Stuart placed the order, wondering why he would think an East Tennessee pool hall would serve liquor.

"You damn Yankees don't know shit. It's a pool hall, for God's sake!"

Stuart said nothing as he passed a cup of Budweiser to my hungry-for-it hand. I chuckled, wondering if the man had ever had a Budweiser in his life.

"A dollar a game?" he asked.

"No way. I'm weird about gambling. See, I grew up thinking it was the work of the devil. My parents are 100 percent against gambling of any sort, even door prize drawings. Mom's father was a compulsive gambler *and* an alcoholic, and she won't do anything he used to do. She had a pretty fucked-up childhood. I guess Daddy just went along with her Goody-Two-Shoes rules."

"Is that why your parents created a fairytale childhood for you? Protected from the big, bad world? Because I can't decide if I should call you cute and innocent, or clueless."

A deep intake of breath, ready to defend myself with anger... with a pause long enough to settle it down. "I am neither innocent nor clueless, I'll have you know. And don't compare me to your New York City girlfriends, big guy. I yam what I yam and I do just fine."

"Point taken." I doubted it, but he stammered to start a light-hearted conversation about the vast differences between East Tennessee and New York City, now complimenting the area and the "friendly, naïve people." *Was that the first red flag, Lela? He's a damn Yankee snob? Pay off the 'little people' and sail through life with high-class charm and manners... is that his schtick?* Whatever his intention, I ignored it, too drunk to stay angry and too interested in him to let the date be over.

"I need another beer, please."

"Coming right up!"

Stuart chose the table in the back, and during the first game, when I hadn't warmed up my arm or focused my priorities, Stuart beat the crap out of me. I took only three piss-poor shots, and he sunk the eight ball with ease.

I discovered more about his past during the game. He had graduated from high school in Geneva, Switzerland... at Collège du Léman, an international school. His pronunciation of the words thrilled me; spoken like a silk scarf rubbing my belly. I made him repeat it over and over. He went to his first year of college in Switzerland, too, he said, at The University of Geneva.

"Why Switzerland? Why so far away?" He explained Switzerland schools are some of the best in the world and he was lucky to have been able to go. "Did you finish college?" I asked.

"Nope. Lost interest. My parents are too damn wealthy and wanted me to come home to run the family foundation, but I bought the transmission shop instead, International Transmission, and worked my ass off."

"That's the other thing... why transmissions?" Stuart seemed way too upscale for car repair, owner or not.

"Most profit, least liability." His answer was quick. "I made the money, but Crazy Janey took it all away."

"Your ex-wife is Crazy Janey?"

"Yep. She screwed me at every turn, all to get my family's money. Mother won't speak her name. There's a lot more to that story, but I'll leave it at that."

Through a laugh, I said, "Oh, I know the pitfalls of ex-spouse bullshit, too. I'll keep mine to myself for now, too." Then a thought hit... a small detail that any date would need to know. "Uh... I guess I should tell you I'm still officially married. The divorce isn't final yet. Doesn't bother me, but it may–"

"Doesn't bother me either, unless he's a big jealous ogre, stalking you."

"No way."

"Does he know you're dating?"

"Miller doesn't *care* if I'm dating. I dated before I left him, actually. Big time. He didn't give a shit then, and definitely doesn't give a shit now. Besides, he's a pussy." I don't know why I said that last line... maybe to stress just how uninterested Miller was, or maybe to express my continuing disdain for him.

"Good. I'll relax," he said. "So tell me about your son."

I sighed. Paused. The mention of Bo seemed to start the process of sobering up. I missed him already, and the last goodbye had been an emotional breakdown for me, literally. My answer was a squeak. "He's fifteen, plays baseball... I can't talk about him right now. I'm still too..." I couldn't finish the sentence; my voice had cracked on the last word. With a deep breath, I changed the subject. "Your turn. Tell me about *your* son."

He smiled, staring through me into some scene of his imagination. "Jeremy. A great kid. Smart. Wild imagination. Loves dinosaurs." He chuckled. There was a long pause. "But his so-called mother has turned him against me so much he hates me. Janey thinks I'm 'a bad influence' and tells Jeremy I'm dangerous. The truth is she just likes to fuck with me."

"That sucks. So sorry th–"

"The bitch demanded *supervised* visitation. I can't see him one-on-one."

"I've never heard of that. And why?"

"She thinks I'm on drugs or something. But like I say, mostly she just wants to mess with my mind, get me in trouble with the law or whoever has authority. And she knows every trick in the book, likes to get the police and the courts involved."

"Oh." I couldn't think of anything more to say.

"So finally, two months ago, I couldn't stand it anymore. Had to leave. I packed a few things, left the business unlocked, and walked away. Started driving north, destination unknown. Just me and my dog."

"Your dog! That's right... we haven't talked about him yet. Your ad said, 'Must love dogs.' That's the reason I picked yours over the others, by the way."

"Good! And yeah, my dog is like my child. I take him to work, take him everywhere. Until Tennessee, his name was Rocky, but now he's Rock-Bob."

I laughed. "Rock-Bob! You're a hoot."

"Something else about Rock-Bob. He likes M&Ms, but only the green ones."

I was laughing hard, cracking up. "You're looney-tunes, Stuart Weinstein." He joined me in laughter and put his hands on my waist, suddenly lifting me to sit on the edge of the pool table. Then he leaned forward to kiss me. I kissed back. Hard.

"Mmm," I moaned, half-kidding and half-serious. "Nice kiss."

"There's more where that came from." He gazed at me... the kind of gaze where they soften the focus in movies. I felt my pulse build as a buzz between my ears throbbed in my temples. I wanted him... wanted him bad.

Stuart held the gaze for what seemed like hours, then sent chills up my spine with wet kisses on my neck, breathy whispers in my ear, ending with the breathiest whisper of all: "Let's go to your house."

"I promised myself I wouldn't get drunk and sleep with you." Stuart looked at me with an exaggerated pout, a frown deep enough to be a cartoon. "But I'll make you a deal."

"The answer will be yes."

"Let's get another beer, maybe two at the same time, and play two more games."

"Done." And Stuart disappeared in a heartbeat, heading to the bar at double pace.

He let me break and I followed up by sinking three more balls, but easy shots. I missed the first one that required a bank shot. "Dammit! That's the only bad thing about being drunk – it makes me a bad pool player."

He chuckled as he chalked his cue and eyed his shot. "I'm going to make you have to lean waaay over to hit the cue ball."

"Cheater."

"I like the look from behind." He did as he threatened; I could've used the bridge, but decided to lean over seductively and cock my leg on the corner of the table. I blatantly teased him and knew it was inappropriate for a first date, but I craved the attention he gave me, feeling alive for the first time in months.

Stuart's eyes lit up and sparkled, glowing from the small pub table in the corner. "Woo-wee! Encore! Encore!" I turned to grin at him, playing my best vixen. I saw his eyes roam the hourglass of my body, head to toe. Stuart's eyebrows moved as he challenged me: "Do it again."

"Well, I'll have to do it again, babe. I guess you didn't notice I sunk the shot."

"I sure as hell wasn't looking at the table. Do it again! Hurry." His knee was jacking up and down on the rung of the stool as he fidgeted to light a cigarette.

I sank three more balls, leaning as far over as I could with each shot, purposefully. He cheered in the background, smoking the hell out of that cigarette and continuing to fidget. Finally, I missed. "Yours. I missed an easy one... too drunk, I guess."

Maybe for the first time in that game of pool, Stuart looked at the table. Four balls left. "Damn, girl! You weren't kidding – you're pretty good."

"No, not just *pretty* good, I'm *damn* good." A glowing sense of power overtook me. I had confidence now... and an audience. As Stuart drew the pool stick backward, I shouted, "Harder! Harder!" He missed the shot. My turn. I cleared the table.

<<<<<<<>>>>>>

When we walked into my house that night, close to two AM, my normally chilled-out dog growled at Stuart eight times. Murphy had never growled at *anybody!* My first reaction was to believe it was a warning, an omen.

I got down on all fours and talked to the dog nose-to-nose, telling him Stuart was okay and it was fine for me to sleep with him. But mostly I was showing off my ass, teasing the hell out of Stuart. I turned to speak to him. "But if Murphy doesn't like you, maybe I should kick you out." His immediate reply was that kicking him out would be a big mistake.

I smiled ear to ear, then turned to tell the dog I wouldn't dare make such a grave mistake. Another growl and Murphy snapped at me, millimeters from the tip of my nose.

"Did you see that? Murphy has *never* tried to bite me! You must be bad news, Stuart."

"Nah, he'll be happy once he meets Rock-Bob. Best friends, meant to be."

"Like us?"

"Exactly. Relax. Take it slow. I'll take good care of you, babe."

My entire drinking career, or maybe I should say my entire sex career, I'd promised to not sleep with somebody on a first date. But I always got too drunk, and only succeeded one time. I tried to "be good," tried to

follow the standards my mom had taught me but I… somehow… just couldn't do it. The thrill of being wanted, the need to be needed and desired – it always won in the end.

I know now that I was trying to create self-worth via others in a way least likely to be successful. Why? Because the Shame of what I'd done, whether admitted or not, always came to bite me in the ass.

The Shame that drove me, drove me to Shame.

THREE DOZEN RED
CHAPTER 11

After Stuart left, I fell into bed and slept for two hours. Around nine, when Caroline came to wake me, she noticed my white jeans on the floor with a huge stain: some kind of black grease. Laundry mistress that she was, Caroline gasped in horror. "Lela! What did you *do* last night?" No answer from me, just a laugh at Caroline being so perfectly herself. She inspected the jeans closer, wiggled her eyebrows, and smiled with an evil essence. "I think I can get that out." Serious as a preacher, she glared at me. "Do you have cornstarch?"

"Yes, I do, Miss Laundry. It's like you live for a homemaker challenge."

"What's wrong with that? Because I always win! Beat those stains, beat those stains!"

"Cornstarch is in the upper cabinet beside the stove."

I lit a cigarette and sipped the coffee my employee had brought. I now kept a vodka bottle in my bedside drawer for my coffee, but that day, I was still drunk from the night before. And still glowing with the effervescence of a wild night of sex and more sex.

Caroline came in to sit on my bed with a scrub brush and the paste of cornstarch. I talked as she scrubbed, telling her all about Stuart and how we met, adding scattered details. The last comment was that Murphy had growled at him; I knew she would find that funny. But she didn't laugh. In fact, she scowled.

"I'd trust Murphy more than a guy I found in a newspaper. Lela, are you sure about this?" Caroline was older than me, and a lot more conservative, so I took her worry with a grain of salt.

"Chill, Caroline. It's cool." Another cigarette; now my hands were shaking. "But I want you to meet him... because we have another date tonight. Oh, Caroline, I like him! A lot. A *whole* lot. And he's rich! Filthy rich!"

"Don't let that sway you, please. I fell for that once and it wasn't pretty. But... what about Logan? What happened to you and Logan?"

"Oh. Shit. So you don't know the story." I paused, feeling the burn of Shame come to my face. "Ask Lola. I fucked up. Got mad and called his wife. Told her who I was." Caroline didn't respond but looked down at the comforter, clenching her jaw.

"That's not good, Lela."

"No shit, Sherlock. Then the wife filed for divorce."

Caroline still hadn't looked at me. Then, as if she flipped a switch, she donned her cheerful happy housewife face and presented the jeans to show the absence of stain. "Caroline to the rescue! No stain can escape my potions!" she said, followed by an evil laugh. Comical... as if somebody or something could fear of a woman as happy and vanilla as Caroline.

She hefted herself off the end of the bed, smacking my ankle through the covers. "Get up! Time for work! Lola made a to-do list for you for the weekend. Do you accomplish anything?" I admitted I had not. The hefty woman sighed, her bosom expanding like a balloon. "Come on... get going."

<<<<<<<>>>>>>

Lola came in early that day. Excited, I repeated the details of my wild first date, despite the snarky look on her face. She wasn't happy. "Lela, you're crazy. You may not know it yet, but he still might be a mental case. A whole bottle of wine would cloud your judgement easily—"

"And a bunch of beer," I added, not realizing I'd added to the bad part.

"Even worse. What if you missed something? Lela, I know you, girl, and you're not such a great judge of character."

Just then, the phone rang. I rushed to answer. "Good morning, sexy lady." Stuart's voice was low and erotic, instantly sending a bundle of butterflies flying to my stomach. A throbbing of red flushed my face.

"Hang on a minute," I said, covering the mouthpiece and whispering to my employees. "It's him! I'm going downstairs for privacy. Don't bother me." As I hopped to the steps, I said, "And good morning to you, sir." First thing, I asked him if he knew how I had gotten black grease on my jeans.

"No clue," he said.

Stuart's voice continued to massage my ego and much more feminine parts of me. He purred, "So can we have lunch together? I can't wait all the way 'til tonight to see you!" I giggled; he continued. "I'd have to make it a quick lunch, but I want to bring something over. For you and your worker bees." Stuart's tone sounded hopeful, almost as if he was begging.

How can I possibly tell him no? He sounds so desperate! I mumbled a non-answer, which he ignored. "Okay, I'll be there at 12:10. With lunch for everybody. Tell them I'm coming."

"What? But–"

"No buts," he interrupted. "Tell Murphy I'm coming and bringing Rock-Bob. He might as well get used to us." Smiling, I sat back, hoping for a long and tender conversation, but a customer had arrived he said, and he clicked off abruptly.

Shocked, I stared at the phone as a rack of emotions pulsated through me. Pleasant surprise... anxiety... eagerness... and a beautifully sneaky feeling, like a teen in love. Stuart's interest in me was overwhelming and ultimately flattering, like he was goo-goo for me already. With a happy smile, I skipped up the steps to the studio.

"Heads up, girls! Stuart is bringing lunch for all of us, so put on your freshest face and sweetest smile." They looked at me, then at each other with mouths agape. I whistled *Off to See the Wizard* as I headed to the shower, feeling on top of the world.

<<<<<<<<>>>>>>>

Stuart brought a family-size container of spaghetti from Olive Garden with all the fixings and a dozen red roses for each of us. As expected, he oozed with charm, working hard to woo the girls. Without reservation, he told Lola and Caroline his intentions were pure and that he, too, had been surprised to meet a normal person via the want ads. I quote him: "I'm crazy about her! The chemistry was instant!" I remember that line specifically.

Never missing a beat, he charmed them as he had charmed me. Slowly, they relaxed, and before the spaghetti was gone, we were all laughing and having fun.

Murphy had stayed by my side the whole time, refusing to interact with Rock-Bob and eyeing Stuart suspiciously. One glance from Stuart brought a series of three growls from Murphy. It became a joke, especially when Stuart growled back and scared the hell out of the dog.

The time zoomed by; suddenly the hour was over and it saddened me. I walked him out, and we kissed while leaning against the Lexus. Then, like "poof!" he pecked a last kiss, rushed to the driver's door, and was out of sight within five seconds.

"Now you see him, now you don't," I said to myself. *But he likes me! He likes me a lot!* A string of giggles continued on my walk inside, eager and anxious to hear what the girls thought about my new prize.

Caroline had been duly impressed with his wit, she said, finding his charm impressive. "I mean... a dozen roses! Who *does* that these days? I'm on cloud nine!" She rubbed a petal against her index finger and smiled ear-to-ear in her farm girl way. "*But* should we worry about Murphy's opinion? Dogs are usually the best judge of character."

"Nah. He just smells Rock-Bob on him or something."

Caroline spat a laugh. "Rock-Bob! It's funny... but a half-insult to Tennessee, don't ya think?"

Lola nodded and opened her mouth to speak, but I interrupted. "Trust me, girls. We had a long discussion about this Yankee versus Redneck shit and I put him in his place." Caroline smiled as if she approved of that.

Lola was a tougher nut to crack. She said, "I'll try to keep an open mind, but I'll be watching his every move. He seems okay, but he was, like... trying too hard. And that makes me worry."

As I shushed her worry, her final comment made me shiver. "And, the dude said he was 5'8" and fit but he's shorter than that and left out the beer belly part. I wonder what else he's lying about."

I blew her off. "What man doesn't exaggerate about his height and the size of his dick? Seriously!"

"True. But please don't fall face-first in love with him, Lela. Be smart."

"You just keep thinking about Logan and comparing. Maybe you think I should be with Logan instead."

"By the way, he and his wife go to court tomorrow. The divorce will be final."

"Already?" My eyes widened. "That was fast!"

"She didn't want to drag him through the mud, though she could have, big time."

My eyes went down as if my feet were of the utmost interest. "I still feel so bad about that. See, I didn't want to... upset his life, ya know? I was just drunk."

"But Lela. It's not really your fault. You weren't the only one. There's been a whole string of Lelas through the years, and she knew about all of them."

"Okay, that proves it: Stuart is better than Logan! Relax and decide to like him."

"Decide?" Lola turned her swivel chair back toward the desk in a swift move. "No comment," she said.

"My overprotective caretaker... I love you, Lola."

"Got to watch out for my girl, ya know. Lord knows *somebody* has to."

GOOSE CREEK INN
CHAPTER 12

For the next three weeks, Stuart and I spent ninety percent of our off-time together. He played the perfect gentleman and shot the moon with the wine-and-dine treatment. As he continued to tell his story, I began a bit of hero worship, admiring his will to survive the tragedies he'd endured.

Stuart was in the throes of bankruptcy, caused by his ex-wife, he said, so he paid for everything in cash. But he was generous with all that cash, leaving large bills lying around my house, intending for me to take them. Once, he left a hundred-dollar-bill on the kitchen table with a note: "Please get some Ritz Crackers and Cool Whip."

Curious, I asked him one night after a raucous round of lovemaking, "So how rich is 'rich' when you talk about your parents? And how can you be in bankruptcy if they're so wealthy?"

"They haven't given me a nickel since I turned down their job offer with the fucking Weinstein Foundation. I don't expect them to bail me out, but I didn't expect them to... like... totally turn their backs, either. Let's just say Mother and I don't get along so well."

I couldn't imagine a riff with a parent. *How sad... his mom must be all kinds of fucked up. To disown your own! Shameful!*

"And she's furious that I didn't throw my weight around and win full custody of Jeremy. Wails about never seeing her grandson again. And it will be her *only* grandchild."

Oh. He doesn't want more children. At least he's being honest about it, UNLIKE THE MOTHERFUCKER EX-HUSBAND. Yes, I screamed in my mind.

"So you don't want kids?"

"Absolutely not."

"I won't ask why."

"Good."

Something hit me, trying to make a joke of what had become a tense moment. In response to his "Good," I sputtered, "Better."

"Best," he said. We laughed and Stuart planted a kiss on my forehead. "You funny lady. You make me laugh."

"Good."

"Better."

"Best." We'd found our first couple joke and paused for the vibrations of love to radiate between us.

When the spell was broken, I continued the probe. "So no children from your sister? In fact, I've never heard you talk about her."

"With good reason. Carla is what they call developmentally challenged. And she's one of the worst. Brain damage from birth. She has the IQ of an eight-year-old at best. Institutionalized in Boston, in a group home kind of thing, six crazies and a 'den father,' as I call him. Mom spends a fortune on that place, I'm sure. See... nobody talks about Carla much. Honestly, she gives me the creeps."

"Do you ever see her?"

"She came last Hanukkah for a few days. Crazy as hell. Brought a chaperone, but she got mad and broke a bunch of Mother's crystal and destroyed most of Elijah's elephant collection."

"Who's Elijah?"

"Mother's husband. A nice enough guy. Old, definitely pear-shaped. He holds the original patent for some machine used in pork processing. Made him rich as shit. I think he's still getting royalties, and it's from the 50s."

"Maybe I'll meet your parents one day?"

Stuart chuckled, his chest bulging in and out and his jaw clenched. "I don't think... I doubt... well..."

"What? You don't think they'd like me?"

"Lela, they don't like anybody outside of the country club."

"Oh." I paused, contemplating the snobbery of that comment but my curiosity remained. "So is Elijah Jewish, too?"

"Yep. Why?"

"Pork processing? It's a joke, right?"

Another chuckle and an eye roll. "You don't know shit about Judaism, Lela. Let's not go there."

"You're right. I don't know a thing. But I like the little cap."

Stuart didn't laugh. His smile had turned into a scowl.

Over the course of the weeks, he told the saga of the breakup with his ex. It appalled me that anyone could treat somebody so terribly. Stuart feared her craziness would rub off on Jeremy; he seemed obsessed with finding something to stop that from happening, mumbling half-baked plans about getting her in trouble... calling the police on her, reporting her for child abuse, calling the IRS, telling the cable company she was pirating HBO... the list of "ideas" was long.

Janey was self-employed as a phone psychic, for God's sake, so Jeremy was always with her. "The real problem," he said, "Is she's an alcoholic. A bad one."

Each time her name came up, Stuart began to fidget. Shaking his leg, bouncing his knee, drumming his fingers on the table; it was always something fast and furious... and always irritating as hell. But I felt sorry for him and said nothing.

<<<<<<<>>>>>>

It was a chilled-out night on the sofa. Stuart had brought two nice bottles of wine and I was already sloppy drunk. But in those days, discovery of Stuart was top priority. "Then why don't you go to court and get custody of Jeremy? If she's an alcoholic, she shouldn't be his primary caregiver!"

I spoke with knowledge and a full cup of been-there, done-that pain. When I signed the new custody agreement, I cried so hard that tears dripped all over the paper. I was embarrassed, and I think the lawyer was, too, but he said it would still be a valid document. Giving up custody was the last thing I wanted, but I knew Andy could have forced it, so I understood how Stuart would do the same.

"Because she's accusing *me* of being the alcoholic and drug addict. Boil it down and it's her word against mine," he explained, "but I have a plan. Soon to begin."

"But, maybe random drug tests, pee tests, blood tests? Surely there is *some* way to catch her! It's not fair to your little boy!" I felt immediate ownership of his problem... that it was my responsibility to help him.

<<<<<<<<>>>>>>>

Three weeks after Bo left, I had an open weekend and planned a trip to Nashville to see him. We stayed at the crappy hotel on his I-65 exit, The Goose Creek Inn.

It would've been a pleasant roadside motel in the 60s, a single-story rectangle with maybe thirty rooms facing a cracked parking lot, but it was way past its prime. Weeds grew in the asphalt cracks and scrubby grass that bordered three sides of the hotel. We pulled in front of Room 14; the warped, rotten-wood door boasted a shiny-new brass knob, but no deadbolt. I knotted my brow, worrying about intruders, but Andy and Ella had deemed it safe. *What the hell... they would know more than me.*

Bo and I unpacked, and I trekked to get ice for the cooler. We drove to the grocery store to get Gatorade and snacks for Bo, and beer for me. On the way, he told me about the friends he had made in his new neighborhood and how he was looking forward to the start of the school. "Tenth grade? Bo, how in the world can you be that old? Seems like it was just yesterday when you said your first word!"

"What was the word?"

I had no idea; booze had eradicated Bo's cute stories. So I made up a tale. "After 'Da-da' and 'Ma-ma,' of course, you learned 'juice.' You said it with a thousand U's." I imitated how I thought a toddler would pronounce it in a high-pitched voice. It seemed to please Bo, which pleased the hell out of me. As nervous as I was... as guilty as I felt... it seemed we would have a nice visit and be "friends."

But everything changed as we chose the groceries.

As I maneuvered to the beer cooler, Bo scowled and begged, "Mom! Please! Please don't buy that!" I was blowing off his concerns quite rudely when I saw a teary glaze cover his eyes. Shocked, I paused, thinking of putting the beer back.

But I couldn't do without, I knew I couldn't. So I used a challenging tone and argued that it wouldn't be long until he was standing in front of the same beer cooler and he best shut the fuck up. I had never snapped at Bo like that and felt instant Guilt, but... too late. It had been said. I quietly put the 12-pack in the shopping cart and kept moving.

On the way back to the hotel, he was quiet, and I had to pry words from him and received one-word answers. We walked around to check out the hotel from the parking lot perspective. Mumbling, Bo admitted that Miller had called four times. I was flabbergasted. I'd called only once... *what the hell is going on?* The realization that I'd lost priority so early in this new arrangement made me furious. I wasn't getting a fair shake from any of them. *They're all against me! And turning Bo against me, too!*

A few minutes later, getting the groceries out of the van, I asked myself why I hadn't called Bo since he'd left. There was no answer. My old friend Shame reared its ugly head, and I lowered mine. *Why hadn't I called my son?* "Here, carry this bag, Bo," I said, but he didn't reach for it. Instead, he stood with his head down, kicking a weed.

"Did you miss me, buddy?" More kicking the weed. I lifted his chin to look at his face. There were tears. I lost it, beginning a dramatic series of sobs and blubbering comments like "I missed you soooo much," and "I feel lost without you."

Bo never stopped kicking the weed, finally speaking above the volume of my wailing. "If you missed me so much, you would've called."

My heart died, then and there. I had failed him. Miserably.

In not knowing what to do, I had done nothing. Feeling a phone call was a lame substitute for a mother/child bond, I hadn't called. So I had already let him slip away from me. *How could you possibly forget about your CHILD? You're the worst kind of mother, an absent one... neglect is worse than abuse, they say.*

It happened in increments; my face crumbled, and I broke down in tears. "Son, go on in and I'll be there in a minute."

"Okay, Mom." Bo sounded like Eeyore.

I sat in the van to compose myself. Each time I thought I'd settled down and could look at him without crying, I stepped out and walked toward the door. Two different times, I made it halfway before breaking down again... then back to the van. Finally, I made it inside and managed a smile when looking at my sweet son's face.

I had never felt so foolish, so ignorant, so inadequate, so much like a loser. My heart broke in knowing I had broken his heart.

I took a deep breath, knowing the subject had to change completely. "Hey! I have an idea, buddy... let's play a dumb game like we used to do." Bo's reply was far from enthusiastic, but I ignored it. "Let's play 'Hide the Cheezits!' Do you remember when we played it with your baseball bat? Just like 'Hide and Seek!'" He looked at me and rolled his eyes but I kept talking. When he realized there wouldn't be a better choice, he shared the nonsense with me.

Bo found creative hiding places, well beyond the typical "under the trash liner" trick. The best one: he balanced the box on top of the door frame in the bathroom. I didn't see it until I stepped inside the tiny tub and looked up. We played "Hide the Cheezits" for almost an hour, laughing so hard we had to crouch over to breathe.

Finally! Laughing again with my son! My precious son I had left behind.

We went out to a Japanese steakhouse; Bo opened up, telling me about his six-year-old brother's craziness. I told him about Stuart; Rather, I tried to. He had no comment. "He wants to meet you, buddy. Maybe the next time you come to town?"

No reply.

After we returned, I brought up Stuart again. I wanted him to be okay with it so obsessively, I pushed and pushed. But through five minutes of my verbal tapestry, Bo did nothing but shrug and mumble. Finally, he grabbed the remote and changed the channel. I felt like he was changing my channel as well.

Overall, the whole weekend was awkward, a fight with myself to minimize my drinking and play the happy, stable mother role. But I squirmed, sitting on my hands and aching for alcohol. I raided my glove compartment for airline bottles and slipped out when I could, barely sipping the beer in the room with Bo. Still, my headache wouldn't stop. I thought I'd fooled him... but no. My son looked at me with pity, seeing straight through my façade.

The conversation was touchy. I'd lost touch with the baseball families and didn't have news... we couldn't talk about Miller... it was awkward to talk about his dad or Ella. Beyond talking about my family, it seemed we had little in common.

I felt like an outsider, a leper. My bottom lip quivered when I said goodbye and I hugged him as long as he would allow, which was a half-ass, one-armed hug also appropriate for a casual friend. *Why doesn't he love his mother? How can he end this weekend so easily, like it doesn't matter? Does he not feel as empty as I do?*

"See ya," he said as I closed the van door, then he began the walk to his brick house without looking back at me.

I cried all the way home.

Leaving Nashville, I felt I'd left my relationship with Bo behind forever, and that it was all my fault. I was an expert at punishing myself already, but failing Bo sent me spiraling down a dirty shaft of Self-Hate and Hopelessness.

If they still call a slide into insanity a "nervous breakdown," that's what happened to me. I fell apart mentally, physically, and spiritually.

My thinking ran this way: I had two choices. I could either dive under the bedcovers and stay there, put a gun to my head, or drink myself to oblivion to numb the pain. I chose the latter.

More drinking created a thick crack in the precarious bond between Bo and me, and it widened more as he grew brave enough to tell me the truth.

He was ashamed of me, he said, and didn't want to be seen with me in his hometown. His comment, "My friends will think you're a loser, Mom," echoed in my brain for the next year and a half.

Even after the blessing of sobriety, it took years for Bo to trust me again. I hadn't proven myself yet... not enough to make up for the pain I'd caused. And I had a lot to make up for.

When I made amends to him, he cried like a two-year-old, also sharing his worst memories... specific situations where I had made him feel Shame and Embarrassment. Daggers, each word. But I promised him I had changed and would continue to. And so I have, sober for nearly twenty years now.

In my mind, as I compared myself with my do-gooder parents, there is nothing worse than believing you've screwed up your own child. Yet I did it; I couldn't stop it.

Now, the things I "can't stop" are quite different... though still quite disturbing. But that's getting ahead of the story.

DAMNING EVIDENCE
CHAPTER 13

Stuart took a day off on Thursday, November 12, 1998, for a "telephonic court appearance." His ex-wife was trying to interfere with his upcoming visit with Jeremy in Florida.

The term telephonic appearance was new to me. Stuart's explanation, "Going 'before the judge' by telephone, because I don't want to use vacation time *arranging* to see him... I'll use the time to *see him in person*," finally made me understand.

Crazy Janey, her even-crazier mother, and her lawyer would be in the judge's chambers in Fort Lauderdale with a speakerphone; Stuart (and me) would be in his lawyer's office downtown with another speakerphone.

The two of us sat in his lawyer's bare conference room with nothing but a soiled beige telephone on a long, scarred wood table. Stuart sat next to the anything-but-suave Garnet Carbell, Esquire with the phone between them. I sat on the far end of the table, there for emotional support only. The only sounds before the phone rang were coughs and sniffs; the silence was deafening. We waited for the call, already ten minutes late.

A secretary slipped in and laid a manila envelope in front of Stuart's lawyer. He opened it and spread a dozen-or-so 8 x 10 color photographs on the table. Garnet Carbell's face burst with surprise, pure amazement... like a cartoon. He elbowed Stuart and looked at him with wide-open eyes. No words were exchanged, just deafening silence.

At just that moment, the phone rang. I heard a gruff voice through the speakerphone, evidently the judge. His garbled words must have been an introduction or something. Then another voice came on the phone and Stuart raised his right hand. "I do," he said.

When I heard Crazy Janey's voice, my jaw dropped. The bitch was British! She didn't speak in the lullaby sound of a happy Brit but in a clipped, snooty, and rude tone. Stuart had told me she was stupid; in fact, he called her a "simpleton," but she sounded smart. Janey said Stuart's name in one terse syllable but drew out a long, three-syllable pronunciation for their son Jeremy. I hated her instantly.

Crazy Janey interrupted her lawyer several times, and the judge admonished her three times for what he called "mindless babbling." Her "babbling" was a string of accusations against Stuart, most so bizarre they were surely concocted in a demented mind. As Janey continued, Stuart's face reddened, brighter and brighter. Finally, he pushed against the table to roll his chair back, hard, and threw up his hands. His lawyer sat in silence, gaping at the telephone.

Janey continued to argue against Stuart seeing Jeremy, insisting he was a bad influence... he'd been a cocaine dealer, she said, smoked cracked in front of his son, and associated with thugs. There was more. She alleged Stuart had left Jeremy with his parents to go to a strip club with his cronies, and that he was being investigated by the IRS. Janey also said Stuart didn't have money to support Jeremy, hadn't been paying child support, and that *he* had been the one to bankrupt his business. Her words: "He put that transmission shop in a pipe and smoked it."

Obviously lying, she ticked off her allegations succinctly in that British-Bitch accent and my stomach rolled. But between each allegation, tit-for-tat, her lawyer presented "exhibits" to the judge – pictures or whatever, things that supposedly backed up her claims. The one I remember best: Janey's lawyer said, "You see here, Judge Martin, Mr. Weinstein with Jeremy and a known prostitute in the parking lot of a gentlemen's club in Boca Raton."

And there were more. Pictures of Stuart and Jeremy allegedly making a drug deal, pictures of the two with thugs, gang leaders, and more prostitutes. A lot of prostitutes.

Garnet Corbell interrupted; he had no choice if he wanted to talk. "Judge

Martin, I have just received a pack of such photos, but I must confirm with my client: Mr. Weinstein, are you aware of these?"

Fidgeting with a paper clip, Stuart sighed and said, "Yes, sir. She mailed them to me last week." The only sound was my intake of breath.

The judge's voice raised an octave. "So you admit the pictures are real, Mr. Weinstein?"

Stuart's voice also gained an octave. "I just don't think they have anything to do with the present time or my ability to father my son! Those are from six months ago, and doctored!"

Stuart jumped out of his chair and leaned forward on the table, shouting into the telephone, "I am a better parent than *she* is! The only difference is I have no pictures of her lying drunk and dressed like a whore! She's an alcoholic! Don't you want to hear *my* side of the story?" Stuart was sweating, breathing hard, his hand quivering as he raised it to rub his temple. The lawyer grabbed Stuart's arm and shook his head furiously, a gesture to shush him.

Such an intense fifteen minutes... such horrible accusations against Stuart... such confusion.

Tears ran down my face. I felt so sorry for him; they were ganging up on him and it upset him terribly!

The gavel fell; the judge had rendered his verdict. Stuart was denied visitation for the weekend he'd requested. Even "supervised visitation" was denied. In fact, all visitation was denied until Stuart met with a court-approved psychiatrist for evaluation and could pass a drug test; a hair test this time, which showed a three-month history. Both the evaluation and hair test had to be done in Florida.

So naïve, just flabbergasted and confused, it never occurred to me that Stuart was wrong. I assumed *she* was wrong... about everything. Crazy Janey.

Stuart had smoothed his way through each accusation along the way, explaining everything as a non-issue, and I believed him.

But afterward, in my living room with Lola upstairs, Stuart ranted. He blamed his lawyer, *her* lawyer, the judge, and insisted Janey was flat out lying, doctoring the photos. "And I bet she wore some sexy, revealing outfit to win the judge over; she does that a lot. Such a BITCH! A WHORE!" He paced around my living room, smoking cigarette after cigarette, lamenting his loss. "Oh, Mother will have a fit!"

With a sudden change of tune, as he could do with ease, he smiled, pulled me into a bear hug, and said, "What the hell, I've already paid for two airline tickets, so we'll go and you can meet my parents." I smiled as if nothing else was wrong. "And for tonight... let's do it... let's go to The Skybox. Surely we can find *something* to celebrate."

Stuart kissed me and patted my head on his shoulder. We swayed for a minute. "Hey, I have an idea, sweetie. We have something to celebrate for sure!"

"We do?"

Looking at the ceiling, he paused for a second or two. "Yes, we do. Because I've realized something, Lela Fox. I love you. I have fallen in head-over-heels in love with you!" *Ah-ha! The "L word" for the first time.* I giggled, snuggling deeper into his shoulder and smelling his clean scent.

"Stuart Weinstein..." I paused, fingering his collar, "I love you, too."

"Aww. We're the Great American Couple. Let's go upstairs, baby, and let me love you more."

It never occurred to me that alcohol and desperation had clouded my judgement. I believed everything Stuart Weinstein said, and thought he could do no wrong. He would use my naivety against me in ways that only happen in the movies. But it wasn't a movie. It was my life... the roller coaster of Lela's life.

Now the plot thickens.

BOOKCASE
CHAPTER 14

I had one concern about Stuart. His New York approach was a little harsh for East Tennesseans, especially at work. As charming as he was with me and those he wanted to impress, when he told desperate customers their transmission needed expensive repair, he offered nothing but facts in a choppy, unsympathetic tone. It wasn't as much a New York *accent* as it was a brusque New York *attitude*.

Overhearing him on the phone one day, I said, "Babe, you need to show a little empathy with these people," My advice interested him, he said, so I continued. "You just don't say, 'It costs $900,' you say, 'Dude, I'm sorry to say... your transmission is ruined, but I think we can rebuild it instead of buying a replacement, and that will save you a bunch of money. So sorry, my friend... I hate to be the bearer of bad news.'"

Stuart found this approach intriguing and pumped me for more information. "So I have to say I'm sorry when I'm not?" I explained how Southerners need empathy when they're being told bad news, and that people would trust him more if he commiserated with them a bit.

I further explained, "To be honest, Southerners hate Yankees, hate everything about them. So you fight an uphill battle every day. Customers won't give you a chance if you're too curt." My boyfriend stared into space, I supposed pondering my advice, and said he would do it my way for a while as a "test."

The tactic worked. His customers didn't hesitate or try to talk him down on the price. Not a single person called a competitor for another opinion; they trusted him to do it and do it right. That night he brought a bottle of champagne home to thank me for my input. Stuart oozed with charm and finesse, the way he always made me feel important and smart.

Still using my suggestion of a more empathetic approach, Stuart had more success stories the next day. He said, "I don't get it. You aren't such a redneck, but you sure know what rednecks want. My cutie-curly Lela Fox will increase my paycheck. Advise me anytime, babe."

"Okay, I recommend using the same technique on your bosses, especially the wife."

Lo-and-behold, the owners began treating Stuart better. Until then, they'd made their hatred clear with nit-picky daily complaints and unfair personal attacks. They didn't like the way his tuna sandwiches smelled, they said... bullshit like that.

With more money in his pocket, Stuart started paying for groceries and household items. One month, he paid the full combo of utility bills. I didn't want to tell him, but my financial situation had changed for the worst. Although the alimony continued, Miller had stopped paying my car payment and insurance, and the cost of my failing business grew exponentially. The money wouldn't stretch the month.

At the apex of my budget worries, Stuart asked, "Why don't I just move in and help pay the rent?"

My heart skipped a beat. "Really? That would really help with my finances, but–"

"But what? Don't you want me here? Please don't say that! Living here would make me even happier, babe... and Rock-Bob wants to stay here full-time. He told me so."

There was no question I needed the money, and it seemed living together was the next logical step in our relationship, anyway. Certainly an expected step if we moved to Florida as planned. "It's no problem to break my lease..." he said in a sing-song voice, "And how many times have I stayed at that crappy apartment in the past six months? It's a waste of money for me."

<<<<<<<<>>>>>>

Stuart purchased boxes from U-Haul despite my plea to get them free from a liquor store. Conservative spender that I was, I found it such a waste of money but Stuart wasted money all the time, as if money was a renewable resource. Clenching my jaw, I realized he was much like Miller about money and that pissed me off to the max. "It's just money," Miller would say – and Stuart said the same. I didn't understand, but I'd never been wealthy.

I insisted, "You could be $20 wealthier if you got free boxes."

"Jeezus! Lay off me, you penny-pinching control freak!" My mind zoomed. *Whoa! Down, boy. I'm just trying to help.* I flashed to memories of the fights Miller and I had, when he stomped my ego on purpose and called me names like that, and radar starting pinging. I wouldn't let another man treat me badly; I'd promised myself that. But I also didn't want to upset the apple cart.

The solution was to argue half-heartedly. "Don't be an ass, and don't call me names. That's how children fight." He rolled his eyes and mocked me. This time I didn't scream – I rolled my eyes, too.

<<<<<<<>>>>>>>

I'd been to his cookie-cutter apartment only once. No personality in 37-C. And I'd never heard of furnishing an apartment the way he did. He'd rented the entire contents: sofa, lamps, framed pictures and all. When I questioned it, he reminded me he'd left Florida with nothing but his dog, a few boxes, and the clothes on his back. "Run out of town by Crazy Janey, remember?"

I had a hard time imagining owning nothing. Over the years, I'd accumulated a double garage full of stuff: Bo's old drawings, his baseball cards, my own childhood memories and yearbooks, endless boxes of craft supplies, and almost every stick of furniture I'd ever owned. Not a packrat, as Stuart had accused, just a "keeper."

There wasn't much to pack at his place, but we divided the task by room. I took responsibility for the contents of the bookcase, also rented, while he tackled the kitchen. I looked at each book as I packed, finding he wasn't much of a reader. There were only a few novels, and none I hadn't already read. The best ones were coffee-table books, three *fabulous* ones, and I got distracted flipping through them instead of packing them. Then Stuart shot me *that* look, and I began packing anew.

A few minutes later, I asked, "What are these doing here?" I knotted my brow in confusion. There were several books on alcoholism, one was a dog-eared book called, simply, "Alcoholics Anonymous." Blue, with an embossed title. A look of panic crossed his face. "What? What's wrong?" I asked, thinking I'd done something to upset him.

Stuart's face relaxed in increments. "Oh, those are just Janey's..." A faraway voice by the end of the sentence.

"So do you want me to pack them?"

His lips were thin, his face angry. "No, put those damn things in the trash. I sure as hell don't need them, shouldn't have brought them in the first place."

The look on his face was puzzling, prompting me to delve further into the mystery. "So, she tried to quit drinking, joined AA or something?"

"Janey quit drinking many times. Went to rehab twice... just couldn't stay sober. She's hopeless." Suddenly, Stuart threw a plastic Corelle plate against the wall in the kitchen. Instant and unexpected anger. *What the hell is going on? Why is he so mad?* "Janey learned just enough to use it against *me!*" His face reddened, leaning against the sink with white knuckles.

He seemed out-of-control angry... and I shied away in fear. *What if he hits me or something? Is he THAT mad?* "Just get rid of the damn books, Lela, *all* the goddamn books!"

I silently set them aside. Stuart hadn't moved an inch, squeezing the countertop by its bullnose edge. Silence. Fifteen seconds, maybe more. Finally, I dared to ask, "Stuart? Are you okay?" My whisper was deafening in the room.

"Leave me alone, dammit!" Like an injured dinosaur, Stuart screamed. Loud. Hoping to console him, I stood to hug him, but his hand raised to keep me back. "Get the *fuck* away from me! Lela, GO! Just GO!" I froze, scared, torn between helping and running for cover. Mostly, I didn't understand what had just happened. *Why is he so upset?*

"Really? You want me to go? Like, home? Without you?" Still, Stuart didn't answer and stayed silent for a tension-filled minute. The silence broke when the air conditioner kicked on. *Why is that so loud?* Confused and scared, I stayed frozen in place. *Should I tiptoe out the door? Would that be... abandonment? Should I stay and help him through this, whatever it is?* I'd never seen him so upset; Stuart was a fairly even-tempered guy.

With a long sigh, I sat back down on the floor, watching him. He crouched over, hands on his knees. "Lela?" His voice was calm, almost ethereal.

"Yes, I'm here. Still."

"Lela, we went together." Stuart's calm voice contrasted with ragged breathing.

"What? Who? To *what?* Together with Janey?"

"We went to AA together."

Taken aback, I repeated, "You went to AA with Janey?" My voice was dreamy, envisioning them sitting together in a meeting like the one I'd attended.

Stuart stood and leaned against the counter. "Yes, I went to AA with Janey. For a while there, I thought... I may... you know, I thought maybe I needed–"

I interrupted. "But of course you needed to be a supportive husband! That's what makes you so loving, babe! Of course you needed to go! Be proud that you tried to help her, but it's not your fault it didn't work." My heart ached for him.

Stuart shook his head, left and right. "No, Lela, I'm an alcoholic, too."

"But... but. Wait! But you *drink,* Stuart! What are you trying to tell me?"

"I can drink now, just a little. Don't you agree that I don't drink very much? I've recovered. A recovered alcoholic, so I can drink now. I'm over it. No problem... I can control it."

I looked at him sideways. *How much DOES he drink? Well, less than me, but how much is that?* I didn't know the answer to that question. "So you won't be a drunk, homeless bum?

A chuckle. "Oh, Lela, you're so innocent it's amazing," Stuart shook his head and continued to laugh.

"Not as innocent as you think, big guy. I've been around the block a few times." But I still had questions; what he said went against what my alcoholic Uncle Jolly had said. "But Stuart, if you're an alcoholic, doesn't that mean you can never drink again?"

"Sometimes, but it's not the case with me. They say I'm an exception to the rule." His body visibly relaxed, also relaxing the tension in my body. I didn't realize how anxious I'd been until I relaxed. *So alcoholics can drink if it's not too much. Hmm. He's a lucky one. And I don't think I could hang out with somebody who didn't drink at all!* "So alcoholic or not, we're still cool, right?"

"Yep."

"Good. But I thought... yeah, I thought alcoholism was a lifelong thing."

"Sometimes." He looked at me and shook his head. "Look, just forget it, okay? Let's just get this shit packed up and get out of here. Right now... I'm freaked out. But now you know. I've told you. Your understanding of it doesn't matter."

As he locked the door behind us, he said, "You're something else, Lela Fox. Damn, girl!"

I smiled, thankful for the compliment after the tension of packing. He put his arm around my shoulders as we walked to the van as Stuart whistled a version of Billy Joel's *Piano Man*.

How could I have been so dumb? It amazes me now, even though I know why I believed him. It was comprehensive stupidity mixed with tonic and lime.

Under the fog of alcohol, I was clueless about Stuart, blind to his lies, and ignorant of the trail of red flags that popped up at every step in our relationship. And I was ignorant about alcoholism; I remained purposely ignorant.

I was under his spell, I guess. Impressed by his money, swept off my feet by his charm, and hopeful for a future where I wouldn't hate myself so much. Stuart promised that life, and I fought to claim my ticket to Shangri-La.

THE FOURTH DIMENSION
CHAPTER 15

Stuart woke up sick on a Tuesday morning. A snotty nose, a cough that rattled with phlegm, stopped-up ears. "I'm dying!" he moaned, "Ohhh-nooo.... I have the flu." He fretted and complained, as men do. But it was just a cold; anyone could tell. Stuart begged me to take his temperature, which I finally did. Normal. Then he begged me to make a pot of chicken soup, purring like a pitiful child.

"It's just a cold, Stuart! Don't be such a baby." But he insisted he would soon die of a rare and horrid respiratory malady. To appease him, I unearthed some cold medicine, poured orange juice into the remains of last night's vodka, and took it upstairs to my ailing boyfriend. The fucking man-flu! But being a "good wife," I decided to baby him, ooh'ing and aah'ing and playing the overprotective mother.

"Sit up and take your medicine, my sweet babe. This is your cure. And I will massage your temples for twenty minutes until it takes effect." Stuart smiled at my overly dramatic act.

"I want to crawl in one of those caves you guys have around here."

"But you need to go to work! If not, it'll cut our trip short."

"Oh yeah, our trip... I hope I'm alive on Friday." The two of us were flying to Fort Lauderdale to spend one night with his parents and two at a five-star resort on Paradise Island, Bahamas. Stuart had connections with a pilot flying a "pond jumper," making the flight from Miami to the Bahamas easy and cheap.

Stuart moaned and rolled over on his stomach. I spoke to his bare shoulders, "I'll make coffee and be back in twenty minutes." His answer was unintelligible.

When the brew started, I put a can of Campbell's Chicken Noodle soup on the stove. Even though it pissed me off, I found it somewhat amusing that Stuart had a bad case of man-flu. *Men! Idiots! Wimps!*

I took the coffee upstairs first. As expected, he lay in the same spot, moaning in the same tone. "Drink this," I said. More moaning, griping and complaining. Then he said he couldn't even taste the bitterness of the coffee. Too sick to drink, he said. Again, I rolled my eyes. "Chicken soup coming up."

Minutes later, he gawked at the soup. "But... but you won't make *real* chicken soup for me?" The pouty lip was out again.

"No, I'm won't! I'm just doing this much to pacify you. You have nothing but a common head cold, commonly called the man-flu. You take what you get."

Stuart was late getting to work and at lunch, he came home to lie down. Again, I went overboard trying to make him feel better. "Come on, babe. Sit on the sofa and put your head in my lap." I rubbed his wiry hair and "petted him," as my Momma would say. After a time, he conveniently "forgot" his sickness and began talking normally. And what he said sent my heart aflutter.

"Do you want to know how much I love you, Lela?"

"Tell me how much, Stuart."

"You have rocketed me to the fourth dimension."

I laughed. "The fourth dimension, huh? That sounds far away."

"But it's true! It's like I have no effective mental defense against you. Lela Fox is my spiritual experience." He wasn't looking at me; his eyes were closed, and he spoke dreamily.

"Aww. Thank you, Stuart. You're making me feel special," I said. And his words had touched me. *See how important he thinks you are, Lela? Why don't you give yourself some credit for making a nice man happy? Seems you have a special talent for it. Then again, Ms. Fox... isn't it because you're head-over-heels in love with HIM?* I reddened from just having the thought.

"I want to retire and take you south... loll in the Florida sunshine with you. Forever."

"Okay, Doofus, you're just being silly now. Quit!" I almost added "unless we get married," which I wanted but would never say.

Stuart's eyes never opened, and I hadn't stopped rubbing his head. He maneuvered to cuddle deeper on my lap. "So I'm going to take a little nap... here in the fourth dimension."

I repeated his first line. "'Rocketed to the fourth dimension.' I like that. How did you come up with that?"

He took a few seconds to answer. "Oh, I don't know... read it somewhere, I guess." I looked down to see his eyes wide open.

"I thought you were going to take a nap!" I tried to shush him, but he was antsy... suddenly anxious.

In one succinct motion, he sat up on the sofa and jumped to stand. "I must get back to work."

"Honey, you've got another ten minutes! Come on... you should rest! Do you want more soup or something?" Lighting a cigarette, I watched the flurry as he re-tucked his shirt into his pants. I asked, "Do they eat soup in the fourth dimension?"

No smile from Stuart, just the irritating fidgets he did with his knees and feet. He turned away quickly, grabbing his keys from the side table.

"Hey, let's go out tonight... get a Monster Burger at Sam and Joe's. I like it there – a good rendition of a deli, but redneck-style."

"Watch it, New York Fucker!"

"Truthfully, I love their burgers!"

"But I thought you were sick, you turkey!"

"I'm suddenly better. It's a miracle, I guess," he chuckled. "But I want to take more of that cold medicine from this morning. Dried me right up."

"It's a twelve-hour dose. You can't take any more right now."

"But I'm going to, anyway. Where is it?"

I sighed. "Men! You're hopeless! Crazy!"

"Just tell me where it is."

Stuart bounded the stairs and immediately returned, walking straight to the front door. *Why is he in such a hurry? What spooked him?* In a heartbeat, he had disappeared. I sat back on the sofa to think... going back through our conversation and trying to figure out what had upset him. *The fourth dimension? Is that where he "got well?"* That seemed right, but I wasn't sure.

I took the steps two at a time. "Lola! Caroline! He loves me!" In my infamous bad-actress character, I sucked an imaginary cigarette holder and declared, "I have rocketed him to the fourth dimension!"

I would learn what book he was quoting in another Lifetime. I swooned as he eloquently spoke dozens of quotables… about joy, peace of mind, brotherly love, and the journey toward a harmonious life.

I thought he was so wise, already in possession of a serenity I had yearned for lifelong.

It was this phrase in particular that put me on a journey with no end, opening my mind to a spirit I am still trying to understand.

COME HOME, STAY AWAY
CHAPTER 16

We landed at the Fort Lauderdale airport and dashed to stand in line at the Alamo Car Rental counter. To prepare for the blistering sun, I had purchased a two-week pass to a tanning bed and my skin glowed the red-brown typical for my fair complexion. My thighs, especially, were an odd shade of Tennessee clay.

Cruising smooth, we drove forty miles to his mother's and stepfather's house. Daphne and Elijah Graning had married two months after Stuart's father died and two years after the Patent Office stamped approval for Elijah's invention.

While income from the pork processing machine added much to the family's wealth, Stuart insisted I know how successful his father had been, too. "Prominence and big bucks go many generations back in the Weinstein family, everybody a power player in the fur and fabric industry," Stuart boasted.

As I formed a reply, we turned into a cobblestone driveway, lined with palm trees and flowering plants. No house in view until we took a gentle curve, then my jaw dropped.

WOW! What a house! Beyond the scope of a "house," it was a contemporary a mansion. "Holy shit! What the hell, Stuart? This is your *house?*"

"What else could it be, Lela?" He laughed, teasing me.

"It's the damn Taj Mahal!" Overwhelmed, my voice shook. Instant fear encompassed me and I didn't want to go in such a place and feel like a

Tennessee hillbilly.

"Nah. It's just a house. People live here. It's all good." Stuart grabbed my hand, urging me forward but my eyes couldn't take it in so fast.

"But look at the garden here! Orchids and... oh, my God!" Massive flowers in bright colors dotted the philodendrons, surrounding massive palm trees and flowering bushes. "Look, Stuart! There's a fucking parrot perched on that tree! A damn *parrot!*"

"Yeah, they always come here. That's just a small parrot, though – sometimes they get huge ones. Those are Silk Floss trees, the gardener calls them, I think."

"The gardener? You have, like... servants?"

"Like... yeah. Duh, Lela. Better get ready." He rang the doorbell.

Before I could freak out, a butler, impeccably dressed in a three-piece suit, opened the door, nose in the air. All business. Before he spoke, Daphne Graning swept into the foyer. "Stuart, good to see you, dear. You look well." There was no smile on her face or in her voice. Dressed in a navy suit and silk blouse with a thin knotted scarf the throat, she was blonde-ish but looked to be in her late 60s. The same penchant for expensive shoes Stuart had, I noticed.

In a voice that shocked me with its formality, Stuart introduced me. His mother's hand reached toward me, but it was the wimpiest "ladies shake" I'd ever had. Her voice was smooth and calm, eerily so. "How do you do, Lela? So nice to make your acquaintance. Please call me Daphne." *Damn, man! Who IS this woman? Is this a soap opera set?*

A 70-ish man in a crisp dress shirt and finely woven gray pants appeared beside Daphne. She turned to introduce her husband Elijah, who shook my hand and repeated, "How do you do?" I immediately felt sooooo small-town and ignorant... overwhelmed by wealth and culture. Stuart's demeanor had changed, too, so I felt apart from him. I was alone, floundering in a world I didn't want to be in, a world opposite of my down-to-earth East Tennessee.

Stuart's parents ushered us into a "den" twice the size of my entire house. Elijah motioned for me to sit on a yawning white-leather sectional sofa. My short denim shorts rode up my crack as I sank into its depths. The butler stood at the entrance to the room and waited for acknowledgement. "Yes, Howard?" Elijah said.

The servant looked at Stuart. "Your bags are in your room, sir."

I blurted, "But how did he get th–"

Stuart glared at me and sternly shook his head; I got the message and shut up. Then he nodded to the butler. "Thank you, Howard." There was an awkward pause. "Okay, Lela, let's unpack." He reached to take my hand and when I stood, he put his arm around me. "Mother, we'll freshen up and meet you for dinner. In the dining room tonight?" Stuart's mother nodded. He nodded back. "Mother." Then an intense look at his mother's oddball husband. "Elijah." Finally, I understood this blank-statement of their names was a way to say "goodbye." Weird. Weird as hell.

On the way down a massive hall lined with expensive-looking art, I tried to tell Stuart I didn't want to be here. "Let's just get a hotel, maybe fly out to the resort tonight. This is freaking me out! I know you said 'wealthy,' but not all this! *Help me!*" He didn't answer. "Listen! I'm just a simple girl from Tennessee!" He laughed but said nothing.

About three-quarters of the way down the hall, he opened a door and motioned me inside. I stopped short. This bedroom was more opulent than the other parts of the house I'd seen. "No. No! I don't want to stay here! I'll break something!"

"It's okay, I understand. Believe me, dear, I don't want to stay, either. They make me feel just as small as you're feeling, though maybe for different reasons. So maybe we'll just stay for dinner, not spend the night. I'll go tell them while you get dressed. You'll need long pants for dinner."

"But I didn't bring long pants, just jeans! Damn, Stuart, why didn't you tell me!" Panting hard, I was frantic.

"Don't worry. We've made the perfunctory appearance. They probably don't want us here, either." Seeming to know how upset I was, he pecked a kiss on my pouty lips.

<<<<<<<>>>>>>

The dinner challenged my knowledge of which fork to use for what, what to say, what to do. This was "charm school" shit, and proper etiquette wasn't taught in East Tennessee's public schools. Though my mom had taught me the basics, I was lost. And the silence in the enormous dining room was deafening.

The cook, or somebody, had cracked and split the lobster tails, but the meat still stuck to the shell and I couldn't get it out. I watched in wonder how they ate it with such ease, using nothing but a tiny little fork. Nobody but me got both hands smeared with clarified butter and white lobster-goo. I tried to keep myself small and said as little as possible.

Throughout the meal, Daphne and Elijah asked what I thought about Stuart's prior life... his education in Switzerland, his marriage to Janey, his transmission business, etc. It left me confused. *Why are they asking ME? And why the distant past instead of our current life, our future life?* It was as if they were testing how much I knew. *And why aren't they asking about MY life, my business, my family? Isn't that the proper thing to do?*

After dessert, Daphne sipped coffee and asked pointedly, "Stuart, when will you see Jeremy, and what time will you bring him here?" She smiled, the forced smile a duchess would wear for a portrait. "I've had Mary make his favorite treat."

Stuart swallowed hard. "Umm, I'm not seeing Jeremy, Mother. Lela and I are flying to the island for a few nights at the Palms." Silence. Long, tense, deafening silence. Elijah cleared his throat, not once or twice, but three times. Then Daphne lowered her cup onto the saucer, rattling it a bit.

"Weren't the courts involved, son? Were you prohibited from seeing him again?" *Again? Janey has done this shit twice?* The sneer made it obvious Daphne already knew the answer... yes, he was "prohibited."

Stuart paused before answering, splashing his face with sincerity and poise. "No, Mother. Janey says he's sick. The flu. Jeremy can't go out." Stuart's lie was easy and smooth. I froze, waiting for another lie.

"That's your story?"

"Not a 'story,' Mother. He's sick."

Slowly and deliberately, Daphne stood and leaned forward on the table, her eyes piercing Stuart's. "You're lying to me again. Pack your bags. I do not want you in this house." She glanced at me, unsmiling. "Be well, Lela. Nice to see you." Daphne left with a sturdy step through the dining room. I stared at Stuart, who didn't return my look, his head down and frozen in place.

A long five seconds later, Elijah stood up with a stumble. "Goodbye, Stuart," he said without looking his way. But he looked directly at me with cold, black eyes. "And goodbye, Lela. Please do not return."

ALL-INCLUSIVE
CHAPTER 17

The private plane rolled effortlessly to the marked spot on the tarmac and a pair of dark-skinned Bahamian men ran to open the doors. One, wearing a bright-colored print shirt, helped me out with a gentle touch. The other man waited for Stuart to exit and grabbed our luggage, singing that we should go inside for "just a little moment." As I found later, all Bahamians speak musically, in a melody that fit the beautiful weather and refreshing breeze.

The "little moment" wasn't even thirty seconds. A uniformed driver of a brand-new van ushered us in, and with a few horns-beeping traffic delays, we arrived at The Palms Resort ten minutes later. The front portico could have been on a brochure cover... opulent, sparkling-clean and welcoming. Not the hoity-toity bullshit of Stuart's parent's house.

The staff catered to us with an honest connection, convincing me they were genuinely happy to help. For instance, the concierge said, and I quote, "Your slightest wish is my greatest desire." The phrase is one my dad once said to my mom in an early romance love letter – it'd been a lifelong family joke – so I laughed, touched. Stuart curtly nodded. As we stood with the blackest-of-black concierge, Stuart fidgeted.

He pulled me aside. "Uh... Lela, give me a minute with this man, would you? Go on up, unpack maybe, and I'll be there shortly.

I rode the gold-mirrored elevator to the fifth floor and threw open the curtains. Aaah! A gorgeous place! Paradise Island had the whitest sand I'd ever seen. The azure-blue ocean swelled calm and inviting, and I watched until mesmerized. "Too bad we couldn't bring any joints," I said to the empty room, then spun around a few times. Freeeeeeedom! "You, dear Lela, are a V.I. fucking-P. in paradise!"

A knock on the door: the bellman with our luggage. Stuart had given me a ten to tip the man, which was too much of a tip in those days, so I thought I was a hot shot and made a request. "Could you send a few drinks up, please? Doubles. Grey Goose and grapefruit, and a Crown and Coke." He bowed and assured me the drinks would arrive in a "little moment." *That phrase again. Love it!*

Outside, swaying palms waved to the sun and massive flowers exploded in a multitude of colors against a tropical field of green. Our room overlooked the pool area, a round pool like a tire... and in the center, a swim-up bar with a long counter and a dozen two-person tables branching off of it. Bikini-clad waitresses swarmed the crowd; it seemed every person had a drink in their hand. On the far side, a dozen-or-so private hot tubs hid under gargantuan palm-frond umbrellas.

Stuart arrived just as I arranged my boobs into the new bikini I'd bought for this vacation. "Ooh-la-la!" he said, wrapping his arms around my back and squeezing the boobs that wouldn't quite fit into the tiny triangles of the swimsuit. "Damn, girl! You are hot, hot, hot!" His eyes were wide watching me, which was my plan.

"I was hoping you would like it, sexy man!" I sang, prancing around the room in a seductive dance. "A white bikini, white sunglasses – exactly like Jenna, my would-be girlfriend from the 'old days.' You remember the story."

"Believe me, I think about it often! The thought of you being with a woman makes me hot."

"That kind of hot is for later! Let's go to that incredible pool and get hot in this gorgeous sunshine."

"I'm game. Give me a minute to dress."

"A little moment only."

I'd never been to an all-inclusive resort and had a hard time wrapping my mind around the "everything's free" concept, despite Stuart's insistence that I pamper myself. "It's a beautiful place, Stuart. Thanks for bringing me here. Wish we could stay longer."

"I like to make my baby happy... whatever it takes."

"You *do* make me happy." I squinted, remembering the pain of the times he'd said things that hurt my feelings and cringed. *But now is not the time to bring up bad things, Lela. Shut your trap.*

After an hour or so by the pool, Stuart excused himself to check with the concierge about "my delivery." His exact words.

"Delivery? From the concierge? What in the world did you order?" Then I grasped a passing thought and imagined Stuart had ordered a shitload of roses for me, as he often did. Exhilarated, I urged him to go check with the concierge... fast.

"Why don't you find us a swim-up table and have a drink or two. I'll be back in a flash."

"Okay, my sweet." I bopped his nose and his face reddened.

"Don't do that, Lela. I'm not a kid."

"It's just something I do to people I love. Enjoy it!"

Stuart rolled his eyes as he threw a towel around his neck. I smiled as he walked away, knowing he secretly loved my silly expressions of love.

I swam to the bar, ordered a shot of tequila and a vodka-grapefruit, then leaned back and let my hair float on the water, straddling the underwater stool. I let my mind wander... enjoying the paradise surrounding me.

Ten minutes later, I sat up, looking for Stuart. *Where are you, ding-dong?* Another shot and another drink later, he still hadn't shown. By the time I returned to the room, Stuart had been gone almost an hour.

The room had no foyer area; when I opened the door, I saw Stuart on the bed, naked and nervous. Startled, he fumbled with the TV remote, opening the drawer of the nightstand and stashing something inside. "What was that?" I asked.

"Uh... just an extra remote," he said. I stopped short because I knew that wasn't true. It wasn't black; it was clear and smaller than a remote.

"Don't lie, Stuart, just tell me. It's not like I'm not the Big Bad Wolf and you're in trouble."

"It's my pipe."

My eyes widened, shocked and pissed, I said, "You didn't share your weed with me? Damn! I could've used a hit or two to enhance this tropical paradise."

I spun around the room, spilling dribbles of my drink.

"Sorry." He continued to fidget.

"Doesn't smell like pot, though. Bahamas pot is different, then? Where is it? I want a hit."

"Smoked it all. Sorry."

"No! You wouldn't do that to me!"

"Yeah, it's all gone. It's what the concierge scored for me. Special, double-duty stuff."

"You mean laced with something? Hell, no! I won't smoke that shit, anyway. What was in it? And is that why you're fidgeting? Damn, Stuart, you shouldn't be doing that! You'll fry your brain!"

"Whatever. Enough about that... I have also ordered a present for you. Another concierge delivery."

"Oh! More weed! Great! But I don't want the laced shit. It scares me."

"No, come here. It's even better than that."

"What?" He wiggled his eyebrows, not saying a word. "Tell me!"

"I got you a woman, baby."

"Whaaaat? Yes! Yes!"

"It's been a while, huh?"

"Oh, honey! You know me so well. That's the best gift ever, like adding a cherry on top of paradise."

<<<<<<<>>>>>>

The main level bustled with noise and action. The casino. Hundreds of people crowded the large and loud cavern, frantic with lights flashing, bells ringing, and people shouting through thunderous music. Still wearing my bathing suit, as Stuart had asked me to do, I paid twenty dollars for a cup of quarters. Beside me, my still-fidgety boyfriend bought high-dollar chips and took off for the Blackjack tables.

I felt guilty as shit for even *thinking* about gambling; the concept gave me the heebie-jeebies but a little lecture to myself convinced me I could handle feeding quarters in the slot machines without the vision of my mother ruining my day.

I would start with a small amount and when it was gone, it was gone. I would *not* lose a bucket of money doing the devil's work, as Mom called it. *And you have an addictive personality just like your grandfather did, Lela. So stay away from anything addictive.*

At six o'clock, my quarters were gone. Perfect timing. Stuart arrived with my last losing spin, having won $540 at Blackjack. "Almost pays for the concierge," he said.

"That much? Jeezus, Stuart! Irresponsible money waster!"

"Hush and go find your date. I'll be waiting..." He sang the last part.

With a shit-eating grin, I sauntered to the Palms Bar and Grille by the pool, sucking in nervous air as I came closer to meeting my sexual fantasy.

Only one stool was occupied at the bar; I ordered a drink and sat back to wait. A blonde bombshell sat at the other end, wearing a black bikini as skimpy as my own. When she caught my eye, I smiled and raised my drink. Then the blonde went back to fiddling with her napkin. *When will my date arrive? What will she look like?* I felt the blonde staring at me and I squirmed, feeling uncomfortable and turned on at the same time.

A vision of my date radiated in my mind: a brunette, kinda short, ultra-white teeth, tiny waist, red lipstick and nails... yep, I was waiting for Jenna.

In my peripheral vision, I saw pale skin as somebody took the stool next to mine. *Why are you sitting so close? There are twenty other stools available. Oh. My date.* It was the blonde who'd been toying with me across the bar. "You're Lela?" she asked.

<<<<<<<>>>>>>

Stuart watched me and the blonde while smoking the pot that didn't smell like pot... the pot that was supposedly gone. The pipe was glass and after taking a hit, he exhaled the smoke into a cup, covering it quickly. Thirty seconds later, he'd inhale the smoke in the cup, then repeat. I wanted to ask what the hell he was doing, but I was otherwise occupied.

A more confident, more sober woman would have understood what Stuart was smoking, seen through his lies to his mother... and run away as fast as she could.

But I was in love with the only man I thought would have me. Or at least

the only one I believed could keep me in top-shelf vodka, kickass weed, and fine restaurants.

Drunken wisdom drove me to stay with Stuart and ignore all facts that pointed off track.

I invented a life with Stuart; I established his personality and imagined the way he would treat me. Anything that didn't fit the mold I'd created... I ignored.

Little did I know how far my perception was from reality, or how close to insanity he would push me.

ANTI-SANTA
CHAPTER 18

I had never missed a Christmas at home, never in my 38 years. Mom and Dad opened the farmhouse to all – aunts, uncles, in-laws, stepchildren, boyfriends, neighbors, friends, and friends of friends. The celebration was huge and the food abundant.

Since Andy had whisked Bo to Nashville, our "split-Christmas-Day" custody arrangement changed; now we'd rotate years... and sadly, Bo wasn't at the Christmas celebration in 1997. I was heartbroken about it, carrying the full burden of Mother's Guilt.

Mom and Dad wouldn't do or say anything to further my Guilt; they actually agreed that Bo should've gone with his dad because they knew I wasn't capable of taking care of him. As horrible as losing custody had been, everybody but me knew Bo would be better off. I still held major Resentments against Andy and Ella – both of them. I even hated their dog.

Despite Bo's absence, the Christmas proceeded as planned; our traditions continued. Only the kids received wrapped gifts; the adults stuffed dollar-store gifts into pillowcases that served as "stockings." I'd glitter-personalized a thrift store pillowcase for each person and we always kept a few extras with a glittered "Visitor" name so nobody was left out. The rule: boyfriends had to attend one Christmas as a visitor before getting a personalized pillowcase.

It was Stuart's visitor year. He'd never been to a "Christian Christmas," as he called it. Religious views aside, I tried to explain our family traditions, many of them silly, like playing charades to Christmas carols, but my mind wasn't clicking on all cylinders. I made us sound like a bunch of buffoons.

A sober Lela would have predicted what would happen and left Stuart at home. Even my scattered, alcoholic brain should have foreseen the upcoming drama based on what he said on the way to the farmhouse. He made fun of the landscape, which is beautiful and mountainous, instead joking about the movie *Deliverance*.

When we reached the gravel road to Mom and Dad's house, he joked about bouncing in the jalopy the Beverly Hillbillies drove. I grimaced but felt compelled to laugh along with him. I remembered not wanting to be at *his* parent's house, either, but I was crazy-determined for him to make a good impression at mine.

Mom and Dad had met Stuart only one time before. In her non-accusing, Southern Lady way, Mom had tucked a white curl behind her ear and said she wasn't sure she trusted him. I was ready for an argument, but she refused to take the bait, adding a knowing smile and patting my cheek.

Daddy, who made it a point to only say nice things about people, asked four times if I was *sure* Stuart was the man for me. "Lela, you always said you wanted to marry a man like your daddy... but that damn Stuart... he's the very opposite of me, hon. Think twice." He squinted his blue-gray eyes looking far into the distance and added, "Actually, think ten or twelve times, then think again."

What do sixty-year-old Goody-Two-Shoes parents know about the ways of today's world? And just because Jennifer doesn't like Stuart... and Karen won't like his attitude, it doesn't mean he's a bad guy. They just don't know his ways. They don't know his heart.

Karen had never met Stuart; neither had her fiancé John. As a couple, they were connected-at-the-hip and in the midst of wedding planning. I found it odd she would marry again, after two failures. *Oh... duh... same as you, dumbass Lela.*

But this time, Karen had been picky and found a good one. A railroad engineer, John was a good guy to the core; he'd proved it many times. Not only did he treat Karen like royalty, even when she was flat-out crazy, but he also treated my parents with the ultimate respect and reverence.

As the only "nice guy" any of us had as partners, he'd been deemed a god.

He once told me he loved Mom and Daddy as much as he'd loved his own parents. With that attitude, he was A-OK in my book, no matter what. I just looked the other way when he wiggled his handlebar mustache; I couldn't help but laugh and think of Dudley Do-Right from childhood cartoons.

If Stuart was in "asshole mode," I knew Karen would have a hard time accepting his in-your-face wealth and know-it-all New York attitude; those traits annoyed me, but they would sicken her. I still yearned for my humble older sister's approval and I knew I was on thin ice. Karen idolized the oppressed and despised the privileged.

On the flip side, Karen was a master of tension-busting humor and used her bubbling personality to make others feel welcomed. I hoped *that* side of her would come forward on Christmas Day, but with Karen, it was always a coin toss.

She lost out on the Fox curly-hair genes but had a beautiful face, a flawless complexion, and deep green eyes that sucked you into her world instantly. But when she squinted those eyes, you knew you were scolded, like BANG!... bullet through the heart.

I knew Jennifer, the sister eight years older than me, would be there with her long-term boyfriend who replaced her abusive husband number two. She seemed happy, but I couldn't be sure; we hadn't seen each other much since the autumn celebration at the farm. Jennifer's kids would also be there, and their father, Les... the "nice ex" my Mom still adored, would come late in the day to pick up the kids.

Three daughters, each with two ex-husbands. Mom joked that she would have the ex-sons-in-law be her pallbearers; she had the perfect amount. With his horselaugh, Daddy said he'd make sure that none of them dropped her. It was a long-standing family joke, but I sensed that Daddy didn't think the joke was funny in the least. When it all boiled down, my dear father blamed himself for his three daughter's multiple failed marriages. Poor guy thought it was something he'd done wrong.

<<<<<<<>>>>>>>

"Helllooo," I said as we walked through the front door of the farmhouse. I watched Stuart's eyes roam the room, taking in the "country-style" décor. A sun-filled home, but with ho-hum mauve and blue wallpaper, lace-trimmed draperies, plaid sofas, matching gold *everything* and a doily on each table. He stifled a giggle, and I bonked him in the ribs with my elbow. The glaring look didn't seem to affect him; he looked at me with a question mark on his face.

Despite the ultra-traditional style of the house, the living room opened to the even-sunnier dining room, creating a two-sided great room. All family and friends on the front side gathered around me for the perfunctory greeting hugs, but Stuart made a beeline for the recliner – *Daddy's* recliner. I broke away from the hugs and sat on the sofa, patting the seat beside me. "Come sit here with me, baby." But he wouldn't move.

"What's wrong with sitting here? It's a Lazy Boy!"

"That's *Daddy's* recliner."

"Except on holidays, right?"

"No. It's *always* Daddy's. Come, sit here." I patted the sofa cushion again.

He raised his voice. "Just a minute. Relax, Lela!" The room was suddenly quiet... eerily so. Nobody – *nobody* – sat in Daddy's chair. It was disrespect to the max in his own house, an unspoken rule. *This is not gonna go well. The whole day... he thinks he's in charge, that we're beneath him.* Then I remembered the first time the ex Miller McKeown met my family. *Repeat. Three-peat.*

With no formal introductions to any family members yet, Stuart snagged a magazine from the end table and studied the cover. Ignoring him, I went back through the hug line. All eyed Stuart and questioned his behavior, but there was one who refused to be ignored: John, my soon-to-be brother-in-law. John walked to the recliner casually, extending his hand for a gentleman's handshake.

Stuart didn't stand, shaking his hand and immediately cranking the handle to lay back in the recliner. The footrest bonked John's shins. Though I saw the steam coming from John's ears, he made a joke to ease the tension... a joke I feared would have dire consequences. "Wow! Lazy Boy isn't lazy when it's time to lie down!" *Don't Stuart! No, he wasn't calling you lazy! Don't give him any shit!*

The tension was as thick as Mom's mashed potatoes.

John walked away slowly, eyeing me sideways. Karen had seen the whole thing and wasn't holding back; the devil's evil eye would have been a kinder look toward Stuart. Then Karen looked at me and cocked her head as if asking "why?" I shrugged. Her frown was ominous.

"Dinner's ready!" Mom's twinkling voice brought the troops to the dining table; the kids were already eating.

Our meal was the famous turkey and dressing, cranberry sauce... the works. Another tradition... we didn't sit at the table yet: Daddy was the turkey carver and, as always, worked the crowd with juicy bites of turkey in his greasy hand. He chose his target and barked the order, "Head back! Tongue out!" Then he'd drop the bite-sized morsel on the awaiting tongue. "Chew three times... swallow once!" The expected response was a stern "Thank you, sir!" with a salute... to which he would reply, "Well done, soldier!"

This weird "tradition" held as long as I could remember. These days, the kids loved it best. Not everybody got a bite, but it wasn't lost on me that Daddy skipped Stuart.

After dinner, the kids opened their gifts, and the adults went through their "stockings" one item at a time, per "our rules."

Like everybody's, Stuart's pillowcase brimmed with the typical silly fare: a kid's curly straw, a toothbrush, Pixie Stick candy, a duet of cheap Christmas ornaments, the world's ugliest oven mitt, a can of black beans (low sodium and expired), wind-up Happy Meal toys, a tangerine, soap balls, and a handful of loose pecans. Stuart didn't understand the humor. As we laughed at the sheer stupidity of the marginally useful but meant-to-be-funny gifts, he said "Thanks, but no thanks."

Again, conversation stopped. John's daughter, about fifteen, was the first to speak. "Alllrighty-then." More silence before I chimed in, "Stuart, you don't get it. See... it's *supposed* to be stupid!"

"And it *is* stupid," he said. Another eerie silence, something that hadn't happened at my folk's house in years.

Mom, ever the peacemaker, broke the tension. "Jennifer! You're next. What silly goodies did Santa bring to you?"

He didn't say a thing as we went through the rest of the stocking protocol, but sat with an erect back and an uninterested expression. I stood. "Come on, let's go smoke a cigarette." He readily agreed and I felt the disgusted looks of my family on our backs.

Safe on the patio, I blew up, telling him exactly what I thought. After the first nearly unintelligible paragraph, I added, "You're acting like a complete asshole, even worse than my ex-husband!"

"Don't you EVER say that to me! Your ex-husb–"

I interrupted, so angry I was shaking. "FUCK YOU! I'll say whatever the hell I want to say! You're being BEYOND rude... like you're WANTING them to hate you."

"Why should I care?"

First, a blast of shock overtook my body. *Did he really just say that?* I blew smoke through my nostrils, willing myself to remain calm, then I let loose. "Listen here you short, fat, dickhead sonofabitch, it's my *family!* So, so different from yours, Asswipe. Flash the Southern charm you use with transmission customers... and why do I even have to tell you that?" I stopped to catch my breath. "Dammit, Stuart... you say you love me, yet you treat me like *this?* How could you?"

I was huffing, my throat the diameter of a decimal point.

Stuart didn't respond, smoking his cigarette casually and shivering when the December wind blew. Finally, he whispered, "Okay, I'm sorry. I'll do better. Please forgive me. It's just that... your family is so different from mine."

"No shit, Sherlock." My breath was ragged with anger and I felt the beginnings of a migraine coming on. "Different, yeah... but I didn't insult *your* family when we visited. I didn't look down my nose at them, that's for sure... and that's what you're doing today."

"But I didn't mean–"

"Shut up and LISTEN! What we have here is what you don't have at your house. We're *real people*... and we have *love*. Absorb it, get off on it. Just don't make fun of it." Taking another hit from my cigarette, I blew the smoke in a plume... as hard and fast as I could. Anything to relieve the tension.

"I'm sorry, Lela."

"You know what? Fuck you. I don't want your apologies." With my hand on the knob going in, I said, "Come in when you want... please don't hurry."

<<<<<<<>>>>>>

I was glad Daddy was in the kitchen when a news-magazine show aired a story about labor unions. The sound was off, couldn't have been heard over the chaos, anyway, but Stuart unknowingly popped a comment about how unions are destroying the U.S. economy. I tried to be the first to correct him, but I spoke too late.

The proud, working-class Fox family was pro-union all the way and vocal as hell about it. John was a union rep for the railroad, had been for years. And Daddy's lifelong career had been in support of the union... from leading a strike in the 60s at Burgess Press, through this last job in workers' rights at Portland Coal Company in West Virginia.

Karen stood, inching toward Stuart. "How *dare* you speak ill of the union in this house!? You best shut the hell up before my Daddy hears you." I can't remember exactly what Stuart said in return; I zoned out, I think, but I remember Karen's inch-by-inch movement toward Stuart... like encroachment. Like she was going to throw him against the wall. The buzz of fear began in my head.

Jennifer overheard Karen's comment and stomped over to join the hullabaloo. "Don't trash the union here, you worm! And my father's not too old to kick your ass."

Shit like this doesn't happen at my house! What has Stuart done to my Christmas? I'm a nervous wreck in my family home!

I interrupted, speaking over the cacophony. "Hey everybody, we're leaving! Got to get home and feed the dogs." Shouts of "Why so early?" and "Don't go yet, Lela!" filled the room.

Without Stuart, I could've and would've stayed 'til midnight. I could hang out with my family and be happy without a drop to drink, for the most part. We were a tight bunch.

Before I half-finished the announcement, Stuart jumped up and grabbed his coat.

"Nice to meet all you people!" he said as if he had truly made an effort to know them. I let a chuckle erupt; it was hilarious how desperately he wanted out of there.

Why didn't you leave him at home, Lela? How will you ever live this down? Your sisters will not let this go. And Mom... Daddy... I've disappointed them – again.

I said goodbye to my niece through a fog... focusing only on my bitter disappointment. *Why did he act so out of character? He's not a negative, asshole guy any other day... why did it have to be MY Christmas Day? It must be some kind of social anxiety bullshit like your therapist talks about… like Miller had.*

I was in the throes of the goodbye tradition for a long while. Stuart stood in the foyer tapping his foot. Twenty minutes later, he caught my eye with a pleading look. Thankfully, he said nothing and I ignored his presence as I finished my goodbyes, albeit shorter ones than I would've normally enjoyed.

"Bye, everybody! Merry Christmas!" I sang, closing the door behind me. Stuart looked ready to explode. He grabbed my arm, rushed me down the ramp, across the driveway, and into the Lexus. I was screaming at him the whole time, not because he hurt me physically, but he had murdered me emotionally.

I let loose on him in the car, cussing him and shaming him, doing anything possible to make him know how mad and hurt I was. He took all I dished out, then calmly said. "I'm sorry, Lela. Honey-bear, sorry if I upset you… because I love you so much! So, so, so much! But they ganged up on me! I had no defense, baby! Please forgive me, please!" Fuming, I didn't respond.

Five minutes later, Stuart said, "By the way, your sister's fiancée… that John guy… is an asshole. He threatened to beat me up, the fucking redneck!"

There was nothing to say. I sure as hell won't bring him back. *I'll find a way to excuse this somehow, or just give it time to smooth over. No… maybe it's best to just stay away from all of them now. Yeah… that's it. I don't like that I can't drink in front of them, anyway. Fuck! Merry Christmas, my ass.*

This was the first time Stuart placed a wedge between my family and me. After years of study in dysfunctional relationships now, I've learned the first goal in controlling the victim is to isolate them from those they love and depend on. He already knew who that was for me.

My family was my lifeline; I had always scrambled to please them… to ease the disappointment I'd dealt lifelong. And I depended on them to feed me morsels of self-worth, to give pats on the back… all the things I couldn't do for myself. Taking them away was the first step in my emotional downfall.

Surely this would have been enough to make me tell him to eat shit and die, or to go straight to hell, right? But I didn't. I clung to the fact that Stuart loved me and nobody else would, accepting the life I was "destined" to live

with the partner I was "destined" to have.

Barely functioning, I knew starting over with another partner would be more than I could handle. And I couldn't imagine living without money, privilege, or someone to take care of me. So I blamed my family for the fiasco, as Stuart encouraged me to do.

Remembering this day remains painful and shameful. I was so clouded by alcoholism that my judgements were just as clouded. To cover my embarrassment in front of my family, I took a step back from them... something I'd never been willing to do before.

As usual, my family members called me the week following Christmas, but if I answered at all, I made an excuse to cut the call short. The only one who didn't call was Daddy. I found out why five years later, in Lifetime Number Six, when I made amends to him.

MOTHER DAMON

CHAPTER 19

I took the week between Christmas and New Year's off from work. After the whirlwind of holiday craft shows, it was a thrill to just sit and do nothing.

My buddy Damon had taken that week off every year for as long as I had known him, and every year, he'd say, "I bet the Post Office can do without me." To appease him, I still laughed at the joke, but it wasn't funny after the first year.

For the last five-or-so years, Damon and I had hung out during that off week. And even if not a tradition, it would be the perfect time to see him; the two of us didn't talk when Stuart was around.

Dialing the familiar number, Damon exploded in joy just from hearing my voice. I barked, "Hey, dude!" as a greeting.

It was almost a squeal. "Lela! I've missed you so much!"

"How was your Christmas?" We chatted about our kids, and how it sucked to split holidays with ex-wives and ex-husbands, blah, blah, blah. Damon wanted to know if Stuart and I had gone to the farm to see my parents. I told him we had.

"So he's now your family-approved boyfriend?"

"Uh... no, not at all," I didn't want to tell Damon anything about the fiasco. "Nah... he was just there, met everyone. It was–"

Damon interrupted before I could stick my foot in my mouth. "Everyone?

So I'm the only one who hasn't met the mysterious Stuart?" I had only talked to Damon a few times since Stuart moved in, and managed to keep them in separate parts of my life. Deep within, I knew Damon wouldn't approve of Stuart; he'd think the love of my life was a New York asshole, rude and not good enough for me. And I didn't want to disappoint Damon.

"You don't want to meet him, Damon. He's stolen my heart."

"You're right. He's my sworn enemy. But I'd like to see *you*, my curly friend. Soon."

"Let's do lunch? Tomorrow?"

"Why not today? Can you force yourself to get ready before dusk? My treat, and your choice of where."

"Sure! Why not?"

"Great! I'll come to get you at noon. And please be ready, Lela. I know how you do sometimes."

"I'll be ready. Can we go for steak? After all that turkey, I'm ready for some red meat!"

"You got it. In fact, I think I'll make a reservation for the round room at Leonard's."

"Oh wow... are you trying to romance me, Damon Toomey?"

"Ha, ha, ha. I wish I could, girl. No, it's just private. This week, everything is so crowded! Maybe I'd just like to hear what you say."

"See you at noon, then!" I said. But he had already hung up.

<<<<<<<<<>>>>>>>

Murphy barked when Damon rang the bell. "Come in, it's open!" I had made a point to surprise him and be ready when he arrived.

"Hey!" Then a long pause. "Lela! What's wrong?"

"Well, it's nice to see you, too, Turkeybutt!" I replied in jest. Thinking again, I wanted to know why he asked. "What do you mean? Have I changed?"

"Lela, you look sick. Or tired. Or both. What the hell?" Damon cocked his head and twisted his face looking at me.

"So I look bad? Really? What *is* it?" Suddenly, I was as concerned as he seemed to be.

"How much *weight* have you lost? Damn, girl. You're a skeleton!"

"But I haven't lost weight! It's just these pants. See? They're baggy... on purpose." I flapped the extra fabric at my thigh. "It's called *fashion,* Damon." Truthfully, those pants helped me hide in full sight; I was self-conscious about my body in those pants took away some Shame.

"Your face... sunken, and you're pale. You're either *getting* sick or you've *been* sick for a long time."

"Damon! You make me feel so beautiful!" I spun a pirouette. "Look! I'm *not* sick. You just haven't seen me for a while. Over a month, in fact!"

"Turn around." I refused, and we verbally wrestled for a bit. In the end, he gave in. "Okay... but for the record, I'm worried. What's this Stuart guy been doing to you?"

"Nothing!" I feigned no concern, but Damon's worry had rubbed off on me. *HAVE I lost weight? DO I look sick? IS something wrong?* I excused myself and stepped to the bathroom mirror. I saw it. Hollow cheeks, my color was off, my eyes were dark, sunken, gray instead of turquoise. *Damn! He's right! I look like shit!*

I stepped back into the living room where I found him messing with the television. "You're right. I don't look so hot today. But I don't know why... it just *is.* So fuck it! Let's have a happy afternoon together, anyway, my sweet friend. Let's get out of here."

"Ready as soon as I find the score of the game."

I ignored him. "And you didn't mention... aren't you amazed I'm ready? Right on time!" Damon obviously didn't hear; he was listening intently to the talking head on TV. I repeated the comment.

He found the channel, nodded, then looked back at me. One more time, his brow knotted. "Maybe you should see a doctor. Are you taking your medicine?"

Sigh. "I take it when I remember." *Why not play the game... let him talk. He's not going to let it drop, anyway.*

"How many different meds now?"

"Six, I think... no, seven," I said, counting on my fingers. "Nope. Eight. Listen to this shit... the last appointment, I told him my sex drive was down, and he added something else! The drug companies must pay him big-time."

"Still taking the Adderal?"

"Dammit, Damon! Are we going or not?"

"But it's way too much medicine!"

"Shut up!" I threw my hand in the air, grabbed my purse, and walked out the front door. "Meet you in the car. Lock the knob, please."

AUNT VAL & THE ZIPPERS
CHAPTER 20

An upcoming big weekend for the Fox family: Aunt Valerie's wedding. Aunt Val, Daddy's older sister and the one who lived with Granny Liz in Lorraine, Virginia for over thirty years, would become a bride at age 55. A spinster, a staunch Christian, a family-focused woman of means, and the one called "Fox National Bank."

When I was young and visiting Granny Liz, Aunt Val was the supposed disciplinarian but we eventually discovered her threats were empty. Then, me, my sisters, and a passel of cousins terrorized her. Once, a group of us topped her mattress with three layers of sharp rocks; she acted mad but laughed about it with the adults.

And even when Karen threw me down the laundry chute, Aunt Val didn't rat out my sister... just comforted me and bandaged my bloody head.

She was the first female Federal Court Clerk in Virginia, a trailblazer, and she was well-paid. And, being a Fox, she pinched every penny and saved every dime.

So, with plenty of money, she shared her good fortune with my many aunts and uncles... randomly and generously. Six times I knew of, and probably more, Mom and Dad received a check from Aunt Val, with a scribbled note, something like... "for the year's mortgage payments," or "Margaret needs her own car," or "for Lela's college fund." She sent money to her nieces and nephews, too, when she smelled a need, though I was never a recipient. At least not yet.

When pushed, she admitted the gifts were payback for her siblings' long-ago suffering; the younger ones "did without" as Granny Liz paid for Aunt Val's education. Forever grateful and gainfully employed because of that education, she felt obligated to repay them. It didn't matter that all the brothers and sisters did okay on their own; she sent them money, anyway.

Single all her life, Aunt Val was now retiring from her post. Ten years prior, she had reconnected with a long-lost boyfriend from high school, the only man she had ever loved, she said. Merritt Sarney.

In high school, she dropped Merritt like a hot potato when she discovered he drank a beer with the boys. One beer. Like Granny Liz, Aunt Val adamantly opposed alcohol (who wouldn't...with an abusive alcoholic father, right?), and she kicked Merritt Sarney to the curb.

But Merritt called 42 years later, now a widower who no longer drank. He asked to see her and romance bloomed. It became a ten-year love affair that brought sudden color to Aunt Val's world. She flitted around in love, comically so, but still 100 percent practical. She'd marry him after she retired, she said, and after Granny Liz settled elsewhere.

The retirement party would be on Friday, the wedding on Saturday; it would be a family celebration with great fanfare. Even the distant relatives would attend, and I arranged to meet Andy halfway to pick up Bo! Oh, the joy of showing him off! And I hoped he'd meet my cousin Dude.

Uh, oh. I hope Aunt Lil won't be there. What if she mentions the drunken letter I wrote? What if she confronts me in front of everybody!? I called Daddy to check the guest list. Good and bad: no Aunt Lil, but no cousin Dude, either.

Bo wasn't so hot about going, being sixteen and flexing his muscles at the girls. "It's not punishment, son! It's family! No matter how cool you are, you still go to reunions, Mr. Teenage King," Bo would resist with his last breath, I knew, so I played the trump card. "It never hurts to get in good with Aunt Val, a.k.a. Fox National Bank."

Stuart had to work and couldn't go: A-OK by me. I didn't want him to uh... "misunderstand" this side of the family, too, and I told him so as he watched me pack. "Stuart, don't forget Murphy's thyroid medicine, every morning without fail, please."

He blew me off while pretending to help me pack. But he wasn't helping me... he was rushing me. "I know how to take care of a dog, Lela! Go! Don't be late!" But something in the back of my mind buzzed. *Why is he so eager for me to go? What plans does he have for this weekend?* I opened my mouth to ask, but he interrupted my thoughts. "Zip your suitcase! Hurry!"

<<<<<<<>>>>>>

A perfect wedding and 100 percent traditional, per my family's oh-so-appropriate moral code. As "Here Comes the Bride" played, I found it both humorous and heartwarming to see the pale Aunt Val creep slowly down the aisle, bent with age. White hair, white dress, white rose... but she glowed with a happiness apparent to all.

Her husband-to-be, dashing in a gray-striped tuxedo, held a charming, toothy smile as love sang its sweet songs in the chapel. And Granny Liz, in a full-length blue gown she had sewn herself, shined as she walked the aisle with Aunt Val to give her away.

All my aunts, uncles, and cousins attended, the only exceptions being cousin Lewis the Dude and his mom, Aunt Lil.

For emergencies only, I took a dozen airline bottles of Absolut. With just a few exceptions, I controlled the cravings. My hands shook, but I was eager to be sober and one-on-one with Bo. After the fiasco at the Goose Creek Inn, I swore I wouldn't drink in front of him again.

Bo must have noticed because the two of us got along beautifully; he seemed happy to be with me.

When we returned to the hotel after the celebration, I said, "Hey, Bo! Want to play 'Hide the Cheezits?'" I hoped to re-invent the game with a sober Lela, but I guess it just reminded him of the horrible weekend. He shut down, and shut me out.

Heartbreak.

I took two Absolut bottles to Karen and John's room and chugged them in the bathroom, spent some time with sis and her hub before returning to the room I shared with Bo.

He was asleep, or pretending to be. Another tiny bottle downed in the bathroom, a little television, a little sleep. I couldn't wait to get out of there. After faking my way through niceties at the breakfast bar downstairs, Bo and I hopped in the van and left before anybody else.

As soon as I dropped Bo at his dad's, I drove to the liquor store. More airline bottles for the drive back to Rockville.

What should have been a happy family celebration for my favorite aunt Val became a weekend with an unwelcome visitor, my old friend, Shame. A weekend guest I could only control with a drink. By then, the Shame that *caused* my drinking was also the *result* of my drinking.

The chicken *and* the egg.

<<<<<<<>>>>>>

I got home on Sunday afternoon, around four o'clock. Stuart sat naked on the sofa waiting for me, with a bottle of wine and a red velvet cake, a fire in the fireplace, lights down, candles lit. *Aaah, what a sweet man! He loves me so much!*

That sweet man rubbed my hair and purred about how much he missed me, said the house had been "lonely and strange" without me. After a little making out on the sofa, I straightened up to light a cigarette. I blew out smoke and asked, "So what did you do while I was gone?"

"Not a damn thing, Lela. I sat here and pined for you. Lonely and sad." Stuart imitated a pout. "But now you're back and I'm a happy, happy man!" His smile warmed my heart.

That night around three AM, after an hour of tossing and turning, I got up with a sigh. Thinking a little vodka would help me sleep, I trod downstairs and saw a new angle of the living room.

Curious... The sofa cushions had covers with zippers on the back. But now, the zippers on two cushions were in the *front*.

Why did he disassemble the sofa?

A ZAP flashed down my spine. *Why did he take the sofa cushions off? He had a woman here! That two-timing mother fucker!*

I bounded up the steps to ask, thinking maybe if I woke him up cold, I'd catch him off-guard and get a straight answer. Wasting no time, I jostled him, shook his shoulder roughly. "Stuart, wake up." He jerked and rolled toward me.

"Wha? What the hell, Lela? It's the middle of the night!" He rolled over again, ignoring me.

By then, my voice had risen an octave and my hands shook with rage. "Tell me, dammit! Why did you take the sofa cushions off?" No response, but I saw his eyes open. Wide. His body froze as he looked into the corner and I could see his wheels turning, searching for the correct words.

He raised on one elbow, speaking with care. "Rock-Bob and I were playing. Why are you so concerned?" His demeanor caused even more suspicion; Stuart enunciated each syllable separately.

"Don't lie to me, you mother fucker! Did you have a woman here this weekend, Stuart? Tell me the truth!"

Again, the slow, almost-staccato speech. "No, Lela, I did not. Nothing happened."

I shoved his shoulder back toward the mattress and stood by the bed, towering over the crumb of a man. "Fuck you! I don't believe you." A vision of his Saturday night burned like a flame in my mind: Stuart and a harlot, some flashy-trashy woman, had a high-volume roll in the hay on my living room floor.

I was *convinced*. "Stuart, you're a liar. You had a woman here! *Admit it*." My voice had risen to a shrill scream but Stuart didn't get mad, continuing in the calm voice, repeating a denial and adding no more detail.

An innocent man would be angry about being accused. What did he do? How could he DO this?

"Calm down. Come to bed! Lela, you're imagining things!" But his face showed just how wide-awake he had become. And he looked scared. *Guilty son of a bitch!*

I left the bedroom in a huff. I remember sitting on the sofa later that night, drinking coffee with a generous mixture of Bailey's liqueur and wondering how I could possibly live without him.

Without a doubt, I was emotionally, financially, and alcoholically dependent on Stuart. And I remember thinking about the pain and uncertainty of starting over to find a new boyfriend who would accept me, as fucked-up as I was. Being on my own was impossible, and I was broke. I needed Stuart in every way.

After three cups of coffee, deliberately drunk, I stomped upstairs again and sat down to play with beads and pewter charms in my studio. My mind wouldn't turn off; I knew I stood at a turning point and something – anything! – must happen.

I cringed, feeling desperate. *I can't let go of him... who will help pay the* rent? *Who will love me?*

Then the other side of my brain screamed: *He CHEATED on you, Lela! He has no loyalty to you, no respect... and doing it once means he'll do it again. Think of Andy when he cheated with Ella.*

Desperate side: *But couples cheat and forgive, then move past it to have a great marriage! And, face it, what solid evidence do you have? Backward cushions?*

Logical side: *He's never taken the cushions off before. Not for the dog or for any reason.*

Desperate side: *But what if he's telling the truth? Then you'd be walking out on a good thing! For no reason!*

Logical side: *Talk to him at length. Get a straight answer. Check his alibi. Follow your gut... and have a plan to leave in your back pocket.*

Desperate side: *But it's just ONE bad decision! Like I'VE never made one! So maybe I'll just sleep with somebody, too... to get even, right? Then we'll go forward as equals.*

At the time, this seemed like a logical solution, but the plans for it perplexed me. *So who can I sleep with? One-night stands suck... you discovered that years ago, right? So... maybe Damon? Would that be bad... to use him like that?*

A pause to think my plan through.

It would sure make Damon happy... and I'm his good friend... one who wants him to be happy, right? What could be the harm? But how? And where?

I contemplated the possibilities. *Well, "where" is easy: throw the sofa cushions on the floor!*

I heard a noise behind me, a croaky voice. "Hey."

Stuart stood naked at the door of my studio, deep blanket wrinkles on his left cheek and his hair askew. "Come to bed. Don't let your imagination get the best of you."

"But... I don't know–"

"Exactly. You *don't* know. So don't let your magic magnifying mind create something that's not there. Come to bed, honey."

I dropped my gaze and looked at his feet on the plywood-covered floor, then scanned up to his knobby knees, swollen belly, muscular arms and shoulders...

and slowly returned my gaze to his face. I stared, wondering how long I should make him suffer.

He spoke again, "Seriously, babe, come to bed. You're safe. We're okay. Nothing has changed."

My bottom lip quivered and the sound of a giant undersea wave built in my ears. The tears that dripped from the outside of my eyes were involuntary; I let them roll down my cheeks as if a faucet had been tapped. Silence. And the moment seemed frozen in time as we stared at each other across the studio.

I was hurt, angry, confused, scared, a flurry of heart-wrenching emotions. Mostly, I was desperate to believe him.

"No sleep for me tonight. Go back to bed, Stuart." I swiveled my chair back to face the desk and strung a glass bead on the necklace I'd been making. About sixty seconds later, I heard his footsteps fade toward the bedroom.

> The weak, desperate, drunken Lela was 100 percent overwhelmed by the whole scenario. I just wanted it to go away; I bargained to find a way to put the puzzle back together the way was before.
>
> To make it go away, I was willing to accept a less-than-ideal relationship as long as I didn't have to be without one.
>
> The desperate, shameful Lela had no backbone; it was as loose as my morals and as transient as my connection to reality.
>
> I decided backward cushions didn't prove he'd done anything wrong. And I bargained again: if he could live with my screwy behavior, I could live with a little suspicion. I remember saying out loud, "At least for now."
>
> The words rolled off my tongue tasting bitter, but I swallowed them anyway.
>
> The logical side of my brain *knew* Stuart had brought a woman into *my* house, had sex on *my* cushions… and I was *incensed!* And the logical side knew I should have kicked him out two seconds after I saw the cushions.
>
> So the desperate side took the logical side downstairs to mix another drink.

ONE ON TWO

CHAPTER 21

"I want you to go to see Kate with me," I said. Kate Cole, my therapist.

"Why? She's *your* crazy-counselor, not mine."

"If nothing else, I want Kate to meet you... the man I've been telling her about." I smiled and fiddled with Stuart's gray cowlick, teasing him.

"Oh yeah?" He cocked his head and smiled at me. "I've seen a few therapists myself over the years, that's for sure. How long have you been seeing her?"

"Years and years. Since before I married Miller. So, that's like... fifteen years, on and off." Kate and I had discussed much, and our sessions were usually quite intense. Like any good therapist, she knew me better than I knew myself. But the problem was I argued with her, especially when she mentioned that I "probably" drank too much.

"Has Kate ever talked to you about drinking? About alcoholism?"

"Why do you ask, asshole?"

"Thought she might have."

"If it's your business... she says I probably drink too much, but I also talk too much, think too much, do too much. Everything is 'too much' according to her." I sighed. "See, even though I've been trying to defend you, she thinks you may not be who you say you are. Because, oh yeah, while I think too much, I also don't think enough." I laughed.

"Then I'll see her. Because I want to convince her I'm the wonderful guy you know I am," Stuart said with a wide and charming smile. "Then she'll quit questioning it. Maybe we can cover some of your other issues?"

Eyes glaring, I huffed. "Like *what* other issues?"

"Your, uh... family issues, dear?"

Instantly infuriated, I screamed, "I don't have family issues! What the hell are you talking about?" *As if he knows the details of my family relationships! He doesn't know shit!* I retorted, "Maybe we should talk about the harlot you screwed in my living room floor."

"Okay, I'll drop it. What time is the appointment?"

<<<<<<<>>>>>>>

I didn't wait long; my perky therapist waltzed into the waiting room immediately after I checked in. I hadn't arranged a joint session beforehand, so I asked if Stuart could come in. "Yes, please," she answered, and as she inhaled him, her eyebrow rose an inch. At last, she turned, swinging her brunette curls.

Introductions. Niceties. Good to meet you, etcetera. Kate put the ever-present notepad on her lap and flashed the friendly smile that welcomed me each week. She had sincerity down pat. "So... Stuart. Tell me about yourself."

"Well... I was born a poor black child in 1932," he said with a straight face. I cracked up but Kate didn't seem so amused. After an uncomfortable silence, Stuart said, "Evidently you haven't seen that movie." Kate didn't answer. "Okay. Well. I was raised by my nanny Tonya in Scarsdale, New York... Westchester County. My dad died when I was fourteen and a girl broke my heart, so I ran away to Switzerland for high school. Also in Switzerland for a few years of college... then to Fort Lauderdale. By then, my parents were staying there year 'round. I floundered around for a while, playing the rich kid. Then opened a business." He cleared his throat. "Which failed. And agreed to a marriage, which also failed."

"Two for two?" Kate asked, being funny I assumed.

"Stuart nodded with a chuckle and continued, "I have a son, Jeremy, almost five. It was a nasty divorce and I'm still fighting for custody. The ex-wife is a bad alcoholic. She–"

Kate interrupted. "Tell me about *you*, not your ex, please." *Wow, a snippy little comment from Kate. What's up with that? If she's going to be mean to*

Stuart, then I'll... My thought dissolved when Stuart began again, continuing to talk about Crazy Janey.

"Well, she went to rehab, but that didn't seem to help. And now–"

Kate cut him off again, still in that snippy tone of voice. "Have *you* ever gone to rehab, Stuart?" My mind was instantly on fire, my arms raised in defense as if fighting off a predator. *Why is she asking him that... and why is she mad?*

Stuart had paused; I supposed he also wondered why Kate had asked the question. Finally, he spoke. "No, not rehab. But back in the day, I did admit I had a slight problem and attended a few AA meetings." *It was Crazy Janey with the problem... Stuart is cured. He's one of the lucky ones. Tell her that, Stuart... tell her!*

"A 'slight problem'? How much of a 'slight problem'?" She gestured air quotes.

"I don't know, really. But I quit drinking for about a year. Felt better. Then my ex relapsed, and so did I. Turns out, nothing changed. I didn't have an addiction problem after all."

"Do you drink now?"

"A little," he answered. His foot began to jiggle. I saw Kate notice it.

"Ever do drugs?"

"A little." The foot jiggled a little harder. Again, Kate noticed.

"What about now? Doing drugs now?"

Stuart uncrossed his legs and stretched. "I smoke a little weed. But you can't report me, right?" A nervous laugh.

"Actually, I could. *Lela* is my client, not you. But I don't turn people in for smoking a little weed." Stuart snorted. I could feel his anxiety building and found it unusual for him to be this nervous, especially about something as innocent as smoking weed. *Something else must be going on. Or maybe this "interrogation" would make anybody uncomfortable.*

Kate wrote something on that damn notepad, not looking at the paper. Then she turned toward me. "Lela, tell me about your relationship with Stuart. How do you two get along? What do you do for fun?"

"But you know all that already! I thought you would ask *him* about–"

Kate cut me off with an instant comeback: "Maybe you'd say something different with Stuart in the room."

Stuttering, I answered, "No, we're open with each other. No secrets," I said.

Kate wrote something on the notepad again. "Stuart, do you agree? No secrets?"

"No secrets," he vowed without hesitation. I nodded at Stuart and again at Kate.

Out of character, Kate sighed; maybe she wanted that topic to continue. "Let's move on." I saw Stuart visibly relax. Then she asked Stuart, "How often do you see your son? Tell me about your relationship with him." He spent ten minutes talking about his horrible situation with Crazy Janey, the bitchy Brit. Stuart told Kate that Janey had insisted he take a drug test that had to be done in Fort Lauderdale.

"Why haven't you flown down there to do it then?" Kate asked, again scribbling on her notepad. *That damn notepad!* I cringed to think there was a permanent record of our sessions.

"I was in Florida not too long ago, but on a weekend. It's not easy to just fly off when you have a job, you know!" He'd raised his voice and my heart rate rose with it. *Please, Stuart, don't lose control around Kate. Stay calm, be nice, be cool.*

Kate didn't miss a beat. "But it seems your son would be a priority if you really want to see him. And, speaking of that, do you pay child support?"

"Crazy Janey had my paycheck garnished," he answered sheepishly.

"Why? Did you not pay on your own?"

"I missed once, *just once*, and she called the state. Plus, she hosed me. I pay *way* more than a Tennessee judge would have ordered."

Kate's face was flat. "That's beside the point, Stuart."

He stared at her in silence for a full ten seconds. Kate wouldn't look away nor lower her left eyebrow. The look wasn't friendly and my blood pressure spiked, scrambling for something to say that would break the tension. Suddenly, Stuart sat forward. "Well, I've got to run! Back to work!" He was unnecessarily cheerful. *What's up with that?*

He took two extra-long strides toward the door, then touched the knob and paused. A quick turnaround, he stepped back toward me, leaning down to peck a cheek-kiss. "See you at home, honey. Let's go out to a nice dinner. You like Altruda's, right?" I smiled but furrowed my brow. *Why is he acting so... cheerful? What's this sing-song voice about? He's acting like he's faking something.*

There was a pause after Stuart left. Kate rearranged in her chair and I did the same. "He's... interesting. Do you have any idea why he was so nervous?"

I answered before she finished her question, in a booming accusatory tone. "Wouldn't *you* be nervous if you were being so clearly interrogated? You treated him like an arch enemy, like a threat!" My eyes flashed at her as I rushed into defense mode. I didn't want to hear anything negative about Stuart from anybody, but especially from my therapist.

Because I felt Kate's crushing disapproval, both professional and personal, I decided at that moment to cancel all upcoming appointments. *She's getting too close. I'm depending on her too much. She doesn't understand my situation. Kate is being too much like my mom, so conservative. She can't possibly understand how I feel!*

My feelings of distress wound to a crescendo, playing the blame game.

"Dammit, I gotta go, Kate. I can't hear you say bad things about him. Stuart is a good man! A *very* good man! And he treats me like a queen! Because you heard that, there at the end! Get off his back!" I stood to leave.

"See you next week?" Kate said as I walked out of the door.

"No!"

<<<<<<<<>>>>>>>

A few days later, I called for an appointment with Kate, forgetting how she had insulted me. As soon as my butt hit the sofa in her office, she brought up the problems she saw in Stuart, but I fought back, finally shouting at her to change the subject.

"Listen! Kate, I have another problem. I want to sleep with Damon." That damn eyebrow raised as she looked at me with an obvious question.

"And why?"

"It's not... well... it's a payback thing and I need your help because there's a chance I'll fall in love with him."

"Fall in love with Damon when you're in love with Stuart?" she asked, scribbling on the notepad while keeping her eyes on mine.

I continued, "It's so easy to fall in love when you're free as a bird, Kate! Don't you know that? And Lela Fox flies by the seat of her pants, more than once falling in love with whoever fell in love with *her*. A man liking me is pretty much the only requirement."

"You're telling *me* this? Lela, I've known you for years... but I'm glad you're now willing to investigate these things *yourself*."

"Investigate? Nah... I'll do that later. Right now I just need you to tell me how to fuck Damon without fucking myself. Advise me, advisor... I don't have much time."

With her usual finesse, Kate talked me out of seducing Damon. But she followed up by insisting we talk about Stuart and my curious dependence on him at the next session.

Denial was my defense, even though I knew it was a sham of an argument, and I made sure I argued until there was no time left in the session. Saved by the bell. I used this tactic a lot in therapy.

Looking back, I now understand my drunken wisdom justified Stuart's "perfect place" in my life. Logic no longer existed in my world of 24-hour drinking; the only wisdom I had was drunken wisdom and that seldom suffices.

Turns out, Kate was right to warn me about Stuart; everybody who tried to warn me was right. In my heart, I *knew* they were right. But I was terrified of being alone... and Stuart was there, money in hand, and his other hand pouring me a drink of premium vodka.

I loved him dearly... before it all crashed. But it took what it took for me to see the truth.

Thanks to Dude, I *did* see the truth. And for that, I am eternally grateful.

But I wasn't finished yet; there was more to learn about myself and the disease, more to help me see the hopelessness I faced. Stuart, in his own blindness, was the one to help me see the light. So I'm grateful for him, too.

Only a sober alcoholic can understand that.

THE SNATCH
CHAPTER 22

Stuart told me all about it. With the usual snotty attitude, his boss had said, "I'll remember this ballsy request when I ask you to take inventory some Sunday." As always, it was like pulling teeth to arrange an afternoon off, but Stuart stood firm in his resolve. The extra hours allowed a 3:25 PM flight to West Palm Beach, arriving at 5:45 with a short layover in Atlanta.

"Just in time for a nice dinner!" Stuart said, leaning over to peck my lips as the plane taxied to the gate. We both had a happy drunken glow, and both struck with the everything's-funny-as-hell giggles.

This Florida trip would be quick but ultra important. Stuart was looking for a job. In two weeks, he'd receive his paid vacation after a full year at Rockville's AAA Transmissions. The plan: we'd spend that vacation week at another Bahamas resort, then return to Rockville for Stuart to turn in his resignation. He had the letter written already, edited by his loving girlfriend the trained writer.

He planned to stay in transmission sales, but didn't want to move to Fort Lauderdale proper; his former business had failed there. So he chose one notch up the coast, West Palm Beach. He'd been doing research, he said, finding the largest independent shops in the area. "No more chain shops," he vowed.

With us going in two directions for the weekend, we'd succumbed to convenience and purchased cell phones. The technology wasn't exactly brand-new, but just a handful of people kept one for personal use. The phones were expensive. Stuart paid for both of ours, and our numbers were sequential, which I thought was romantic and sweet.

"Let's synchronize our watches!" he said, opening his flip phone. Animated and playing with our new toys, we mixed drinks, clicked a toast and had another two drinks before going out to dinner.

On the way to the car, I asked, "Are you okay to drive, Stuart?"

"Of course. Why would you ask?"

"Cuz' I'm drunk on my ass. And hungry! What's this place?"

"Brook's Garden."

"Sounds like a tourist spot with flowers and ivy and shit."

"Five-star French restaurant, babe. Totally understated, obscure even. You'll see it and think... 'What *is* this non-descript place?' but you just wait! You'll freak! Is it safe to say you've never been to a *real*, five-star restaurant?"

"Uh... remember, hon, I'm just a country girl. But why are you spending this much money on food? I mean, it's just tomorrow's poop."

Stuart laughed. "The tab will go on my mother's account by default."

"Stuart, that's not right! She wants nothing to do with you!"

"Lela, you don't understand rich people. Relax. Let me handle it."

Stuart was right; I didn't understand rich people, and I didn't understand what a five-star French restaurant was all about, but I was soon to discover the mystery. It was the kind of place with six spoons and a dozen forks at each place setting, more silverware than I had ever seen. I flashed back to the dinner at Stuart's mother's house... if I thought *that* was confusing, this was triple the complexity.

After two courses, a menu and new glass of wine for each course, my memory fades. But one thing I remember is somewhere after the main course... looking in the ladies' room mirror, examining my soaking-wet silk shirt. And I remember trying to get the bathroom attendant to laugh about it, but she was like a stiff Buckingham Palace Guard. All I could see was the hair in her upturned nose.

When I came back to our table after the restroom fiasco, Stuart gawked at my appearance. "What the hell happened to you?" My only answer was more laughter; I couldn't stop! He led me out of the restaurant, to the car, and opened the passenger door for me. Limp, I fell into the seat and passed out before he walked around the car to get in.

<<<<<<<<>>>>>>>

I woke up with my seat belt buckled. In a parking lot, beside a light pole with a flickering bulb. I blinked, trying to figure out where I might be. *Stuart. Right... I'm with Stuart. Rental car. West Palm Beach.* My head pounded and my mouth tasted like I'd eaten raw earth. *Oh, God! The French restaurant! Oh, how drunk am I?* "Pretty drunk," I said out loud, or at least I tried to say it. *Oh man, you can't even talk!*

Sitting up further in my seat, I looked around. Plenty of cars. A lot of pickup trucks. A neon light flashing nearby, bathing the pavement in moments of yellow and green, then blue and red the next moment. I unbuckled, sat up and felt for my purse on the floor, relieved to find it there. I found a cigarette and lighter inside.

Inhaling deeply, the smoke caught in my throat and I choked. Coughed, gagged. Coughed more. A deep sigh.

I rubbed my eyes, finding the goo of sleep boogers. Then I flipped down the mirror and screamed *"Oh my God!"* followed by laughter as I remembered the bathroom scene in the French restaurant. The left side of my make-up and my hair were trashed, but I still looked okay on the right. The word "half-baked" came to mind.

More internal laughter... which jostled a part of my brain wanting to be still. It demanded silence, and I gave it silence. A wave of dizziness caused me to close my eyes. Woozy, I felt the car was fading in and out of existence. Pulsating. *Oh, God, Lela, are you going to throw up?* I popped my eyes open, and the dizziness came to a sudden stop, jarring me. The flashing neon continued its dance. It was the buzz of the flickering light on the pole above me that sliced into my head. *Where AM I? Where is Stuart?*

I opened the door to throw out my cigarette and felt a rush of cool air; I hadn't realized how hot it was in the car. *Wish I knew the time. Oh! I have a phone that knows the time!* I pawed through my purse. 2:41 AM. *My Lord, what time did we leave the restaurant? What the hell?*

Though I was seeing double, I punched Stuart's number on my phone's keypad. Five rings, then a beep. Furious, I barked a message on his voice mail, demanding to know where in the hell he was and how dare he leave me alone.

It was the first time I discovered how dissatisfying it is to hang up on somebody with a damn button instead of a slam onto a wall unit.

What am I going to do? Is he in this building beside me? And I have to pee, bad! Slowly, I stood in the parking lot, hearing creaks and pops from my joints. I felt like I'd run a race or been in a wrestling match. Even my hair hurt. Out loud: "Well, I've got to go in there, to pee if for no other reason. What *is* this place?"

I lit another cigarette; I heard somewhere you can use a cigarette as a weapon if you're jumped. Then I grabbed my purse and closed the car door quietly, leaving it unlocked. Half-limping, I walked around the corner of the building. There, the neon sign came into view. "The Snatch, A Gentleman's Club." *Oh my God! A strip club! I can't go in there! Why did HE go in there? Lela, get him out of there! And get YOURSELF out of here!*

Scared, I froze in my steps. People came and went, both men and women as I stood in place near the door. *But if I don't go in, I'll just have to go back to the car and wait. What has he done?* Again, I dialed Stuart's number. Again, no answer.

No, don't go in. Find another way to the hotel. Fear pounded in my head as I reluctantly walked to the curb, looking up and down the main boulevard for something that might be open at that hour. No gas stations, no drug stores, no nothing... just darkened signs and iron bars on the storefronts.

At first, I was shocked he would bring me to a bad side of town, then realized most strip clubs would be in such neighborhoods. *How can you do this to me, Stuart? Leave me stranded and confused... drunk and in danger! What have you done to me?* I groaned, walking back to the club entrance.

Okay, your options are limited, Lela. Think! The only solution that came was to ask the hostess to page him or something. Further, I knew the chance of finding a women's restroom in a "gentleman's club" was slim so I'd have to pee in the parking lot beside the car. *Ha! If this wasn't so horrible, it would be funny.*

No, not funny at all. *How can I get out of this?* Stunned and confused, I stood frozen, racking my brain for another option. A man exited, gave me the once-over, and walked past. *Right, dude, I'm a dancer. Ha!* Grinding my cigarette into the pavement with my high-heeled sandal, I held my breath and entered the club.

The music was loud, with a booming bass beat. Lights swirled in the dark. To the right, I saw the flashing floor of the dancer's stage, two women twisting on the same pole. The sight of it brought a sick feeling in my stomach, a bend-over-to-breathe feeling of utter tension.

A mountain of a man stepped in front of me. "Ladies free," he said, "But I need to check your bag." His flashlight danced inside my purse.

Yelling to be heard over the music, I leaned close and asked, "Can you page somebody for me?"

He chuckled with the answer. "No way, man. No paging." I didn't move, afraid to go all the way into the place, hoping the burly man could protect me from... everything. "The bar is to the left. Free drinks for the ladies."

"Oh! Free drinks!" Well, at least there's that. I'll have to walk around and look for Stuart; might as well carry a drink. The black light at the bar caused the lacy white in my top to glow. I thought I saw it pulsate. *But that's not possible, Lela. Hallucinate much?*

"Vodka-tonic, please," I said to the topless bartender, "Make it a double if you can." The woman nodded, adding the liquor to my glass with a flourish. She looked at me with eyes that brought a shudder. *Oh my God, you're in a strip club, Lela. Alone! What the hell? They think you're on the prowl!* I sat on the stool in front of me to gather my bearings. Waitresses rushed in and shouted orders to the bartender who moved at double-speed. I noticed how little alcohol she added to the drinks. *Rip-off place, too. Jeez.*

Before I stood to go, a waitress scooted next to me. "Looking for a date?" When I didn't answer, she asked, "You want one like me... or one like them?"

Shocked, I answered staccato, "Neither, actually... I'm trying to find my boyfr–"

She cut me off sharply. "Good. Because if you want one of *them*, you're taking money out of my pocket and that's not cool." She bonked my nose. "You're cute but you're rolling the dice in here, honey. This isn't a place to for a nice girl to hang out."

"I'm looking for my boyfriend," I said.

The woman laughed with a wide-open mouth. "Aren't we all, honey. Aren't we all!"

Okay, Lela. Walk. Focus. Head up, don't be shy. Look only for Stuart, not at the people looking at you. I knew he had on a red shirt, so I looked for that.

No faces. I started in the back-left corner section, walked all around the place, and just before I gave up, found him in the back-right. Stuart sat at a table alone with what looked like a scotch-neat on the table. He didn't see me but watched the stage with a scary, intense stare. Carefully, I slid into the seat beside him; he casually looked over. Doubletake. "Oh, hey, honey! You woke up! Hi! Glad you're here!" Way too fucking cheerful. Then his fidgeting began.

"Get the hell out of here, dammit! Get *me* out of here. How *dare* you leave me in a parking lot!" I raised my voice, loud enough for other patrons to hear. There was a response from the men in the crowd, a mixture of "Leave him alone!" and "Get outta here, bitch!" A Double-D topless waitress walked by and the men quieted down.

Stuart stammered, "But I can't leave... and you can't either. I have a surprise for you!"

"What surprise?"

"Hold on, we need a table on the other side." He took my hand and led me in front of the stage and around the corner.

I tried not to look at the other people, men who hooted at Stuart, saying, "You got her where you want her now," and a full array of comments that made me feel sleazy and dirty.

"Stuart, I want to *go*. Go back to the *hotel*." I was screaming over the music but he was too far ahead of me.

He stopped at a table for two, surrounded by a barrel-booth with puffy cushions. Moving like a hummingbird, he rushed me, "Here, baby, sit here. Oh... you already have a drink. Well, hold on. Don't move; I'll get you another. Drink up! Sit here, baby." He was nervous, shooting words like bullets. Reluctantly, I sat, feeling sheepish and hopelessly embarrassed. Stuart said, "I'll be right back!" and disappeared.

Desperate, I yelled at him, "No! Don't leave" When he didn't stop, I fumed. *How dare he leave me here alone! Oh, please God, get me out of here!* I turned my drink up and drained it. It seemed to be the only solution.

At that specific moment, a big-haired blonde waitress appeared and placed a drink on the table. "Double vodka-tonic, right?" I didn't answer, kept my head down. "Ladies drink free," she said, then disappeared into the crowd. *What the hell just happened? Am I in a dream or something?* I saw Stuart speeding by, chasing a brunette waitress. He caught her, but they talked for too long for a simple drink order. He slipped her a bill; I couldn't see the denomination, then he rushed back to the table where I sat so carefully.

"You have a drink, baby? Good. Are you having fun?" He continued to bombard me with short questions and answer them himself, speaking so fast and fidgeting so hard... I knew something was seriously wrong.

"NO!" I screamed. It stopped him.

"What? What's wrong?" he asked, still fidgeting.

"What's *wrong*? You don't understand what's wrong with this picture?"

"But wait just a minute baby! Understand! I have a surprise for you. But you may want to finish your drink first," he said. "Hurry!"

"Stuart, what the hell? Please, let's just go. NOW. *Goddammit!*"

He touched my arm, ran his finger down the outside of it gently. "I bought you a present. Something you've always wanted. But you need to finish that drink."

Tired of his insistence that I drink fast, whatever it meant, I turned my drink up and drained it, just as I had the previous one. "Good girl!" he said. Then Stuart looked around frantically, flagging down the same waitress he had cornered earlier. He pointed to the top of my head, his fingernail pushing through my curls and into the meat of my scalp. Minutes later, the waitress placed another drink on the table. Stuart gave her a twenty and said, "Keep 'em coming."

"But ladies drink free!" I insisted.

"Forget it, Lela. Hush! Relax." I sat back. Two quick drinks, actually four since they were doubles, warmed my insides, and I did relax a little. But Stuart's foot was jacking up and down; he was fidgeting much worse than normal.

"What's got you all tied in a knot?" I asked. I realized then I had re-entered the drunk zone and scolded myself internally. A woman interrupted our would-be conversation, a dancer. She stood over me, straddling my feet, wearing nothing but a thong and a pink boa around her neck.

I shook my head to make sure I wasn't seeing things. Her breasts were at eye-height and she was shaking them, rubbing them, just inches from my face. I began to speak, "What is..."

Stuart interrupted, "Chill, baby. Enjoy your gift." He sat back into the depths of the cushions, grinning, hands behind his neck... settled in for a show. I turned back to the woman to tell her to move, to leave me alone, but as I did, she straddled me, knees on either side of my hips, undulating to music that couldn't be heard, only felt in a pounding beat.

"NO!" I said.

Like a vixen, she said, "But yes, baby, yes!"

"HELP! GET OFF!" I screamed!

"I'll help you get off, baby," she whispered, twisting and grinding inches from my body. The woman rubbed the boa against my face, snatching it back and forth.

"NO!" I tried to stand to get away, bumping against her.

"No, baby, can't touch. It's the law." She continued to grind on me, without touching. There was no place to go; she had pinned me against the seat. With a rat-a-tat heartbeat, I closed my eyes, seething in anger, refusing to believe Stuart would do this to me. *Liking women to be with women is WAY different than this public humiliation, dingbat! This isn't a gift to me, but a gift to YOU! YOU are the one who gets off on it.*

I opened my eyes, only to see hers, glitter on her eyelids, eyelashes four inches long. "No, please, don't do this!" I begged, tears welling in my eyes.

"Relax, baby. Hot little mama. Let me love you." She stuck her finger in her mouth and used its wetness to rub her nipple, daring me to watch. I closed my eyes, willing this to be over. I felt two inches tall, mortified. The woman paid no attention to my further pleas, continuing her erotic dance. As I turned my head to glare at Stuart, my nose brushed against her bare breast. She arched her back to get away. "No touching, baby. Just love me. Dig it, baby, dig it."

I collapsed into myself like a rag doll. It was my way of running away, I guess, blocking it from my mind. The world blacked out; my mind shut down, and all sound stopped. I was alone in my humiliation. But there was also something sexual to my collapse, I knew because the release was total. Complete exhaustion... the same breathless exhaustion an orgasm brings.

Tears stained my face. When the dancer saw tears, she jerked back, jumped up, stumbling on my sandals. "Are you okay?" she asked frantically. It was like I suddenly disgusted her. I closed my eyes and soon my shoulders hiccupped with sobs. Shame. Guilt. Embarrassment. Total humiliation.

I saw her reach to Stuart and take a bill of an unknown denomination. Then her black spike heels clicked away.

Stuart's voice was loud in my ear, full in volume and full of glee. "I guess you *really* need a drink now, huh?" The sonofabitch was giddy, oblivious to my pain and unease. "Let me find her... I'll get you a drink, baby. That was fantastic..."

"Shut the hell UP!" I screamed. Stuart's face fell, clueless.

"What? What happened?"

"Asshole! I'm leaving. Follow me." Though I said it through a clenched jaw, I spoke with brute force. Anger. Fury. Rage.

When I stood, the table of men to my left also stood, applauding and cheering. "Whoa! Hot Mamma!" and "Lap-dance girl!" and the loudest, "Whores love whores." I put my head down and walked as fast as I could to what I thought was the exit, but because I was looking at the floor, I veered way off to the right, dead-ending into a multiple lap-dance group. "My" girl waved, blew me a kiss. I corrected my angle and walked fast enough to call it a run and I didn't stop until I reached the car. Thank God, I had left it unlocked!

I peered into the backseat to make sure there was no boogie man and reached for the door handle. Still shaking, I didn't have the strength to open it and had to use both hands. Weak, breathing hard and now sobbing uncontrollably, I collapsed into the passenger seat and pushed the lock. My breaths came in ragged gasps and I could feel every heartbeat in my eardrums.

I counted to twenty, then used controlled breathing to bring calm. *Deep breaths, Lela. Long, slow, deep breaths...* Little by slowly, my anxiety eased. I breathed, slow and deep, and I waited.

And waited.

And waited.

And waited.

I wanted to get out and walk, find somewhere safe, and call a cab. It was now 4:37, and the morning traffic was picking up. With shaky hands, I lit a cigarette, the first since I'd come to the car. *Maybe places are open now, or maybe I could call a taxi.* Still in the trance of humiliation, I realized it would be crazy to walk around in the dark; I would be mistaken for a prostitute.

I'll wait 'til dawn... until then, find something positive.

PANIC IN PALM BEACH
CHAPTER 23

I felt somebody shaking my shoulder and reaching over me to unbuckle the seat belt. Stuart's voice. "Wake up! Lela, we're here. Wake up, honey!"

"Oh! okay!" *Wake up from your dream, Lela.* Stuart's face was close to mine as he leaned into the car. He looked like hell. *Was it a dream?* I couldn't tell. "Where are we? What time is it?"

"We're at the hotel and it's almost six o'clock. Hurry! Get up, sweetheart!" *Oh my God... it wasn't a dream.*

My gruff voice came to full volume in a heartbeat. "Sweetheart, my ass! Stuart! HOW could you do that to me? How could you HUMILIATE me like that?"

"Okay, come on, Miss Prude! Hearing that, I growled, deep in my throat, feeling the ache of *hate* rise in my throat.

"ASSHOLE! GET AWAY FROM ME, YOU PERVERT! First you leave me alone in a parking lot and THEN you... you...

"I thought you'd like it, baby! Everybody likes a lap-dance! And I know you like women... like them a lot! I've seen it happen!" Then he offered his baby-talk "pretty-please-forgive-me" voice. "Oh honey, baby! Don't be mad at sensitive little Stewie!"

Still laying down, I shot him a look that could kill, prompting more gushing and self-defending. "Seriously! It was supposed to be a gift! Something special for you! Because we're on a special trip here, you know. Please don't be mad at me! Lela, please don't..."

I took a deep breath, ready to resume my screaming. Then, like a thunderbolt, I felt my throat close, my heart race. As if my brain was in a blender, my thoughts became a snarled mess. Panic. *Oh, here it comes again. I'm going to lose my mind!* Tears rolled and my entire body began to shake, hard enough to rattle my teeth. All-out panic. Drooling, I couldn't remember how to swallow and my breaths came in gasps as I reached to claw my throat.

Stuart dove into the floorboard and dug around in my purse for the vodka. "Here, drink this. Calm down! You're scaring me." With no hesitation, my shaking hands grabbed the mini bottle, and I threw the cool contents to the back of my throat. I felt the warmth hit my stomach and spread... *ahh.* Another few breaths, feeling quieter, I drank the other bottle in one swallow, too.

A full-blown panic attack, the worst one yet. Slowly, I smoothed my pants down, noticing a stain that looked like a dollop of butter. *Yeah, from the lobster, I bet.* My mind jumped to the *other* end of the night and I stopped. NO! I jumped out of the car. "Let's go," I said, not waiting for Stuart to follow. Somehow, I had a room key in my hand.

When Stuart came in, I was in the shower. His supposed-to-be-funny callout, "Lucy! I'm home!" did nothing but piss me off. With the water as hot as it would go, I tried to scrub off the *dirty* off of me.

Overall, I felt like a slut, at a new level of low. *Has it really come to this? Is this the best I can do?*

I sighed... the answer seemed clear. It *was* the best I could do. *Accept what he gives you or accept you'll get nothing at all. This... is all you have. All else is out of reach. Yep, I'm stuck. Drunk and stuck. Your mother is ashamed of you... your father has turned his back. Lela Fox, you'll rot in hell!*

A cool draft sliced through the steam. Stuart peeked his head inside the shower curtain, trying to be cute. I screamed and covered myself, bending my knees almost to the floor. He raised hell, yelling "Lela, Jeezus! It's not the end of the world! You act like I've murdered you or something!"

"GET OUT!" Full volume.

"Quit that shit! Look at you... you're alive and beautiful. Plus, I don't want to fight in a hotel. It's not proper."

"PROPER? PROPER!? Oh my God! You DARE to talk about PROPER?" I knew he would never understand, never. There would be no apology even if one would have helped. Another clueless man. *Why do I get all the stupid ones? The mean ones? Surely this is more than my fair share! What am I doing wrong?*

I shivered and cried until Stuart left the bathroom. Once out, I stared at myself in the mirror for a solid five minutes. *Just get me home, God... home in one piece. Then I'll never drink again. I'll never do anything except the things you told Jesus to do. I'll go to church, quit smoking, do charity work, ANYTHING! No, EVERYTHING. Just get me home and out of this hell.*

At long last, I tiptoed into the bedroom, heading straight for the dresser and my cigarettes. "Did you drown in there?" he asked.

I stared him down, glaring. Seconds passed. "I wish I would have," I said.

"What does *that* mean?" Stuart asked.

When I didn't answer, he walked to the window and leaned against the frame. "Going to be a nice day, they say," he said. *Ha! I got him! He's nervous!* Then I realized... what's the point in making him feel bad? Is that going to make *me* feel better? A big, fat NO.

I dug another mini vodka bottle from my suitcase but paused before taking the drink, knowing I was trying to obliterate the pulsating Shame I felt. *What the hell? What ELSE are you going to do?* I turned it up to my quivering lips. The promise I had just made to God would start when I got back to Rockville, I decided.

Wowzers! Vodka burn, burn! Jeezus, Lela, you could've mixed it this morning, dumbass. Did you forget you bought tonic? Stuart's back had been toward me during this action, but he knew what I was doing. "Do you want me to pick up another case of those today?"

"Are you going out?"

"Yeah, I've got job interviews, baby. You know that."

"Didn't know if your plans had changed. I've never been to a job interview after staying up all night, snorting coke and groveling with the lower echelons of society."

"Shut up, okay?" he said. It was a statement, not a plea. *So, you got my answer to that: he DID snort coke last night. That's why he was so fidgety.* In an abrupt move, he turned and put his cigarette in the ashtray. "I'm hitting the shower."

It was easy to turn away and climb under the covers, thinking a few hours' sleep would offer a clue about how I should proceed. Before this shit happened, I had big plans for the mall while Stuart interviewed. That's one reason we needed the new cell phones... so we could separate and hook back up later in the day. But everything had changed.

I felt manipulated, misunderstood and used as a toy for his enjoyment. He didn't get that lap-dance for ME! He probably had the guys at the surrounding tables in on it! I felt the panic begin to rise, and I stopped... *Breathe, Lela. Don't go there. Don't let him do that to you.*

Tears poured from the depths of my soul as I prayed and cried out for my friend Lola. And I cried for my Mom, my dear, sweet Mom. *Oh, dear God! To hear Momma's voice... to hear Daddy tell me it's all fine. "Never fear, Dad is here," right?* My tears became racks of sobs.

In complete despondency, I broke down, wishing my Daddy was there to scoop me up and wipe my tears. But I was alone. Stuck here. With HIM. *Even worse, I'm stuck here with ME.*

I dozed and awoke startled, with Stuart's face inches from mine. "Are you going to shop or sleep?" he asked.

"Sleep."

"Well, if you change your mind, it's here, on the dresser." He wanted me to see it was not one, not two, but *three* crisp hundred-dollar-bills. The door closed behind him.

<<<<<<<>>>>>>

He woke me up at two in the afternoon. "I got a job."

Sitting up, rubbed my eyes. "Where? Tell me about it."

"Ace Transmissions, right on the main drag in town." I scowled, remembering that "main drag" from last night.

"Are there strip clubs all the way down that boulevard?"

He didn't react to my obvious reference. "No, just the part north of town." He stifled a yawn. "Besides, we want to live in Wellington. I've been driving around, even looked at a place."

Silence from me.

Stuart powered on the TV, clicked through the channels, turned it off. "So you're not talking to me?" Silence for another full minute, then I threw the covers back and swung my legs out.

"I'm going to the pool," I said.

"I'm going to bed, then."

"Good."

"Better." It was a challenge, our everyday back-and-forth joke.

I couldn't help it. I finished the phrase. "Best." And tears came to my eyes.

With tonic this time, I mixed a drink and threw a few tiny vodkas into my beach bag. I took my swimsuit to the bathroom to change. Stuart was snoring when I left, fully clothed, with the remote in his hand.

<<<<<<<>>>>>>

The flight back was non-challenging with no drama or delays, just as a person wants a flight to be. But there was no joy in coming home and tension between us was high. Mostly, I felt sad... just plain sad. I refused to talk to him.

Back in Rockville, as we hefted our luggage into the trunk of the car in long-term parking, he pecked a kiss on my cheek. I stopped and looked at him, incredulous. A glare followed; I wiped the kiss off as a child would.

Stuart stuck his bottom lip out in a mock pout. "Lela, please... let's kiss and make up. I hate being mad at you. It doesn't feel right. We're young and in love! Nobody died, we made it back alive. Please, Lela. Be my girl."

He did a silly soft-shoe dance, around in a circle, and then gestured as if tipping his hat. When I didn't smile, he repeated it. And again. "Besides, I didn't tell you the best part about moving to Florida."

Still refusing to speak, a question crossed my face, enough to encourage him to continue. "My salary... and one helluva bonus system, I'll be bringing home six-figures-plus. You can be a lady of leisure... you don't have to work at all." I looked down, contemplating this glorious fact. "You can play with your crafts as you like, decorate the apartment on an unlimited budget, babe. We're rich!"

When I still didn't respond, he repeated the silly dance in a circle, this time adding lyrics and rhythm. I remember every word. "Oh, my baby... she's going to be free... free to be... whatever she wants to be... she'll have fun... in the Florida sun... every day... hey, hey, hey."

It was so silly, so much of a show to soften me, I finally smiled. "Stuart, you asshole, I love you so much it hurts."

"I love *you*, babe. From the bottom of my heart, and I can't handle it when you're mad at me."

With a sniffle, holding back the tears of a thousand emotions running through my heart, I said, "I don't want to be mad at you, either. You're my man."

"And always will be."

"But–"

"But nothing! Come here and hug me. Let's kiss and make up." The hug lasted many minutes. I cried, and he held me as we swayed back and forth. After a while, he held my shoulders and eased his body away, checking for tears. "Are you okay now?"

I nodded. "Stuart, you're all I have," I said.

"I'm all you need," he answered. Then he chuckled, "Me and a fifth of vodka, right?"

I did love Stuart – heart, soul… and hook, line, and sinker. I had always loved with great passion and, so far, always to my detriment; each partner was a worse-than-before choice.

Determined this time would be different, I invented a personality for Stuart that met my lofty ideals of what a "good man" should be. Period. Nothing could veer me off course, and I guess that's why I could overlook the bad stuff.

Stuart was slick; he knew when he had pushed me too far or made me too suspicious and immediately backed down, changing his tactics. I was on a perpetual roller coaster designed by a man who knew I was a helpless drunk.

I guess, deep down, I knew about his evil, lying-sonofabitch ways because I remember hiding such distasteful incidents from Lola and from my family.

Despite the man I had created in my mind, I knew his mistreatment of me wasn't right. I felt Guilt for letting it happen to my father's favorite baby daughter. And I cringed with Shame because I couldn't stop it.

The only cure was one more drink.

THE FIZZLE SHUT-DOWN
CHAPTER 24

Monday morning broke with a bright orange sun over the spruce tree in the front yard. The sun spilled in my window and I blinked my eyes open... then closed them again, not looking forward to the day. But it wasn't the sun that awakened me; it was the squeak of the front door opening. Caroline. I heard her doing her thing downstairs; greeting the dog, turning on the water in the kitchen with a blast, and a few minutes later, bounding up the steps and into my bedroom.

"Rise and shine, gal o' mine! Here's your coffee!" Caroline placed the mug on my bedside table. "So how was your weekend? Sunny? Funny-sunny?" She giggled. So damn chirpy.

"Caroline, please, cheer down." On one elbow, I reached for my cigarettes. "The weekend was fine. And whatever was on the agenda for today is *off* the agenda. Stuart got a job."

She asked strings of questions slowly... as if in a dream state. *Fine with me; at least she's not chirping.* "But a job in Florida? I guess that means... oh, my God! You're moving!?"

Not letting her mystic sadness affect my happiness, I chirped back to her. "Yep. West Palm Beach. There's an apartment in Wellington, a suburb, that looks promising."

"But..." her words trailed into the air. I knew it would be a surprise for her; I'd told Lola of my plans to close the business but kept Caroline in the dark.

151

This may not have been the best way to tell her, but fuck it. Whatever.

Alarmed, I snapped my head to look back at her when she began to wail. *Yes, a fucking wail!* "So I don't have a job anymore?" A tear tracked down her right cheek.

Oh, Jeezus! No way I'm going to babysit her today. I have too much to do. I threw a little empathy in my tone but spoke directly to her. "Right. No more job, Caroline, and I guess this is your notice. But you don't have time to cry yet, sweetheart. It will be a while counting down to zero. I need your help in closing everything down, counting the inventory, organizing a yard sale, helping me sell personal and business stuff. Even better, I'd love your help in packing the house. If you can stay to do it, I'll pay you for the week between, when Stuart and I will be in the Bahamas. Lola will work that week, too, and she'll guide you.

"So Lola already knew... and you didn't tell me?" Caroline's lower lip stuck out a full inch, like a pouty child.

"I didn't want to say anything until everything was confirmed! And please don't cry. It's stupid. Anyway, you have about three weeks' notice, and remember: it could be no notice at all."

Caroline appeared to be in shock. "But Lela, this business... you have shows scheduled, with inventory ready. You still have things on consignment in... what... *eight* places? Even Boise! How are you going to–"

I interrupted, "That's why I need your help. Now let me get up and get busy. Much to do!"

Raring to go, I started the day with a hot shower, not my typical beginning. There was much to manage with a cross-country move, closing down a business... a dying business. *No, face it Lela... a dead business, complete with a dollar-sign toe tag.* I owed my suppliers thousands of dollars, especially my main supplier, Quest Cast, and I had no idea how to pay them. The only way I knew to handle it was brutal honesty; call Jo and tell her I'd have to pay in installments. *But how can I muster the guts to do that?*

I put it out of my mind, continuing the shower with a long mental list of things to do. Caroline stuck her head in the bathroom and asked what I wanted her to do first. I yelled through the curtain, "Count stuff that's ready to sell. Downstairs and on the shelf. With the codes." That would keep her busy for a few hours.

Later, dressed and sitting at my desk, I wrote out the to-do list. *Wow!* The list was long, overwhelming. Downstairs for another cup of coffee, I added the vodka this time.

Freaking out now, I looked at my list again, hoping to set priorities, but that nauseous feeling returned. A cure: I slipped downstairs for another cup of coffee.

When Lola pulled in at one o'clock, the garage door was open and I was tugging on a box, sweating in the cold. "How was your weekend? Did he find a job?" she asked, walking into the dark-ish garage.

The two of us walked inside to the kitchen. "Sit down, Lola. Here's the deal: Moonlight Jewelry is no more."

She threw her purse on the table, staring into space for several minutes. "Damn! Lela, we've had a nice run. But I'm so, *so* sad. Like I've lost a child or something."

"But Lola, there's a few things you don't know. First of all, I'm broke. The business is costing way more than its making – and that's been the case for a long, long time. I'm in debt up to my ass."

"Oh. I... I... didn't know."

"Some things I hide." I stood, paced the length of the kitchen three times. Since coming inside, I had toyed with the idea and decided to go ahead: I snatched the bottle of Grey Goose from the counter and opened a new bottle of tonic water. I made the drink strong. *What the hell? Why not?* Somehow mixing a drink so early was "worse" than continuing to spike my coffee and I shuddered.

Lola remembered what I'd told her months ago: she'd be in charge of "The Great Shut-Down," and she wasted no time. "First, I'll make a list for *you*. And on your favorite purple pad."

I smiled, knowing my responsibility for the day was over. Lola, to save the day. Again.

<<<<<<<<>>>>>>

"How many swimsuits do you *need*, woman?" Lola asked as I handed her another; the skimpiest one I owned. A week after telling the girls Moonlight Jewelry would close, I asked Lola to pack my stuff for the week-long Bahamas vacation, the one Stuart had earned after one year at his crappy job. Lola would be house-sitting, dog-sitting, and continuing to pack my personal belonging for the Florida move. Caroline would help, in her usual twelve hours per week.

Thanks to Lola, things were perfectly organized; everything about the move and sale of Moonlight Jewelry assets was happening as she had planned. "Lola! You are my *savior*. No way I could've managed all this. Thank you so much... now I can be on vacation and genuinely relax."

My organized friend checked her clipboard, made a check mark somewhere, and spoke with a pencil behind her ear. "Okay, I got the second estimate for the moving truck, and they also said you'd need the full tractor-trailer, too." She passed the paper to my hand. "Here's the full estimate."

I didn't look at the total, passing the paper back to Lola. "Hopefully, it's less than the two-thousand estimate from Allied Van Lines! I about shit when I saw that! I know it's a long way, with a lot of stuff, but you've labeled everything now, making it so easy for a mover. Don't they consider that in the price?"

"This guy said something, so maybe. Do you want me to move forward... book the cheaper one? The prices are within a hundred bucks of each other."

"Then book the one you feel the best about. Lola, your judgement is better than mine. They'll need a deposit, I'm sure, and my Visa card number is written on the—"

"Lela, don't you think I know that already! By the way, it's been seeing a lot of action. It's cool to keep charging?"

"It's cool."

Lola switched topics abruptly, first building a dreamy smile. "I envy you being in the good weather. Winter is getting old, my friend." It had been frigid that week, much colder than normal for East Tennessee.

"The Bahamas are beautiful, Lola. Temps stays about 85 degrees year 'round. The ocean breeze... and sand that's as white as a dove's ass. Throw in a steel drum band and you're in paradise."

"New place, right? Not the one from before?"

"Right. It's supposed to be bigger and better... but it's *not* all-inclusive. They'll probably nickel and dime us to death."

"Watch your Visa, then."

"No, this one's on Stuart. All of it, he promised." I cocked my head, thinking. "Unless I want to buy clothes or a purse or something."

PRAYERS & TALL TALES
CHAPTER 25

My jaw dropped and goose bumps covered my skin, absorbing the warm and inviting opulence of the lobby at Reef Atlantis. "Stuart, this is *by far* the nicest place we've stayed!"

"Awesome isn't it!"

"Incredible! It reeks of the five-star rating." I swiveled my head, noticing details, every one of them more impressive than the one before. "Oh, and I haven't asked, but surely you've received the trust fund payment by now because you haven't—"

"Nothing to worry about, baby. Especially not now. The trick here is to gamble a lot so they comp the room, maybe send us to the penthouse *and* comp it. I've got it covered."

"But wouldn't the gambling cost *more* than—"

He interrupted with his index finger wagging at me. "As I said, there's nothing to worry about."

After an easy check-in, the concierge was Stuart's first stop. The bellman rolled our luggage in that direction and smiled, waiting patiently... but I was impatient. I called over my shoulder, "I'm going on up!" Deep in conversation, Stuart didn't reply. I looked at the bellman and shrugged. "He'll find me. Let's go."

In Suite 812, the happy bellman threw open the curtains to a spectacular view. The night was ebony, but low-wattage string lights twinkled everywhere, bathing the pool area in soft light. He opened the French doors with an old-Hollywood flourish, and I laughed. *He's cute.* Then I heard the rhythmic steel drums at a pool party below and laughter from a tent gathering by the shoreline. I could see a few feet of lighted turquoise water before it faded to black.

Like a NASA photo, the moon glowed with deep contrast between a hundred shades of white, silver, cream and glazed pearl. It blazed, a throbbing, pulsating orb in the sky, mingling with a zillion sparkling stars.

A breeze, laced with the distinct scent of tropical flowers, filled the room and an involuntary *"mmm"* escaped my lips. I couldn't take my eyes from the sight before me; it was like a drug I couldn't stop taking. *One more time, you're a V-I-fucking-P in paradise.*

The bellman cleared his throat, shaking me from the scenic trance. *Damn, my wallet has only twenties! Too much for a tip, but what choice do I have?* Hesitating, I handed a bill to the bellman. His eyes widened. I cringed. *Too much! Too much money!* But Stuart would applaud; he'd always said large tips paid off in the end. My conservative, penny-pinching childhood teachings screamed every time I spent money, but I had gotten used to spending Stuart's money with ease. Just not mine.

We had arrived at the Nassau airport at 11:20 PM, so there'd be no partying for me that night. Just the right amount of vodka on the flight... a common little buzz, perfect for sleep. I assumed Stuart would agree, so I put on my new, lacy lingerie and slipped between the covers. *Aaah... luxury sheets, too.*

My mind wondered as I waited for Stuart to arrive, wondering what "arrangements" he'd made with the concierge. And I still didn't understand how or why Stuart had declared personal bankruptcy and still had all the money in the world at his disposal. It would not compute in my mind, though Stuart's many explanations made sense... kind of.

As always, Stuart ended those discussions with the truth: "You just don't understand rich people," and he was right. I'd never known a truly wealthy person until Stuart. And if we followed through with his plan of marriage, I'd be truly wealthy myself. The thought of it gave me chills.

<<<<<<<<>>>>>>>

I awoke with a start. The clock glowed 5:05 AM. A sleepy-slur of "Honey, what's going on?" brought no reply so I cocked my legs to kick him awake. The bed was empty; Stuart's side was undisturbed. "Stuart?" No reply from the bathroom. To be sure, I got up to check. No Stuart.

I guess he's gambling downstairs, that fucker. Now he'll sleep all day when I want to play on the beach! Shithead! I lit a cigarette and crawled back into bed, turning the TV. Two channels, both fuzzy and half-pixelated. The third channel played a film broadcast from the resort itself, highlighting each of the ten restaurants and dozens of activities, all saying "For a small additional fee…" *Yeah, but I bet nothing around here is a SMALL fee. My bet is that it's expensive to breathe the air in this place!* The film was on a loop, and my thoughts swirled through six repeats.

Where is Stuart? Sonofabitch! In my imagination, I saw him with crazy-red eyes amid the flashing lights of the casino, his foot jiggling, his hands fidgeting at the Blackjack table. The next moment, I envisioned him with a different wild look, whooping it up at the craps table, throwing $100 chips around as if they were pennies.

After nearly an hour tossing and turning, I got up and put on my new swimsuit.

The hall and elevator were eerily quiet, but when I turned the corner to the casino section, the noise was just as loud as it'd been at eleven o'clock. Bleary-eyed gamblers roamed the interior, shirttails stained and shoes untied. I saw one guy with a blown-out flip-flop, shuffling toward the exit. As he passed, he warned me, "Odds are with the house, man, and they're fucking thieves!" The comment and the sight of the rumpled-and-drunk young man brought a chuckle. *Maybe his girlfriend is waiting for him upstairs like I've been waiting for Stuart.*

I searched all twenty Blackjack tables, looking for my runaway boyfriend. Then I veered to the side section where crowds still cheered at the craps table and roulette wheel, even at this hour. I walked the four long rows of slot machines seeing no one with mostly gray hair. Then I remembered he had on a bright blue shirt and walked back through the twists and turns of the place searching for shirt color. No Stuart.

Desperate, I stood by the men's room and asked the next guy going in to look in the stalls. The man came out shaking his head. I went down the retail hall, snaking through each shop, and did the same bathroom request at another location.

"Where the hell *is* he?" I spoke out loud as I walked back toward the casino. A waitress met me at the mouth of the loud room.

"Mimosa, ma'am?"

"God bless you. How did you *know?*"

"Half price because it's the last one on the tray."

"Sold!" I grabbed the flute and took a sip. *Weak, watery, but delicious.*

She stood frozen; a pen poised above a small notepad.

"Oh! Room 812. Weinstein."

"Thank you. Have a lucky day!"

Have a lucky day! What a great line for a casino server! I walked back through the casino looking at my feet, not caring if I found him now. *Asshole. How dare you disappear and leave me alone on a damn island? How DARE you?*

A buzz between my ears pushed at my temples and tears burned my eyes. *How can you let me down time after time after time, Stuart? Why do I let you do this? What's wrong with ME? And what's wrong with YOU? We've gotta fix this, dammit, especially if we're going to get married like you say.*

The lobby's back door whooshed open as if by magic, leading to the pool area. I looked at the distant ocean and my jaw dropped – the sun was coming up over the water, brimming the horizon with a brilliant orange glaze.

Below, a uniformed man arranged the lounge chairs around the pool, creating orderly rows as he softly sang an old Bob Marley tune. Slowly, stress melted with the memories of the music of my youth. Another resort staff member, sporting a tropical-print shirt, slid open the woven shades of the poolside bar, now open for business. Perfect timing!

I sat sideways on the center barstool. "Good morning, sir! Special deals for your first customer?"

"Welcome, beautiful ma'am! Always special deal on mornings like these... what can I mix to please you?" The man's voice was like silk, gracious and sincere.

"A screwdriver, please. And make it a double. You guys make the drinks too weak."

His white teeth glowed in sharp contrast to the ebony face as he sneaked a smile. "I fix you up! Yes, I will!" The first sip proved that he had, indeed, mixed a strong one. Of course, the orange juice was fresh squeezed, but the vodka overwhelmed that strong taste, too. *Kick-ass!*

"Do you have coffee out here, too?"

"I wake you up! Yes, I will!" The repeat and his lilting accent made me smile. He pushed a receipt toward me; I signed to add the charges to our room. *Here we go... over twenty bucks in less than ten minutes.* My fear, instantly, was that Stuart wouldn't show up in time to pay the hotel bill. *But I'll just have them put it on the credit card he used for the reservations. I hope he has the headroom on that card.*

This headroom was a practical concern because Stuart only had a pre-paid credit card, an account opened in an effort to up his credit rating after bankruptcy. Perplexed, I'd never heard of such a "non-credit credit card" but Stuart seemed to know all about it.

Taking the steaming mug from the bar, I said, "Thank you, sir. Don't worry, be lucky."

"Yes, ma'am. Be lucky today!" With a nod to my happy friend, I walked toward the pool in the growing light.

A contoured poolside chair offered the best view of the sunrise. Mesmerized, I sipped my drink while watching the impossibly yellow sun rise over the horizon. First, just a peek of yellow, like a slice of cut toenail, neon against a navy-blue sky. Slowly, the yellow orb rose to its full brilliance, and the sky turned a blue too bright for my eyes. I squinted against the dazzling color, wishing a gnome would appear with my sunglasses in hand. No such luck.

By 7:30, the sun washed the beach with the happy glow of daytime and people began to stroll around the grounds. The people-watching was intense entertainment; I suppose I stayed another half-hour before I couldn't bear the lack of sunglasses.

In the elevator, I rode alone to 812 to get my shades. Still no Stuart. His absence stopped pissing me off as worry took over. I stuffed a beach bag full of mini liquor bottles, sunscreen, and such, and headed back to the pool. *Thirty more minutes... I'll wait for thirty more.*

The sound of the casino called to me and I turned, again walking through the labyrinth in search of Stuart. Nobody resembled him. One more time, I asked a man to check the bathroom; he wasn't there. He wasn't anywhere.

Are you hurt? Dead? Or are you in some other woman's room, laying drunk, you sonofabitch? How DARE you ruin my vacation, you little fuckwad? What has happened to you?

The pool area was busy by then; laughter filled the air. I ordered another screwdriver at the bar, planning a walk on the beach. *If he hasn't shown up by the time I return, I'll call the police.*

<<<<<<<>>>>>>

The sand was soft and sugar-like, warm but not hot. *Aaah* – the first step in the water was the best... warm sand and cold water. The ebb of the first wave tugged at the fine-grained sand under my feet, sinking me down a half-inch. I stood in the gentle waves and watched as the sand covered my feet a half-inch at a time. Mother Nature, doing her work.

My shoulders glowed, warmed by the morning sun as I looked at the sky and incredible beauty that surrounded me. Out loud, I said, "Beautiful place! Thank you, God." I startled myself: *Thank you, God?? Why did I say THAT? I don't talk to GOD!* Then something happened, something surreal... something snapped in me and I felt a rush of overwhelming gratitude, love, peace, calm, happiness, all of it mixed together.

At the moment, I froze, joyful and scared of the joy. I felt anxiety rise... then peacefully ebb.

Tears poured down my cheeks as I turned to face the ocean... so peaceful, but too big, too scary, too intimidating, an ocean of confusion. The peaceful feelings twisted backward and I suddenly felt 100 percent vulnerable. I screamed, alone in the dawn, "Oh, God! Help me! Can you? *Will* you?" My screams became quieter wails as my throat closed with more intense crying. "I'm so screwed-up, God! I'm sure you don't mess with people like me, but..." *But what? I have no idea.* "I BEG YOU, GOD! I beg you to hear me somehow!"

Then I spoke with vapor, as in a dream. "I wish I could be one of those people you bless... like *every day*. Whatever 'bless' means... I always thought those people were weird, but now I wish I could be one of them."

As I sunk to sit in the sand, my heart also sank. Unable to speak through the tears, the prayer continued in my addled mind. *God, I wish I could do better. I wish I could just do something to make you part of my life. What could that* be? *Just believe in you, like they say? Just take this... "whatever it is" feeling and run with it? Or would I have to quit drinking and spend my days and nights in church? On my knees, singing hymns?*

Out loud again... "But those damn church people only believe on Sunday mornings! Parading around in their fine clothes! I don't want to be that kind of bullshit hypocrite, God!" *No... church people aren't the blessed. They're not the generous, kind souls who make the world a better place. Those people matter. Those people... you live in their heart. I believe that.*

My throat closed, tears choking me. *Wait! Don't leave me, God! Just tell me... how can I get you to come inside my heart? What do I do? What am I supposed to believe? Please, PLEASE tell me!*

I thought of my sham of a baptism years ago, my fight against the priest who laughed at my idea of skipping the Jesus part, going straight to God – a God I thought I understood. *So am I not a Christian, then? I'm afraid to be one because... what if the Bible's stories are lies? And I'm afraid to NOT be a Christian, too. But I just want to believe in you. And I want you to believe in ME. Help me, God! Please help!*

Looking at the sky, now blazing-blue, I again felt an overwhelming, all-encompassing feeling of peace. I whispered, "Thank you, God, thank you, thank you. Thank you a million times."

With my head between my bent knees, I sobbed. The next time I looked up, the sun had moved and now shone nearly straight overhead. Suddenly, a wave knocked my screwdriver backward into the sand and splashed salty water in my face. The spell was broken.

I walked waist-high into the water, trying to analyze what had just happened. *I don't believe in God, so why did I talk to him? And why do I feel so damn peaceful and free?* I didn't even get an answer to the most basic question. But the lack of answers didn't upset me. I had brought my glass into the water and played games with it, filling it with water then pouring it out... like a child plays in the bathtub.

I lost track of time in this mindless activity, shaking myself out of the trance when I heard laughter from the sand. Dozens of couples and family groups had set up umbrellas for a day on the beach. Feeling apart from my body and mind, my legs went through the motions. I walked to the Atlantis Reef and pressed the UP button on the elevator.

Maybe Stuart will be there. Maybe this peaceful feeling is God-trick so I won't kill him.

<<<<<<<>>>>>>

Alone in the elevator, I downed a mini bottle of vodka, cringing at the taste. *Lela, you've got to stop drinking those damn things! They're killing you!* But I needed liquid courage in case Stuart had returned. I had my confrontation speech planned, at least in outline form. Things would have to change.

The door to our room was wide open and the taste of copper rose in my throat. I tiptoed into the foyer and called out, "Stuart?" The reply was a snore as he rolled over in bed, fully dressed. *Why is the door open? What the hell is going on?*

I closed the door, stomped to the bed, and shook his shoulder hard, six or seven times. He roused, mumbling variations of "leave me alone," then snuggled in deeper with his hands clasped under his chin, as in prayer.

"Stuart! Where did you *go* all night! You left me alone *on vacation!*" Another push on his shoulder.

His eyes opened wide as his body stiffened. "Lela?"

"Who else, Asswipe?"

Stuart rolled over onto his back. "Hey, baby. I'm tired."

"Where the hell have you BEEN?" It was a scream.

"Calm down, dammit! You're out of control!"

Nothing could have pissed me off more than being told to calm down, no matter what. "Calm down, my ass! Where the hell did you go? WHERE? And why did you leave me?"

"I didn't mean to leave you. In fact, I was trying to *find* you when it happened."

"You would have found me right here, asleep! And what's the 'it' that happened?"

"Oh, Lela, it was awful!" He patted his shirt pocket and removed a pack of cigarettes.

"Don't start that shit. I want an explanation and I want it *now.*"

"Oh, don't be so upset! Trust me, I'm more upset than *you* are, baby!"

"How dare you 'baby' me? That shit won't fly, asshole! TELL ME WHERE

YOU WERE, GODDAMMIT!"

Stuart calmly lit a cigarette as if nothing was wrong. His clothes were wrinkled but he seemed bright-eyed and in control. So he must have slept... but where? *Probably with some fucking harlot, a waitress from the casino or some shit like that. Who? And WHY? How could he DO this to me?*

"So here's what happened..." he began.

My butt found the other bed, but I sat forward, ready to hear Stuart's bullshit lies. "I can hardly wait to hear *this* story. Must be a whopper."

"Actually, it *is* bizarre. I'm not sure exactly how to describe it."

"Just spit out your lies, Stuart. Starting NOW."

"Honey, well..." He looked at the bed, his head hung low. "A fucking cocktail waitress sexually assaulted me, Lela, held a knife to my neck and forced me in this, like, tiny dressing room with her. A small sofa and nothing else in there, nothing at all. Lela... it was horrible!"

Purposely aloof and calm, I spoke as if uninterested. "Right. Horrible, I'm sure." I tapped my toe on the carpet. "I'm sure you're traumatized. Scarred for life."

"I am! Listen! She had some bizarre fetish, and I was her *victim*. Her eyes were scary-crazy, like a maniac's eyes. Lela, oh God... I know this sounds crazy."

"Uh... yeah." Smartass remark. Sounding crazy was a laughable understatement.

"The bitch pulled out a vibrator for herself and licked my feet. My *feet*! For *hours*, Lela, moaning and shit. Oh, God! Finally, she straddled my leg and fucked my damn foot! All of it! Inside her! Can you believe that?" His face was white, and the fidgeting began. "Lela, I've been... raped!"

Again, calmly and purposely, I said, "Do you honestly think I believe *that?*"

Stuart's face was red and the rapid-fire of his words increased. "But it's true! It happened three times, all night long. Finally, she fell asleep, and I escaped. No shit, Lela! I reported her to the front desk and the manager... or whoever he was... said she had done it before! They called the police!"

"What a dumbass, *stupid* lie. Who do you think I am? Do I *look* stupid enough to believe that?" I blew a shrill laugh. "I mean, why didn't you choose a more believable story... like the Mafia robbed you at gunpoint, you were run down by a car, eaten by a shark, or maybe you stubbed your toe on the craps table and spent the night in the hospital. You know... something an *intelligent* person would believe." I was breathing hard, so angry it hurt.

"What can I say, Lela? It's the truth. I feel like a dirty slut or something."

"I don't give a shit *how* you feel. But what am *I* supposed to do, huh? I want out of here! I don't want to be here with a *liar!*"

Stuart picked up the hotel phone and thrust it at me. He was so excitable, his words shot saliva on the handset. "Here! Do it! Call the desk and confirm it! Lela, I'm telling you the truth! Please, baby! Believe me! I would never have left you alone if it wasn't true!"

Snatching the phone from his hand, I pressed zero for the front desk. A woman answered on the first ring. I began, "Yes, this is Lela Fox in 812 and I need to speak to the manager on duty, please."

"One little moment," she purred.

A short pause later, a melodic voice said, "This is Cyril Pinder! How can I make your day lucky?"

"Yes, are you the manager?"

"Yes! Cyril Pinder, ma'am, at your service."

"Okay, well... this sounds quite bizarre, but was there a complaint this morning about a waitress who, um... sexually abused a guest?"

"Oh!" I heard a gulp. "Uh, yes, ma'am, I'm sorry to say. The police are taking her as we speak." His sing-song words ran together, but I caught a few: "Why do you ask? Is there another problem? Did she attack someone else? You? Oh, ma'am, I apologize deeply! This sort of thing doesn't happen at the Atlantis Reef!"

"What did the man look like? The man who complained?"

"Oh... no. I should not share that information, ma'am. We treasure privacy for our guests."

"Did he have gray hair and a royal blue shirt?"

A pause. "How are you involved, ma'am? See, I hesitate to ask, for I treasure your privacy as well."

"I'm his fiancé," I lied. "He's... uh, very upset and I'm calling to make sure the problem is... uh, that the woman is under arrest. So I need to know: who complained?"

"Your fiancé, you say? Tell me your name, please."

When I told him, there was a pause as if he was checking a list or writing it down. "Yes. Ms. Fox... how can I make your day lucky?"

"Don't start that shit with me! Just tell me right now – did the man who complained have mostly gray hair and a blue shirt? Tell me!"

"Yes, ma'am. I'm sorry to say but it was Mr. Weinstein. He insisted he was okay and simply wanted to report the... intrusion. Is he no longer fine?"

My heart sunk. *It's true. Poor Stuart was attacked by a sex freak! What the hell? And I've been mean about it. I bet he feels, like, dirty and scared. Poor man!*

The manager's words interrupted my lament for Stuart as his voice took a turn toward pleading. "Please note, the resort will make sure Mr. Weinstein is well-compensated for the inconvenience."

"Inconvenience!? I'd say it's a bit more than that!"

"Yes, yes, I understand, but he will be compensated. Promised by Cyril Pinder, ma'am." His voice trailed off into silence.

With nothing further to say, I readied to disconnect the call. "Thank you for the information. That's all I needed to know."

"Can I get you something else? Room service? More towels?"

"No, we're fine. Thank you." I hung up the phone, shaking my head in disbelief. There were no words.

Stuart interrupted my ponderings. "See? See? I told you it was the truth!"

"How the hell did you pull *that* off, Mr. Weinstein?"

"Pull it off? No! It's the truth! Lela, you heard him... and *I* heard him through the receiver! Damn, Lela." His voice changed from pleading to a more tender tone. "I mean... give me some credit for being honest about this humiliation. I've been sexually assaulted! Put the shoe on the other foot."

I snickered at the analogy but Stuart didn't seem to get it.

As the silence built, I willed myself to keep calm and not let my rat-a-tat heartbeat zoom higher. I refused to give in to the anger and scream my ass off or, even worse, to cry from the overload of emotions I felt. Instead, I stated firmly, "Fuck you. I'm going to the pool." After a few more seconds of staring at Stuart's pitiful eyes, I left the room, leaving the door open.

<<<<<<<>>>>>>

I'd doubled the vodka in four drinks, adding an airline bottle to each. The sun beat high overhead, but the sweet ocean breeze kept the sweat at bay. The steel drum band began, serenading a happy drunk day for me. For the past hour, I'd run Stuart's story through my mind a thousand times, still in disbelief. *A foot rapist?! What the hell... how can that be right? How does that happen? Dammit – that DOESN'T happen! Was the manager lying? Did Stuart pay him to lie? Who else is in on this? Am I being watched, too?* Paranoia took over; I snatched my bag and rushed toward the beach.

With the plan for a long walk, I hoped I'd meet God again.

I walked for a half-mile before finding the perfect spot to sit. I spread my towel. "God, you there?" No reply. "Did the foot fetish thing happen? Is he lying? Am I stupid?" Nothing, no bolt of lightning or harp music. *So, ask yourself, Lela. DID it happen? Can you prove that it DIDN'T?*

I sheltered a lighter within my beach bag and lit a cigarette. After fifteen minutes of watching the turquoise water undulate, feeling the peace of the beach, my senses expanded. No, it wasn't God... it was the realization I'd never be able to confirm *or* disprove his story. The police wouldn't talk to an interested tourist; that would be the only way to confirm it further. Stuart wasn't acting quite normal, suggesting he was upset by something "new" and the manager of the hotel offered the only proof I'd get... which I had no reason to doubt.

So why do you still doubt it?

Okay, Lela... say it DID happen. Is he suffering? Traumatized? Am I being insensitive? And wouldn't it be even more shameful for a MAN to be raped?

Then the most insensitive thought: *If it's true, the trip will be free and we'll maybe win a lawsuit or something. All good things. Seems like they're trying to pay him off first, though, as Cyril Pinder said: He'd be "well compensated."*

Those thoughts brought more pangs of Guilt, knowing I hoped to profit from Stuart's rape (and "rape" would be the word, I realized). So I'd been an asshole to a man in distress. *You're an ass, Lela! You're just what you accuse him of being.*

A tall, tan twenty-something man with a rock-hard set of abs came into view, walking fast. He eyed me and smiled, but kept his eyes drilled into me too long for comfort. Fear spiked, my heart pumping hard, then just as instantly, the fear abated as he looked away. *What if that guy raped me, even with his foot? Wouldn't that traumatize the hell out of me?*

I stood and walked the half-mile back to the Atlantis Reef.

Stuart was in the shower when I returned and an idea struck; I called room service to order us drinks, hoping to help Stuart relax. The service was lightning-fast, and a tray arrived a minute before Stuart entered the main suite, wet and wearing a towel. He rallied when spotting the drinks. "It's like you read my mind, dear." He sipped the drink and made smacking noises. "Mmm! So good!

I looked him in the eye, my brow wrinkled. "Do you... uh... need to talk about it? Process your feelings? I'm sure you're overwhelmed with emotions, maybe you feel... dirty, or at least that's how I felt."

"No! I don't want to talk about it at all. Not one word! Because I want to forget it happened... forget it forever. I'm good at that kind of thing, anyway."

"Denial?"

A pause; Stuart cocked his head. "Yeah, denial. I'm good at it." He turned to the mirror and ran a brush through that wiry hair, changing nothing. Then he put on his watch, noticing the late hour; it was almost four. "So what have you been doing, anyway?

"I've been at the pool and took two long walks along the beach. It's beautiful here, Stuart, and the sunrise was gorgeous." I paused to look at my hands, clasped in my lap as I sat in the puffy side chair next to the window. "But that was after I searched for you in the casino, the men's rooms, and everywhere. Twice!"

"Oh baby, I'm so sorry. Believe me, I wish you could've found me and helped me escape!" A visible shiver racked his body, the poor man. It struck me how he easily changed his tone... back and forth from happy to upset, then back again. *Which was it?*

But *I* needed to talk, to tell him about my experience with God that morning; in fact, I wondered if the two might be related. "Well... something funny happened down there on the beach." I said, keeping the volume of my voice low.

As he continued to dress, he appeased me, seeming upbeat and interested. "Tell me what 'funny' happened on your gorgeous day, dear."

I hesitated, not knowing how to phrase it. "I was just thinking about the natural beauty of the place and I said, 'Thank you, God,' like without even thinking about it!"

"What's wrong with that?"

"Nothing, really, but it... it just surprised me. I haven't thought about God in years, much less *talked* to him! And after I said it, like a long prayer-thing, I got embarrassed. I'm thinking... why would God want to hear from *me?*"

"Maybe he thinks you're important. Don't ask me this stuff! I'm a fallen Jew... what do I know?"

True... maybe he doesn't believe in the same God I do. Then a thought struck: *I just said I believed in a God.* As quickly as I could, I erased the thought by putting it in words. "But do I even believe in God anymore? I doubt it or I wouldn't act the way I do."

Stuart huffed a laugh. "You're no angel, that's for sure."

"And that's what I'm saying! Mom would say God wouldn't forget about me, but I've forgotten about God, turned my back, whatever you call it. He doesn't want to hear from a 'sinner' like me."

"Lela, you had too much church as a child or something. You're fucked up about this. Why are you talking about it, anyway?"

"Because it surprised me. I mean... I *prayed,* Stuart! I fucking *prayed!* What if there *is* a God, and he's really pissed at me? I mean, I do *everything* wrong... according to, uh, Methodist rules."

The ear buzz started anew, and I felt tears well in my eyes. The one-sided conversation had caused a rise in my blood pressure and my body naturally rose to meet it. A sigh. "God doesn't like me at all! Why would he? I don't want to sound melodramatic, but I have failed God. Big time. My mother, I'm sure, believes I'll go to hell. Daddy, too."

"Lela, drop it. You're getting weird. God, no God... what does it matter? We're on vacation! Don't screw it up by getting down on yourself." He picked up the remote and turned the TV off with a click. "Shut up and finish your drink. You're worrying me."

Stuart had stopped the conversation in its tracks, but in my mind, it was far from over. *Maybe I'm too sober, beating myself up about being a lush.* I laughed at myself, at my own thought. *Way to go, Lela. Avoid it.* But my forehead creased to half its height. I didn't know what to think.

I closed my eyes, squeezing a few tears on my cheek. *Do I believe in God?* The best answer I could figure was "maybe." I knew this beautiful world couldn't be explained just by science, scoffing at the "Big Bang Theory" all by itself. *But then… what? The original question was "do I believe," but maybe that's immaterial. The real question: does God believe in ME?* I pondered that question and shuddered. *No, he doesn't. Why would he?*

I drained my drink in one swallow, taking a small piece of ice to chew. "Fuck it. If there was a God, I wouldn't be so drunk right now."

The "God Thing" stayed on my mind the entire week of vacation. I couldn't put my finger on what was making me feel so weird and guilty. And I fought to hide from one specific feeling: my old friend, Shame. Shame about the way I lived, how much I drank, how I'd attached myself to Stuart so desperately.

I knew God didn't approve of me or how I was living, but I found change overwhelming. I only knew how to stay in my lane, keep doing what I did and continue the lifestyle I'd chosen. Or rather, the lifestyle that had chosen me.

Twenty years later and sober, I know the reason for the Guilt and Shame. Simply put, I wasn't yet willing to change. I hadn't met my bottom yet.

As for Stuart's tall tale, I had doubts. But all the evidence, including his shivers and odd behavior, were signs of trauma… the exact kind *I* felt after a sexual assault. I dared not share my empathy or my doubt, so I tiptoed around his emotions, afraid to rock the boat.

It was the first time I remember stepping back and questioning him. I asked myself directly if I trusted Stuart, then ran from the negative answer that roused. His story was either too bizarre to believe or too bizarre to *not* believe. I couldn't, or wouldn't, decide which way to turn.

But I got an answer at just the right time, if you consider "God's schedule" the right time.

THE COST OF PARADISE
CHAPTER 26

I fed the one-armed bandit with fury. Stuart was in the lobby, talking to the concierge again and I wondered why. *Is he buying that drug-laced weed again? Buying me a woman? Telling him about the rape by the cocktail waitress? What?* The thoughts disappeared when the bell above my head clanged and deafened me as the red light flashed and whirled. *Yippee! I won sixty-three dollars!* Quarters spewed from the machine as I hooted with joy. Not a shabby payout for a quarter!

Scooping the winnings into an empty cup, I ran to the cashier's window for bills. No more quarters. Adapted Fox Family gambling rules: I'd spend forty bucks but when I made my money back, that was that. I'd spend the extra on that nice beach wrap I'd seen in a shop window.

I stuck the bills under the elastic of my bikini bottom and walked into the lobby to find Stuart. Ta-da! We met head-on as he walked into the casino. "Come on, I've got something to show you," he said, his cherubic face alight.

"Right here, babe! Let's play." I'd never played the Roulette wheel; Stuart explained the no-brainer rules. With his direction, I bought chips: five white ones, a whopping five dollars. I put two chips on the Red. Stuart bought sixty bucks in chips from the man and spread them over several numbers. "What numbers?"

"Jeremy's birthday, always my first bet," he said. I smiled. *How sweet is THAT?*

He lost. I won.

"Oh well," he said, spreading chips on other numbers. I put my dollar chips on the numbers of Bo's birthday. The wheel spun; neither of us won a thing. No pressure involved, we played for a while with no success. Stuart bought another sixty-dollars-worth of chips and led me to the Blackjack tables.

"Oh, no, Stuart; I suck at Blackjack."

"No worries! I'll coach you. Free drinks for Blackjack players, you know?"

"Really? Well, hell! Let's play!"

As usual, I lost hand after hand after hand. Disgusted. Bored. "I'm a loser. This sucks, so I'm going up to change for dinner."

I showered with hot, hot water. When I came into the bedroom, Stuart was sitting back on the bed, his legs bent, and one crossed over the other. Without looking up, he quickly put something in the nightstand's drawer, then fumbled with the remote. His foot was pumping up and down, shaking. "What are you doing?" I asked.

"Nothing," he answered before I finished my question. *Have I caught him doing something? What?*

"Did you win anything down there?"

"A few hands. Not much. Wasting money." All clipped phrases and without looking me in the eye.

The hair on the back of my neck stood out as my eyes narrowed. "What are you up to, Stuart Weinstein? Obviously, you're hiding something from me." The comment was three things – a question, a tease, and an accusation.

His laugh was quick, fake. Like Woody Woodpecker. The fidgeting had reached a fever pitch. Scrambling for the remote, he awkwardly clicked through the channels, finding nothing but fuzz. And his foot kept jumping and pumping. I stared at him for a while. *He's up to something all right. Maybe he has a surprise for me and he's doing a bad job of hiding it. Must be something like that.*

There was a knock at the door. Our drinks. Stuart had piled five-dollar bills on the table beside the door, specifically for tipping room service guys. I grabbed one from the top of the pile, thanked the man, and brought the tray into the bedroom. "We're building quite a tab already, Stuart. You cool with that?"

"Don't worry about shit like that! You know better." I *did* know better, but I worried every time. The working-class girl in me was ashamed to spend money, even too ashamed to approve of my boyfriend doing the same. It ate at me daily. But I still let it happen all the time.

Dinner at the on-site Asian restaurant... feeling no pain with a dozen cups of rice wine in me, we killed some time in the room before hitting the casino again. I sat at the end of the bed and heard the click of Stuart's lighter. But what I smelled wasn't a cigarette.

He had a glass pipe in his hand with the bowl of the pipe consuming the flame. His normally chubby cheeks were hollow with such a deep draw on the pipe. Finishing the hit, he looked at me with a sparkly smile in his eyes.

"What's that?" Stuart didn't answer, holding in the hit he had taken. Then he motioned me forward, pointing to my lips, then his.

"Oh? Like a shotgun?" I asked. He nodded, still holding the smoke in his lungs. I assumed he'd use the pipe to blow a shotgun, but he'd set it aside. Finally, with his face fire-engine-red, he put his lips to mine and blew into my open mouth. Leftover smoke. I inhaled, tasting something acrid, chemical.

Stuart sat back, smiling. "Hold it in for as long as you can, babe." I felt confused; where was the smoke? And why did this pot taste so funny? After a few seconds, I blew out the hit, slow and smooth. There was no smoke!

"What the hell, Stuart? There's no..." Then a feeling like I'd never felt hit like a wave, spreading prickly heat to the end of my fingertips and toes. The most pleasant feeling ever! I fell backward on the bed slowly; I didn't want to waste the energy it took to fall and bounce.

The euphoric sensation lasted a full sixty seconds, during which Stuart remained silent. I rolled over on my belly; in my head, the action followed me a few seconds later. *Wow. This is the best pot I have ever, ever smoked.*

The sensation ebbed, and I rolled on my side, facing Stuart. Without moving, I said, "Damn, man! What kind of pot *is* that! So I guess it's laced with something... or something?"

"Laced with cocaine," he said, lighting the pipe again. "Again? Not for me, I'm too stoned." *Ha, ha, Lela... how long has it been since you said THAT? A* true statement, because I was suddenly sober. I didn't like that. So intensely, acutely, and totally *aware* of everything around me... amazed by the slightest twist of air floating in the room.

As he held his breath once more, he pointed to his lips and mine again, as if asking a question. I shook my head no. A disappointed look covered his face. Stuart closed his eyes and leaned back against the headboard in slow motion, spreading his legs wide on the bed. I guessed the overwhelming sensation was hitting him as it hit me and it was spooky to watch it happening. Spooky enough to send a shiver down my spine. *I hope he's okay! That shit is lethal! And I'm pissed it sobered me up, sonofabitch.*

My drink; the ice had melted, but it would do. In my mind, the umbrella accent became a full-size umbrella and the rain fell in buckets... it was a momentary vision. Another blink of my eyes and the umbrella returned to its normal size... and I became mesmerized by the faint printing, by the shape, the point of the toothpick. I studied it as a scientist would study a new specimen, in pure and child-like wonder.

There was a high-pitched buzz at the top of my head. I felt smart. Genius. *Maybe because you're sober, Lela.* Then a sudden inspiration: *Or maybe because you just smoked some cocaine-laced marijuana.*

I pointed to the glass pipe, wanting another exhale. That one was even better, an incredible rush, lasting longer. I saw an aura around my body, like air with ripples in it. Strange...

But enough was enough. The shit scared me. "I can't handle any more of that shit, Stuart." I jumped; my voice echoed in triplicate within the room and felt like an album running on high speed. A click on my tongue turned into a horrific case of cotton mouth.

Stuart put the pipe in the drawer and we sat in silence for a long while. He stared at various spots in the room, especially mesmerized by the triangle where the ceiling met the corner walls, where the light played tricks. Still speaking fast, and now an octave higher than normal, I urged him to get up. "Let's sit on the patio, baby. Please!"

"But you're naked."

"And I can feel every square inch of my body touching the air in this place. Let's smoke more of that pot."

<<<<<<<<>>>>>>>

Saturday. Our last day. As yet-another treat, we had pre-ordered a V.I.P. room service breakfast. When I opened the door, I straddled the envelope that had been slipped underneath, the final bill I assumed, and grabbed two fives from the foyer table to tip the man. A bottle of champagne, eggs Benedict, a gargantuan bowl of fruit, the works. Stuart and I ate the decadent breakfast while lounging in bed.

"They slipped the bill under the door, honey. Make sure they comped the room." I had no reason to believe they wouldn't have; a crime had been committed against Stuart and he'd lost almost $2,000 in the casino, he said.

"In a minute," Stuart said, leaning against the headboard with a full flute of champagne. We kissed and slowly made love. Then Stuart got up and skipped to the foyer. He was a gone a long time then burst into the bedroom and sat on the club chair with a plop. "Uh... Lela?" He drawled the words out. I assumed he was making fun of my accent.

"Yeeeeeeah?" I could drawl, too.

"Uh... I need your credit card."

I snapped. "What? *WHY!*"

"Simply put, they didn't comp the room."

"Well, that's just a simple call downstairs... to Mr. Silver Tongue Cyril Pinder." I smiled, pouring the last of the coffee into my oversized mug. "He said you would be well-compensated. Surely that includes something he's free to give away in the first place." No worries on my end, I smiled at Stuart and hoped this talk wasn't making him feel the same "dirty" all over again.

"That's the thing. There's a note with it, from Cyril Pinder, the manager." Stuart's voice was dreamy but his eyebrows smashed together in worry.

"And what did the silky Mr. Pinder have to say?"

He looked at the stapled stack of paper, scanned one by one, then flipped back to the front page. "It says: 'A check will be forthcoming in U.S. dollars, as our bank deals only in the native currency.'" Stuart let the papers drop to the floor.

"Let me see that!" I bounded from the bed and snatched the bill from the carpet. Sure enough, an oversize yellow Post-it-Note lay on top, written in scribbly print, saying exactly what Stuart had quoted, and more. I read the rest of the note, incredulous. "And you have to wait two months! That's insane!"

"*Totally* insane."

With a sigh, I put the paper on the desk. "Well, hell! You'll just have to pay it, then. But that sucks."

Stuart paused, looking away... looking at everything in the room but me.

"What, Stuart? What's wrong?"

"Lela, I don't have the money."

Shocked, I sat back on the corner of the bed. "What? What the hell are you *say*ing? The bill is more than $5,000!" My face drained of blood and I felt my stomach turn, churning with an unease that was sure to release my gourmet breakfast.

"Stuart, you put it on your credit card when you made the reservation! And you got a check from the trust, you said! What the hell? You best have plenty of explanation, buddy. This is bullshit! Total BULLSHIT!"

Stuart simply repeated his previous sentence. "I don't have the money." Flat, without emotion or inflection.

"But I don't understand! And I don't have the money, either! This will put my Visa over the credit limit, *which I just raised to pay for the move, you sonofabitch*." Growls of frustration exploded within me; anger blasted from every pore.

Stuart's eyes glazed with tears. "Honey, it doesn't help to yell at me. All I can say is I'm sorry. *So* sorry! Do you want me to yell back at you?"

Exasperated, I fell backward on the bed, pondering the situation... wondering if a toll-free number would work on this island. Another call, another credit increase, but no increase in income – a DEcrease, in fact. *What the hell are you going to do, Lela Fox? You may be rich later, but you're not rich now.*

When I rose halfway, Stuart was at the desk, scribbling as left-handers do... like he was retarded and wrapping his arm around the trunk of a tree. Without looking up, he said, "Okay, I think I can pay some of it. Hold on and I'll tell you exactly how much. Unfortunately, I gambled all the cash I had planned to use, but I have some left... and a little headroom on my pre-paid MasterCard."

With a laser focus on the notepad, he wrote numbers, then ran to find last night's pants, pulling his fat wallet from the back pocket. "How much to get out of long-term parking?" he asked.

"Hell if I know! What the fuck? Are you cutting it that close? You're crazy!"

"Why not? There's money in Rockville, a full paycheck waiting on me."

"Good, then you can use it to pay me back."

"Not if we want groceries. And the rest of the stuff to move."

I screamed again in frustration. *GRRR!* "How much did you spend on that pot?" The laced shit... the kind that makes you hyper as hell? I bet *that* wasn't cheap! And how could you gamble all your cash away? HOW? Even better, WHY? Stuart, you can't possibly be so stupid, no matter how traumatized you are!"

Stuart's face was red, growing darker with each sentence I yelled. "Shut the fuck up! And you did your fair share of gambling, too, young lady."

My voice squeaked high in response to this ridiculous comment. "Because I thought it was all going to be *free! Of course I thought that!* And what I don't understand, Stuart... you're rich as hell! You have money coming out your ass! This is a sham! You're trying to fool me, you little fucker!"

Silence. Stuart turned to the desk again, apparently checking his numbers and ignoring me. Then he turned slowly to face me, panic in his eyes "Okay, I can pay some. And of course, I'll pay you back. Lastly, don't call me a fucker – that's not fair."

"Fair? YOU are the one who's not being fair!

"Stop."

"No. I can't. I won't."

"Stop. Stop yelling. Breathe, Lela! In through your nose and out through your mouth. This is not the end of the world, just a little bump under the rug."

Flustered, pissed, distressed... my hands were shaking as I picked up the invoice once more. I flipped through the multiple pages. Drinks, dinner, more drinks, chips at the casino, more chips, more chips, room service – dozens of those. Oh, my God! The bar tab! Probably a thousand bucks there. The words and numbers on the paper started to run together. "I can't pay this," I said in a voice barely above a squeak.

"I can pay $812."

"Big whoop. It's $4,900!"

"Jeezus, Lela, I'll pay you back!" A hateful tone this time.

My heart was beating like a gong on steroids, and the fear of another panic attack was building fast. *Breathe, Lela, breathe.* I forced myself to settle down, to relax. Breathing deeply and purposely, I sat in silence for a full minute, trying to focus on anything other than this insurmountable problem.

Words spilled from my mouth; I could not control them. "But... but..." I couldn't finish the sentence. Confused. Lost. Deflated like a tire. "Stuart... I am stunned. And I'm so pissed. So you've been... oh, God, you've been lying to me all this time!"

Stuart rushed to my side, smothered me with kisses. "No, baby, I was not lying to you. I would never, ever lie to you." More kisses. He rubbed his forefinger on my cheek. "Baby... I love you. And we'll be okay. This is just a little hiccup. Believe me, it's all okay. Don't be upset!" He went on with kisses and promises, and professions of his love. "Here, more champagne." He fumbled for the flute and the bottle, acting very nervous.

"What's wrong with you? You're a wreck!"

"Just trying to calm you down. And I don't want you to have another panic attack. Here, drink this," he said, passing the flute. I eyed him, still suspicious, but drained the glass.

"Whoa! I needed that!" I said.

"Another? There's a bit more." Not waiting for an answer, I snatched the bottle and turned it upside down.

Tears stung my eyes; that sad, flat feeling returned. *I've been screwed. See, God, you wouldn't let that happen if you loved me! You motherfucker!* A deep sigh. "Get in the shower, Stuart. We don't want to miss the flight."

<<<<<<<>>>>>>>

The airport on Grand Bahama Island was small and filled with slot machines. We passed through customs, lying about what we had purchased because we couldn't afford the tariff, even as small as it would have been. I wasn't speaking to him beyond the necessary grunts of "yes" and "no."

As the small plane landed in Fort Lauderdale just minutes after taking off from the Bahamas, I stepped outside to smoke while Stuart went to the restroom. When he joined me later, his nervous tics were even worse; he hadn't stopped fidgeting and jiggling the entire morning and it was driving me crazy.

With just an hour layover, we had to high-tail it to the gate for the Delta flight to Atlanta. In flight, we couldn't afford to buy a drink from the beverage cart, which pissed me off to the max. He was still trying to woo me, going above and beyond to lure me back to coochie-coo with him. I must have heard "Please, Lela, don't be mad at me!" a hundred times.

My jaw ached from clenching it so tight. Gathering my things to deplane in Atlanta, I realized I had lost my passport. "But Stuart, you picked up both of ours at the customs counter. Do you have *your* passport?" Yes, his was where it should have been. With a *hmpftt*, I continued my silent treatment until we landed in Rockville and entered the long-term parking garage. I hoped somebody had stolen his car, or another catastrophe would happen to him.

In the car, I took a deep breath and blew it out with a sigh. "Home, James," I said.

"Yes'm, Miss Daisy."

I don't know the going rate for passports, but I'm pretty sure he sold mine in the Fort Lauderdale airport when "in the bathroom." It's long-expired by now, and I've never had the balls to apply for another. Now I worry that he sold it to a terrorist or an underworld criminal and I'm on some kind of international "Most Wanted" list.

But at the time, I forgot about it once I had the next drink.

I believed in Stuart Weinstein, thought he had a good heart and trusted that the two of us had a good future. There were a few doubts about his truthfulness, but I forced myself to see only the good in him... and there was a lot of that. No shit.

Mostly, I believed I had no other choice. I stayed drunk enough to be happy and only cried when I thought about how much I was disappointing my Daddy.

WELLINGTON

CHAPTER 27

"Anything in this pile is a dollar. The other stuff, just ask about the price." It was a one-on-one yard sale with the handyman who came to tear out the countertop and cabinetry in my studio. I meant to have an official yard sale, advertised and etcetera, but it was too cold and I was too overwhelmed to get it priced and sorted.

Lola offered to help, of course, but she was already doing so much... practically everything. Frustrated, I threw junk in the car and took it to Goodwill. The last of it I left on the front porch, leaving a phone message for the Salvation Army to come to get it.

It was New Year's Eve when I left Rockville, about 200 miles ahead of the forty-foot moving truck. They kept loading and loading; I couldn't believe I had that much stuff! I threw away as much as I could, but I had a houseful and I wasn't willing to part with it.

The movers charged by the pound, and I had overshot the estimate by a thousand pounds, costing $300 extra. I hoped Stuart wouldn't mind the addition to the bill. He'd promised to pay me back, saying, "Just add it to my tab." The comment sent my stomach to the floor, desperate for the payment and not feeling so sure it'd be coming this month. Too many moving expenses.

Stuart had been in Florida for ten days, had already started his job. I hadn't seen the apartment, which made me anxious, but there was no other way to do it. I didn't trust Stuart to make this all-important decision, and spent the last three days on the phone with the landlord, asking for details. The man finally got pissed and told me to call when I saw it.

<<<<<<<<>>>>>>>

The movers had a hard time navigating the bedroom; it was tiny. *Not* what I would have chosen, but the living/dining room was huge and with a high ceiling to maximize the expanse. It separated from the kitchen with a breakfast bar on an island. The kitchen was okay, big enough for our not-so-gourmet needs. And, as I had specifically requested, it was on the ground floor.

The backyard was a dream. A sliding glass door opened to grassy stretch, then to a pond filled with white ducks... mommas and babies. Stuart said the quacking was driving him nuts, but I thought it would be worth a little noise to be living among wildlife inside the city.

Worrisome, the gate for the complex held back no one. It was wide open every time Stuart passed, he said, as it was when I arrived and when the truck passed through.

I figured out the furniture arrangement on the fly, but I was on-target. The bedroom to be Bo's was the same size as the Master. It broke my heart to see it so empty. I had promised to fly him down, along with his best-friend Bryce, for a week-long visit on spring break. It seemed ridiculous for a sixteen-year-old to have a bunk bed, but also ridiculous for me to buy another for an occasional visitor. *Occasional visitor. Oh, that makes me cringe.*

I felt like a crappy mother most of the time if I thought about it. So I tried not to think about it.

Bo and I talked every other week, or when I remembered to call. But he was a busy kid, breaking records on the baseball team and with honor-roll grades. Andy said he had "a thousand friends" and he hung out with good kids. "Bo isn't trouble, and he's not making trouble. I think he's really happy here." Andy's comment was an assurance, but it panged me with Guilt and Shame. *Lela Fox, you still can't give him what Andy and Ella can. You're still too fucked-up to be a decent mother. What's WRONG with you?*

Murphy strolled into the living room to break my thoughts. "So what do ya think, Murphy? Will this be a happy home for a good dog like you?" The poor dog seemed confused and disoriented. I sat on the sofa and rubbed his belly for a while after the movers left.

Then I called Stuart at work. "Movers are gone. The place is a wreck. I have a lot of work to do, but I'm looking forward to it."

"Well, don't *you* sound upbeat! A little manic, my sweet Bi-Polar girlfriend?" It was a tease, not an inquiry of concern.

"I am, I guess. It's a new adventure, ya know? As much as I hate to pack up, I like to *un*-pack and put things up all neat and organized. The furniture fits fine. Except for the bedroom. Why didn't you tell me it was dollhouse-sized?"

"Sorry, babe. I can't think of everything."

"Okay, for now, I just want to find a glass and the vodka."

"Got to go! Bye!" Stuart answered four lines at the busy shop. And every call was a potential commission. Evidently, West Palm Beach residents had a lot of transmission problems.

I scrambled through the cabinets and saw the two glasses he had brought with him. I chuckled. Two glasses. I'd seen Lola pack more than twenty! But a huge bottle of Grey Goose vodka was on the counter; that's what mattered the most.

Drink in hand; I sat down at the breakfast bar with the phone book. So thick! I got lost in the yellow pages, amazed by the choices available just in the small burb of Wellington. *Florida is WAY different from Tennessee, girl. Ready for some culture shock?*

I started work in the living room, loading the entertainment center with videotapes and CDs. Holding my breath, I turned on the TV. *Great!* The power and cable came on instantly. *Good job, Stuart.* He had arranged all the utility connections and I applauded the follow-through.

Thirty minutes later, I was up to my elbows in details. But I seemed to be able to handle things a little better here, much better than when I was leaving Rockville. I missed Lola, thinking I'd much rather sit back and watch her do all this work.

Another box of CDs, which again made me wonder why Stuart had none. Not a single one. But he arrived at the green house with very little. Everything in this Wellington apartment, with few exceptions, was mine.

I freshened my drink and took the kitchen by storm. The phone rang and startled me. I answered, "Stuart and Lela's place!"

"Aww. Isn't that cute!" It was Stuart. "How's it going?"

"Okay. Tired already, but the living room and kitchen are mostly done!"

"How's Murphy? Does he miss Rock-Bob?" As always, Stuart took Rock-Bob to work with him, sharing his lunch and the after-lunch M&Ms.

"Murphy isn't looking for Rock-Bob. He likes the ducks too much."

Stuart said, "I called about dinner." *Just like him to think about food.* "Takeout tonight. Chicken? Steak? Fish?"

"Don't care. Food."

Stuart bounced in around six o'clock with two, huge Boston Market meat-and-three boxes. I was working in the bathroom, unpacking a ridiculous amount of cosmetics. With just a single sink, there wasn't enough room, but I found a way.

"Want a drink? I'm playing bartender," he said.

"Absolutely."

Around midnight, I fell into bed, feeling at home. I awoke when Stuart joined me two hours later. We hadn't made love since returning from the Bahamas, so I assumed our first night in the new place would be a given, but Stuart made no moves and didn't respond to mine. I instantly knew something was wrong; even after all the time we'd been together, we were still in the rabbit stage. *Could it be because of the foot assault? Oh, hell! Will I have to coach him through that?*

The next morning, I got up with Stuart, even though he left early for work. I chased him around as he darted from the bedroom to the kitchen to the living room. *What was I going to say? Something to remind him of...* "Oh, honey, that huge credit card bill came in the last Rockville mail delivery. It's in the little organizer by the phone. Pay it off, all of it, like you promised, right?"

"Right. I'll have to get a money order. No checks yet, I assume?"

"I'm going to the bank today so it will be another week, at least."

"I'll take care of it, babe. No worries," he said. I noted a strange squeak in his voice. He pecked me on the cheek and dashed out the door. I sighed. He didn't take the credit card bill with him.

I added a splash of vodka to my coffee and unpacked my office; I put the desk in the dining room so household headquarters would be front and center in the house.

Organizing my desk took quite a while because, as always, I created a "happy place" to work. I surrounded the work area with a variety of... stuff. I liked everything in view: notepads, colored pencils, pictures, kitschy toys, random shit... and always, my coveted calendar. The same kind, same brand each year and specific formats for specific tasks and appointments.

For a lousy drunk, I was obsessively organized.

Errands. I headed out to open our bank accounts and rent a safe-deposit box. I drove around to explore the town a bit, ending up at Stuart's shop. *Is it okay to just show up, to surprise him?* A bell tinkled when I walked in the door. *Oh, my Lord!* The waiting room was clean as a whistle. Upscale, with upholstered chairs in designer fabric, nice artwork, the works.

"Impressive, Stuart. And you sit here on a throne."

"King of the transmission business."

"Har, har."

"Don't complain, my lady of leisure."

<<<<<<<<>>>>>>

On the way home, I realized how long I'd been gone. In the green house, and for years before, I'd been home to let Murphy out several times a day. Immediate Guilt. After letting him out, I mixed a quick drink and made a fruit salad. I was zooming around the kitchen... *uh, oh.*

That's when I realized I hadn't taken my medicine... not since we landed in the Bahamas three weeks ago! I pawed through my bathroom bags and found the pill case, counted out the correct combination, and downed the pills with a fresh vodka-tonic. I hoped it wasn't too late to stop a manic swing.

But I knew the truth. It was too late to stop it; it had already taken over my body.

Might as well take advantage...

Over the next few weeks, I ran on 100 percent adrenalin, exploring my new hometown in all nooks and crannies. In a frenzy, I tackled the apartment décor, adding details of every sort and shopping for artwork and antiques in the many boutiques of West Palm. I also drove to the beach each day. Floating in the water was the only time I could completely relax... paddling out and letting the peaceful waves wash me to the shore.

Stuart continually fed me hundred-dollar-bills, and I continually spent them. We hung out with Stuart's mother and Elijah a lot; she'd forgiven him or given in to the pressure to what Stuart called "the nanny syndrome." Sundays were often nights at their country club, where the food ran the gamut from burgers to Beef Bourguignon, and the drinks were free.

It was a happy, carefree time of my life. Stuart and I got along like new lovers; it was as if he'd become himself again... and that refurbished self treated his girlfriend with respect and care.

Months passed, and during this time, I even started to like myself, maybe even respect myself. For the first time in... ever... I thought I was worthy and deserving of this good life.

Looking back, I wish those good feelings would've brought a decrease in my drinking. Though I thought I drank more in periods of self-hate and low self-esteem, I realize now I'd crossed that line, too. I drank with the good and the bad.

I remember talking to myself about it, urging myself to slow it down... maybe wait later in the day to start, or quit earlier in the evening. For a while, I put doubles on hiatus and created rules to trick myself into drinking less.

Of course, none of these tactics worked; I'd only made myself feel stupid for bargaining with something so "harmless," as I thought of it then.

I continued with what I considered to be a normal life. The new normal. Which was not normal at all.

SHINING LIMELIGHT
CHAPTER 28

Eventually, I got bored.

On Tuesday, my day at the spa, I realized how few people I'd spoken to beyond a word here and there with a store clerk, waitress or my masseuse. During my facial appointment, I asked about the "happening spots" in Wellington where I might find friends, and the technician rattled off a few.

She told me about Limelight, just down the street. I went there immediately. The place was a dead-ringer for the bar in *Cheers*, the ultimate neighborhood hangout. Brick walls, funky décor, and the soft glow of a circular bar in the center. Intimate. Friendly. I fell in love with it before I sat down.

Slipping onto a stool at the bar, I ordered a glass of wine and perused the lunch menu. All-American fare with a Florida twist. I ordered a bowl of tortilla soup and a second glass of wine, chatting it up with the bartender, Barry.

Stuart and I have to check this place out, and soon. But I found no "friends" in that friendly place. The big sigh that followed made me think my manic swing was soon to be followed by a depressed one.

I hated to leave... to go home with nothing to do. *I need a job. Something little, even if it's just part-time.* On a whim, I asked the bartender if he knew anybody who needed help. "Something interesting," I specified.

"The term 'interesting' can be a lot of things, Curly."

On my way out, in the vestibule, a newspaper box held the *Palm Beach Post*.

Aha! I thought it was an omen... a thick newspaper full of job listings. *I'm supposed to look for a job today!*

Home, I spread the paper on the coffee table, circling possibilities with a fresh, red Sharpie. First, I focused on writer's jobs. Just a few listings, but all display ads with corporate-looking logos. *Do I really want the pressure of an ad agency again?* My experience at Sturbridge in Rockville had tainted me. So I crossed those off the list.

Here's one, a manager at a dry cleaner! It's been years, but my first job was at a dry cleaner. It's something I know. I circled it. The location was perfect, just a few miles from home. I scoured the ads for hours, remembering the ad that led me to Stuart. It was a nice memory.

Stuart breezed in a bit after six o'clock. My first comment to him: "Did you get the money order?"

His face froze. "Sorry, honey, I forgot."

"Dammit, Stuart! You promised! Like you've promised for months on end. And if you remember, you promised to pay the full amount right after we got back! I'm without a credit card!"

"You've had handfuls of hundred-dollar-bills! Quit your bitching."

"I'm not bitching! You're an asshole."

Stuart sighed, detailing each piddly payment he'd made month by month... as if he remembered each penny. Tiring of his bullshit, I shouted. "Pay it! The interest is stupid and I'm getting really, really, really angry at you." My intense glare drilled through his thick head, I hoped.

"Just give me the damn bill. I'll take care of it tomorrow," he said, stomping to the mail organizer by the phone.

"No, I'll tell you what. Publix, open all night, and they sell money orders. We're going tonight. I want this taken care of!" He threw up his hands, arguing. But my determination won, and he promised.

I flipped the mood. "We'll do it on the way to this great place I discovered today! Dinner out, baby?"

<<<<<<<<>>>>>>>

We sat in the back corner booth of The Limelight, one of eight that lined the side of the bar. The menu featured specialty pizzas, a new thing... off-beat ingredients on a pizza crust. We split the "Love Pizza," white cheddar, spinach, and sun-dried tomatoes. It was as good as I hoped; Stuart agreed. "'Love Pizza' makes me horny," he teased.

Instead of going along with the joke, I took the opportunity. "Being horny is something I wanted to talk to you about, too."

"What do you mean?"

"Stuart, I'll be blunt. Our love life is waning. What's up with that?" I tried to act casual, but this was serious business to me.

"Uh... we're in public, Lela. Don't you think–"

I interrupted. "Maybe ten people in this place, Stuart. Private enough... even my mother would think this is a good time to talk. And we *have* to talk. Honey, we used to be crazed sex fiends, and suddenly – no, not suddenly, since the Bahamas. You seem... uninterested, preoccupied. And why so damn fidgety?"

"I don't know, Lela. Maybe it was the foot rape thing. Or maybe things just change. So what if we're not rabbits anymore? We are now like... ducks."

"Ducks." I challenged him to explain, but it turns out, he was just making a joke to avoid a serious discussion.

"I am a little preoccupied, I guess. Let's go home," he said.

"Not yet. Am I...? Is it...? Is it me?"

"No, baby. You're awesome. You're sexy. But I *will* say..."

"Go on..."

"Well, you're pretty drunk by the end of the night. Sloppy sometimes."

"Oh." In that instant, my body felt incredibly heavy. The weight of Guilt.

A long moment of silence as I kept my head down, fidgeting with the seam of the napkin. "Fuck it. Let's go."

We slid into the car. Before he could turn the key, I leaned forward for a kiss. A quick peck on the cheek. Nothing more. He didn't respond.

"Sorry, not in the mood, woman. What's gotten into you?"

Crushed, I closed my eyes as a loud buzz began in my head. After a pause, I decided it would be best not to push it. "It's the 'Love Pizza,' I think." He spewed a nervous laugh and started the car, turning toward our apartment before I stopped him. "No, Stuart. To Publix. The money order."

"Oh, yeah. No problem." I stayed in the car while he went inside the store, realizing five minutes later that he didn't know the exact amount. *He'll get close enough, I guess. He looked at the bill.* Minutes later, he hopped in the car, all smiles and happiness, then leaned over to give me a long, deep, and sensual kiss. *Maybe we'll have sex tonight after all.*

As we walked in our front door, I asked, "Where's that money order?"

"In my wallet." He sat on the sofa, not offering to stand up to retrieve his wallet. *Just as well. I'm too drunk and too disheartened to handle it tonight, anyway.* I passed the Visa bill to Stuart. "We don't have stamps. Can you handle that tomorrow; just mail it from work?"

"Free stamps at work. Why not?"

DRAGON MAD

CHAPTER 29

I took a deep breath and dialed the number. For the second time that day, I put on my best face and gracefully stated my qualifications for a job, ending with a request for an immediate interview. I must have played my cards well because that was the second of two job interviews scheduled for the next day... one right after the other.

Happy as hell, I dashed to Publix, buying ingredients for a surprise dinner. I intended to consciously watch my drinking that night and be sober enough for raucous sex later, so I mixed a weak drink and rattled a few skillets. Veal Parmesan.

Stuart called about 4:30. "I have to go to Fort Lauderdale after work. I won't be home until 7:30 or eight."

"Why? What's in Fort Lauderdale tonight?"

"What are you, my mother?" His laugh afterward said he was teasing, but the tone had been sharp and snippy.

"I'm cooking a special dinner because I have good news to share."

"Oh, yeah? Tell me."

"Not 'til dinner. I can hold it until eight. But no later, please."

"Okay, see you then."

But Stuart didn't get home until after nine, finding a ruined dinner and a dragon-mad girlfriend. He made it worse by not offering an apology. In fact, he side-stepped my questions of who/what/where, saying only that his mother's cook, Mary, had made dinner for the two of them on a whim.

"Not Elijah?"

"Out of town, seeing his nephew or some shit."

I was too drunk to push for more details. I hated feeling suspicious or distrustful, so I decided to play dumb. It was just easier that way.

<<<<<<<>>>>>>

I told them I got lost. *Damn! Ten minutes late for a job interview. Not good!* I don't know why I got so behind that morning; mismanagement in general, I suppose. It was the dry-cleaning company, Mr. Clean Jeans, with the opening for a manager. The couple who conducted the interview were sharp, prepared, and charming. They offered me the job on the spot and I accepted. *I'll just blow off the other interview and have lunch at The Limelight.* A few glasses of wine sounded nice.

I swung by Ace Transmissions and entered an empty waiting room. No Stuart. "Hello?" I hooted. Stuart rushed down the hall with a frantic look, guilty as hell, and not happy to see me. "Why are you here?!" It was a combination scream/question, emphasis on the scream.

"What the hell? Are you busted or something? Sleeping on the job, in the bathroom?" I laughed. He fidgeted.

A rash of nervous laughter blasted from Stuart, like Woody Woodpecker reincarnated. I was used to his fidgeting, and he was doing plenty of that, but he was acting odd. So nervous!

"I got the job. I start Monday," I said.

"Well, good, hon. Proud of you. But if you don't mind, I'm busy."

My brow squeezed together. "You're kicking me out?"

"Yep." No explanation. In the past when I dropped by, we laughed, hung out, and shot the shit for a while.

"Well, I need a pair of sneakers for work. You have cash?"

"You know it, baby." He reached back to his wallet in double-speed. Concern came to the forefront. *Why is he so nervous?*

"Are you okay? You're so fidgety today!"

"I'm fine. See you later." He handed me another hundred-dollar-bill.

"Okay. Well, thanks." I headed for the door.

"Oh! Lela! I forgot..."

With my hand on the door, I stopped. "What?"

"Gotta go to Fort Lauderdale again, but it'll be quick. Be home by 7:30, no later."

"Again? What in the holy hell is going on?"

"Surprise!" He beamed with a smile that warmed my heart.

"Okay, see you then." I crossed the cracked parking lot and headed to Bealls Outlet, my favorite shopping destination.

Errand complete, I swung by The Limelight, thinking I'd model my new shoes for my favorite bartender. Barry had my wine poured before I sat on the barstool; I didn't have to order. *Good bartender.* With nothing exciting at home, I stayed longer than usual, maybe four hours. I left when the dinner crowd arrived, feeling no pain.

"I should just start a charge account here, Barry. What's your interest rate?" He laughed. But that jarred a memory. I wanted to make sure Stuart had mailed the Visa payment and that it got there on time. I made a mental note to call their toll-free number when I got home.

RED-HANDED

CHAPTER 30

"Visa customer service, your name please." I stated my name and account number. After a few clicks, the operator said, "How can I help you, Ms. Fox?"

"I just want to make sure you received my payment on time. It was a big one." I waited while she clicked. I heard a beep through the line.

"Yes, ma'am, we received a payment on the seventh for one hundred dollars. There is no late fee."

"Wait... did you say a hundred dollars?"

"Yes, ma'am. On the seventh."

"Then what's my balance?"

"She clicked more buttons and said $4,897.12."

My face fell. "Uh... are you sure about that?"

"Yes, ma'am. Is there something else I can help you with today?"

"No, just... uh, thank you." I didn't hang up the phone, but let it drop to my lap and sat in silence. Angry. Furious. Confused. Amazed. "Why?" I said out loud. *He'll be home in an hour. I'll hit him in the head then. Why would he lie to me? What's the problem? What's going on?* I realized he didn't have the exact amount when he bought the money order, but a measly hundred dollars? It made no sense.

At eleven o'clock, I went to bed. No Stuart. I fell asleep hard and woke up at 4:32. Stuart's side of the bed was undisturbed. I lit a cigarette as tears took over and my shoulders racked with sobs. *He'll probably say he was raped by another cocktail waitress, maybe a hand-job rape this time. Sonofabitch!*

Then I heard Murphy barking. *What's wrong with my dog?* In one svelte motion, I hopped out of bed, dashed through the living room and slid the backdoor open in a rush.

Stuart. Holding that glass pipe he used in the Bahamas, with eyes as wide as frisbees. His head jerked in four directions as he lurched to hide the pipe behind his back, all this as he flashed his million-dollar smile. "Hi!" he said.

"WHAT IN THE HELL ARE YOU DOING?"

He shushed me. "It's the middle of the night, Lela. Don't yell!"

I ignored him. "WHAT ARE YOU DOING?"

He looked down, stammered, shifting his feet. "Nothing, man. Calm down."

"WHAT THE HELL ARE YOU SMOKING?" I cleared my throat, lowered my volume. "That's not just that laced pot, Stuart. You're hiding something else. It's what you got in Fort Lauderdale, right? TELL ME, DAMMIT! What are you smoking?"

"It's just crack, Lela. No big deal."

"Whaaa…" I staggered back, shocked. *Crack? Stuart is smoking crack? That's what derelict drug addicts smoke! Oh, my God. Smoking cocaine… that must be crack. Oh, my God. I did it, too!*

But in the middle of the night… all his fidgeting, no sex, he's been doing this all along. Crack! Addiction. And not paying my Visa! He's spending all that money on crack. Crack! I couldn't wrap my mind around it, but I knew it was bad. Beyond bad. This was a life-changing discovery.

He's been lying to me the whole time! And if he's addicted… surely he is… it will only get worse. Still on the patio, I spoke in a half-dreamy voice, "I've gotta get out of here. I can't live with an addict." I realized my life had changed completely. In one instant.

"Yeah, just leave me be, as the rednecks say in Tennessee."

"LIAR! LOSER! You have screwed me royally! I guess you've been screwing me over for a while. Maybe the whole time!" A heavy tear dropped from my jaw, making a splat on the patio. Then more splats. I stared at him, trying to drill a hole through his heart.

"Lela, don't get all dramatic and shit! Chill out!"

"FUCK YOU! I'm calling your parents… they'll help me."

"DON'T CALL MY PARENTS, PLEASE! Jesus, Lela, they don't need to know. Hey look – I'll pay your credit card off, every cent! Just don't call! *Please* don't call my parents."

"Okay, then we're going to Publix for a money order right now. Right this minute!"

"Well, not NOW, sweetie. I'll have the money in two weeks, easy."

"Don't 'honey' me, you asshole. LOSER! DRUG ADDICT!"

"We're calling names now? Okay, so you're an alcoholic without a lot of room to criticize me."

"THIS IS DIFFERENT!" I was screaming so loud that saliva spewed.

"Lela, please, keep your voice down."

I took a breath. He was right; I didn't want to wake the neighbors. I paused to let Murphy in the door. He was scared of all the yelling. "Stuart, now or never. Money order or not?"

"Next Friday, I promise."

"Nope. Not good enough. I'm outta here. But I need money, so I'm calling your parents. They'll help me, because I guess you're lying to them, too. Let me guess… it's not the first time."

My footsteps followed Murphy's inside the apartment. Stuart stayed behind; I saw the lighter flare. Stomping straight to the phone, a moment of clarity hit. *I can't call them at 4:30 in the morning!* The frustration I felt… the angst… the defeat; my knees suddenly couldn't hold the weight of my body.

A grip on the kitchen island stopped my fall. *Deep breaths, Lela. Then you need to think… think, think, think.* I mixed a drink, a strong one, and moved to the sofa. My hands were shaking; my whole body was shaking! On overdrive, my mind replayed the scenario, realizing I had also smoked crack – that's what the "laced weed" was in the Bahamas. I remembered the euphoria I'd felt, understanding how a person could become addicted. It's just that it had scared me, made me sober. I hadn't liked it, but Stuart sure had.

Now look what it's cost you. And how will you pay? His parents… I will ask for their help with the move. But I need money in the meantime with a credit card maxed out. Mom. Damn. Calling Mom again. Isn't she tired of me and my drama?

A vision of my sweet, Goody-Two-Shoes mom brought a rack of sobs. I had leaned on my parents so much, time after time after time. *Oh, my poor mother! But she'll help me if I tell her the truth. SHE doesn't accuse me of being an alcoholic like Stuart did... like Miller did... like Andy did. Oh, Lela, you ignorant soul... will you ever grow up?*

I collapsed, falling sideways on the sofa and wailing a literal 'boo hoo' noise. Twenty minutes later, sobbing the entire time, I realized my vision was blurry already, and my eyes hurt. *That's what happens when you cry too much, Lela. So stop! Girl, you must be strong now. Starting NOW.*

With a sigh, I finished my drink, poured another, and walked to the bathroom for a face-full of cold water. I looked in the mirror and had a long talk with myself. Then I tip-toed to my desk for a pen and notepad, returning to sit on the bed. A list. Thinking it through. Options, plans, what if's.

At seven o'clock, I walked to the phone in the kitchen. The second I removed the handset from the wall, Stuart begged me not to call her. BEGGED! I questioned the extreme amount of fear he displayed. *Calling them means something more than I know. Will he be disinherited or something? That's what he's acting like. So be it!*

I dialed Daphne Graning's personal number. "Hello?" she asked in her clipped New York accent. The conversation was short. I was factual... told her what happened, told her what I wanted, and she agreed in a voice totally void of emotion. I arranged the details on when and how to get the check. And that was that.

At the conversation's end, she surprised me with a comment that sounded genuine. "I'm sorry my son is such a problem for you, Lela. You're a nice girl and don't deserve that." The phrase echoed in my mind. It would repeat for years. Somebody had been nice to me, empathetic even.

MOMMA FOX

CHAPTER 31

I was the walking dead. Stuart had left just after seven, while I was chatting with his mother, pausing only to throw a handful of clothes in his Louis Vitton suitcase. That day is still mostly a blur; I couldn't move forward in my thoughts... couldn't stop raving about how I'd been screwed by Stuart Weinstein. *And it happened right under your nose, Lela! Wake up! Sober up! How did you not see this coming?!*

Between sobs and hours of staring at the walls, I continued making the list of things to do... but only two check marks dotted the margin. I was still in shock, I guess. Confused and frozen in purgatory.

My intention was to stay sober the entire day, but I knew the headache and shakiness would come soon. *Deal with that later, Lela. First, call the movers and get the final cost... go to Ft. Lauderdale to get the check from Daphne... call Mom.* The passing thought of Mom, and especially Daddy, brought buckets of tears. *Lela, you've fucked up again and here you go asking them to bail you out one more time. Dammit!* I wept with Guilt, Shame, and Remorse, not yet knowing the significance of those words.

But the result of spending a morning sober brought the first-time-in-a-long-time realization that I drank too much. The buzz between my ears that pushed my temples out, the sinking of my stomach, the fear that sent my heart rate to the stratosphere... even the thought of cutting back on the drinking was too much of a challenge to deal with, I decided. But I promised to delve into it very soon... *maybe with my therapist's help, since I hope to see Kate ASAP. But for now, Stuart is doing much-worse things and I've got TOO MUCH to do!*

The day and night passed with only two tasks accomplished: I booked a mover and got the check from Daphne. I'd picked up the phone a dozen times to call Mom, but chickened out each time. The movers would come the next day at a "rush rate" which was almost double but Daphne didn't bat an eye and kept shushing me when I apologized and/or thanked her. It was as if she didn't want to talk about it.

I understood; I didn't want to think about it.

The next morning, the movers woke me at 8:30. They worked efficiently; I paced the floor, accomplishing nothing except to put Stuart's things on the left side of the closet, the only things the movers were to leave. It was a pitiful pile of nothing. He owned only one item. One not-so-big TV. He'd brought it to the green house to replace my smaller one. The problem was that I donated the old one, leaving me with no TV and no money to buy a new one. I was damn-determined to be fair, but decided I must take his TV and risk his wrath. *He owes me much more than that, by God!*

I thought about calling to get more money from Daphne, realizing getting home would be a squeeze with so little headroom on my credit card. But I put my head in the sand on that one, knowing now that calling Mom was a do-it-now necessity.

Getting a job in Rockville was also an immediate need. I'd been out of the advertising field for so long that technology had taken it to a new plane; I was too old and too out of the loop to go back. The weight of hopelessness sent me to bed as the movers packed the kitchen, but I couldn't sleep. *You can't put it off anymore, Lela.*

The phone only rang once on the other end. "Mom?"

"What's wrong, Lela?"

"How do you know something's wrong?"

"A mother knows her baby daughter. Spit it out – what's wrong?" Impatience screamed in her whisper.

"Well, Mom," I paused to sob. "Oh, Momma, I love you so much! Thank you for loving me even though I keep screwing up!"

Switching to a more staccato, more demanding voice, she said, "Tell me what happened. Be clear." Obviously, she wasn't interested in my frothy crap.

"Well, Stuart is smoking crack, he... he... stole money from me, Mom. So, I'm calling to ask..." Sobs took over again. I did *not* want to ask my mother for any more financial help. But I had to have a place to live in Rockville and I had no money for a deposit, or the first month's rent, or utility hook-ups, nothing. And since I had no job, nobody would rent to me. I'd need to borrow her impeccable credit rating, too.

A wave of misery shook me when I realized I had no money. None! After the unending supply of hundred-dollar-bills, after the six-figure income from years of freelancing when I first left the agency, I was broke and jobless.

Mom didn't waste a minute in responding though she seemed to be crying herself. "Baby, you don't need to ask. I'll help you without question. Whatever you need. Money, anything... *everything!* Your dad and I can come to Florida... is that what you want?"

"No, Mom, the movers are here packing everything. Stuart's mother is paying for me to move back." A new string of my blubbering began. A painful combination of Gratitude, Shame, and Fear.

"Move back where? Come *here*, Lela. Come to the farm."

"No, I can't do that, Mom! I need to a job, get my shit together..."

"Language, Lela!"

"Sorry... get my *life* together. But I'm running in a circle. What to do?" Tears spewed. "Uh... I'm not... doing so well, Mom."

"Have you been taking your medicine? Is that it, too?"

"Well, until yesterday, I would have told you I was manic. But now I'm frozen. Stuck. Stupid. I've got to find an apartment and a job and it's like I've... forgotten how to do stuff like that. I can't stop crying and start doing." There was a pause. "Can you help me, Mom? Again?"

"Do you need me to pay your rent for a while?"

"No, but... the deposit, maybe. The utilities. I have no money in my pocket. It was all Stuart's."

"How much money did he steal from you?"

Oh boy... I dreaded telling her. Hiding the details, I kept it simple. "Well... he maxed out my credit card. Can't use it now, not even for gas on the way home."

"Maybe that's easy to solve, Lela. Simply call and ask for an increase in your credit line. That will take care of that. Have you been paying the bill on time?"

"Uh... until lately, I'd paid the full balance every month! But even these small payments were made on time." *Aha, there's one thing you've done right.*

"Happy to hear you're being responsible, Lela."

My body jerked with a chuckle. *Responsible? Ha ha ha. Lela Fox, you fucking nitwit! You don't know how to solve a simple problem!* The familiar shaming self-talk chattered as my shakiness began in earnest. Like the day before, I'd skipped the vodka in my morning coffee. My head screamed: *but morning vodka doesn't count! It's medicine.* I decided to believe that voice and carried the phone into the kitchen, dodging the movers to locate the tall bottle of Grey Goose.

Mom's even-paced voice jerked me from my spaced-out thoughts. "Then the Visa people will grant a credit limit increase easily. That'll get you home, but you'll soon have to budget for paying it off. It's not good to carry a balance, of course. It's expensive and bad for your credit rating, dear."

Thanks, Mom, a lesson on credit rating isn't what I need right now, please!

She continued, plotting a plan for me, or at least asking questions to help me make a plan. "Then where will you live? Have you found an apartment?"

I'm going to explode if you don't shut the fuck up, Mom. A deep breath in, blown out slow.

"You can't afford to be too picky, Lela." I heard the scolding rise in her voice and rolled my eyes. *I can't handle being slapped on the hand right now either, Mom.*

"Well, I gotta go now. Calls to make! Bye, Mom!" She was wearing me out. *But watch yourself, Lela. She's also BAILING you out. you irresponsible scumbag!*

I heard her signing off without hearing her words. "Wait, Mom!"

"What, baby?"

"I love you."

"And I love my favorite baby daughter."

Tears of overwhelming Gratitude marked my cheeks. I closed my eyes, thinking about the good in my parents and how lucky I was.

B-4 ABODE
CHAPTER 32

As the packed-and-ready moving truck sat in my driveway overnight, I stayed up crying, wringing my hands, and willing Stuart to stay away. At 3:00 AM, I gassed up the van and began the long trip to Rockville. I could tell Murphy was as freaked out as I was. After an eye-opening scare falling asleep at the wheel, I pulled over at a rest stop to sleep. A dozen tractor-trailer trucks blocked me in during the hour I slept, then Murphy's bark and a peck on the window woke me. I rolled down the window to find a greasy-haired, drunk trucker inquiring about my services.

Back on the road, mile after mile. Angry, ashamed, painfully sad. My eyes still brimmed with tears and my heart weighed a ton, heavy with remorse and bitterness.

Over and over, I chastised myself for smoking crack and not knowing what it was. At the time, I assumed the "laced weed" was something like the Thai sticks I smoked in high school. *But Thai sticks aren't addictive as hell! And think of all you could have avoided had you'd known he was a crack addict... all the trauma and heartache, all the money you would have saved.*

I only stopped three times for paper-bag beers; maybe I wanted to feel the full pain of my stupidity. Because somewhere deep down within me, I feared I may be a laughable hypocrite. *If you're an alcoholic, Lela... which you're not... but if you were, then you and Stuart are both guilty of addiction. How can you judge him when you're in the same boat?*

<<<<<<<<>>>>>>>

In Rockville, Mom and Daddy met me at the apartment office about three hours before the truck was due to arrive. Mom signed the lease, and wrote separate checks for the deposit and pet fee... the list went on. In front of the rental agent, Mom veered out of character and glared at me with the instruction that I would, *without fail,* pay next month's rent on my own. "On time, Lela. No way you're ruining *my* credit rating. Do you understand?"

"Yes, Momma, I promise." The truth was, I was at her mercy... and ashamed of it. For some reason, my mind couldn't wrap around the fact that I needed a job. I didn't know what kind of job I could get, or if it would pay enough to allow for the rent payment, but I promised her and I meant it. I *had* to mean it.

But that was before I knew how screwed up I'd be in my residency there.

It was a two-bedroom place... ground floor, apartment B-4. The second bedroom was for the storage of my washer and dryer and a guest room for Bo, should he be able to visit. One more move for the bunk bed.

This time, I placed my desk in the dining room, a 10-by-10 square that straddled the kitchen and living room. "Downsizing" exaggerated, I'd packed the entire apartment with furniture and excess. Cringing, I realized "packrat" *was* the word for me. Yep, a packrat with a penchant for the weird and impractical.

The movers were full service, so they UNpacked, too. I paced the apartment, accomplishing nothing that day... or the day after. But the next day, I wasted no time in starting my job search.

It was in there somewhere, I knew. Yep... in the second-bedroom storage, I found my portfolio and dusted it off carefully. My goal was to re-establish my advertising career; the only way I could afford to live alone, I reasoned.

First things first: I wrote a powerful letter to Barry Sturbridge, president of the largest agency and my former employer. I knew Miller McKeown, husband number two, had left to open his own studio, so why not shoot for the top job, right?

Too impatient to wait for the mailman, I drove the letter to its destination, five miles from my B-4 abode. The receptionist said Barry was in and assured me the letter would be on his desk by lunchtime.

Later that afternoon, I followed up with Barry by phone. Yes, he'd received my letter. As expected, with his effervescence still front and center, Barry gushed with congratulations for getting back in the business, but... he had no need for a writer at the agency. "Fully staffed, Lela. Sorry."

Bummer. But I willed myself to keep a stiff upper lip, to keep hope alive. I wrote letters to the heads of a few other local agencies, most of them I knew already. To the post office to mail them ASAP. I was on a roll.

Who else to call? I drew a blank. So much time had passed, so many bridges burned. There was nobody. *Oh! Augie Highfield.* I wondered if he was still directing awesome video production. Augie and I had developed an uneasy sexual tension when we'd worked together before, but he was a respectable "in" to the best in the business. I picked up the phone.

"Lela who?"

"Not funny, Augie. You know good and well who I am!"

"Of course I do, but it's been so long! So you're back from jewelry... and from Florida? So much has passed you by, Chickadee."

"Like what?"

"Um... let's see... the entire industry. You missed the digital revolution, girl. It's a whole new ballgame from my end."

"But not from my end. There are no digital writers, Augie. So who do you know in need of a damn-good copywriter?"

"Sorry to say, but you picked a bad time, Lela. My business is down... everybody's is. You'll be hard-pressed to find an advertising job in this economy. Sturbridge actually laid off a few folks." With a thump, my heart fell to my stomach. I had been full of hope, full of confidence.

"Okay, then... who's doing the Connor Health stuff? Please tell me my former largest client is still using freelancers."

"Bad news there, too. They've grouped everything and only advertise corporate stuff. Done mostly in-house."

I'm sure Augie heard the depth of my sigh. "Augie, I'm in dire straights, in need of the tiniest freelance project."

"I may have something for you later."

"*You?* You're taking direct clients?"

"Yep. It's become the 'new normal,' and to have a kick-ass writer like you would be a big sell. I don't care how long it's been, Lela... you're still the best."

"Well, thank you." I blushed.

"And still the best looking, I'm sure."

"Sex, sex, sex. That's all you think about!"

"Some things don't change."

I laughed... *that damn Augie. Half sexy, half sleazy, 100 percent fuckable.* His voice interrupted my thoughts. "Seriously, there may be a video script coming up... are you game?"

"Hell, yeah, even if I'm full-time elsewhere. I'd love to work with you again, Augie. We're good together."

"But no more elevators crushing us."

I smiled at the reference to our old award-winning projects. "We had some fun, huh? Made kick-ass TV... and I'm fired up to do it again!" The truth: I was exhausted, not fired up about anything, scared as shit about delving into something I hadn't done in more than a decade. But saying those things wouldn't get me a job.

Augie didn't share my enthusiasm. "Be prepared. There's a flood of unemployed writers now. Sorry, kid." I had no reply. I heard Augie's deep intake of breath. "Oh! Maybe you know... but Miller's gone from Sturbridge. They fired his ass."

"Whaaat? Bo told me he'd quit!"

"Fired with no notice. Too many complaints that he was an asshole. He became the meanest SOB in town, Lela. Snooty. Thought local talent was beneath him. Dashed to Chicago for a simple photo shoot."

"He *always* did that! And that's how we traveled so much. But... so everybody figured out what I knew all along, Augie. He's just plain mean. *So* self-absorbed."

Augie continued. "If you remember, I felt the same. But he's got it bad... lost all his friends and vendors here, pissed off hundreds of people. He tried to freelance but failed. Filed for bankruptcy, I'm told."

I felt like dancing a jig! He got what he deserved! I also felt shameful... it's devilish to be happy about another person's ill fate. I shook myself from analyzing everything and asked for more news. "Did he get married again?"

"Yes, and I thought of you. Big wedding to a hot, twenty-something first-timer. Fancy wedding, ultra old-fashioned. But they're divorced now."

"Wow. That's divorce number *five* for him." Augie laughed. Who wouldn't laugh? *FIVE!* "It's so shameful it's funny."

"Lunch sometime?" Augie offered.

"Sure!" But I knew it wouldn't happen. "Let me find a job first and we'll schedule a time."

"Good talking to you, Lela. And I still love you, ya know?"

"And I love *you*, Augie."

I hung up the phone and stared into space for a while, biting my fingernails absent-mindedly. *Another opportunity pissed away.* But I had kept my secrets quiet; I hadn't told him the yucky stuff I'd been through since leaving the advertising business. I'd avoided talking about the failure of Moonlight Jewelry and my most-recent failed relationship, and I didn't share details of my bruised ego. Correction: crushed, black and blue, totally *destroyed* ego. I felt as low as I'd ever felt. And so alone.

With a sigh, I picked up the classified ads and a Sharpie. A job for Lela, ASAP. Drink in hand; I tried to decipher the small print. There weren't many choices.

<<<<<<<<>>>>>>>>

That night, I signed onto AOL with a cranky and slow DSL connection. Drunk and alone, I was pouting, feeling sorry for the fuck-up I'd become. I clicked to join a chat room for Rockville singles, thinking it would be a joke. But a dozen "men" were on me like stink on shit.

With my screen name "Granny Liz," they all wanted to know if I was, indeed, a Granny. I confirmed it, screwing with their twisted minds, and giggled over the banter until "George Washington" entered the chat room. Drunk, I flirted with him as one would when hidden behind the black curtain of anonymity.

For the most part, I was honest in describing myself and told him my goal was a purely sexual relationship. He wouldn't let it drop. I continued the tease as long as I could. "George Washington" wanted me to come to his house, even gave his address... and he lived not three miles away.

I considered it but decided I was too drunk to drive. Resigned to be alone tonight, I signed off but knew I'd go back to that wickedly alluring chat room. For an hour, I hadn't been lonely.

FRAMED

CHAPTER 33

Two minutes late, damn! But better than your last interview... for the job you never started in Florida. And this job was more suitable, tapping more of my creative abilities. A frame shop, a franchise location of the parent Square Shoppe, was opening in a month and needed a manager.

The shopping center was a busy one and within a five-mile drive of my apartment. At least it was something familiar, no matter how long ago... when I'd helped my sister Karen with her frame shop in high school and college.

I planned to call Karen for tips on what to say about the management end; I'd only been the designer and finisher. Karen's shop had remained a destination in Jackson City, unaffected by the economic slump. And even after all these years, Karen was happy with her work and elevated status in the city's business community.

My fingers cramped dialing her number; I'd avoided Karen for almost a year, hadn't called much since the fiasco with Stuart on Christmas Day.

The tension of our phone call eased after five minutes or so; Karen and I would always share a strong bond. She was "sorry it hadn't worked out in Florida," but happy I "came back in one piece." Thankfully, Karen didn't scold me. She had insecurities of her own and knew better than to point out mine, but big-sister bossiness reared its head sometimes and we would butt heads.

I heard through the grapevine that she feared my temper and didn't trust my judgement, so I can't say I was 100 percent comfy in talking to her. Then again, I rejected anybody who knew the ugliness of how I lived my life. That left few people to trust.

Clever and sneaky, I thought I'd successfully hidden the bulk of my drinking from my family. But with so much to hide by that time, it was hard to have a close family relationship, even with Karen.

<<<<<<<<>>>>>>>

Determined to skip the vodka in my morning coffee, I was worried my "new boss" would smell it on my breath. The shakes began an hour after I woke up and applying makeup with shaky hands called for a talent I didn't have. I cussed the unfairness of having to choose, but I couldn't have both. The vodka won. Then, after a few sips, I cussed the vodka for being so necessary. "Damn you, Grey Goose. You suck!"

I chanted positive, confidence-building mantras on the way to the interview.

The storefront door was dirty glass, the inside still in construction phase. A loud knock brought the owner to the door. Maybe I could fool this guy, I thought. He sounded like a nice guy on the phone... genuine and with a positive attitude. I held my breath, ready to meet the one and only Roman Painter. It was a strange name, but with no accent to determine its origin.

I passed my résumé across the desk to Roman. I'd struggled to customize it, highlighting long-ago experience and covering my yawning gaps in employment. After all, it had been almost two decades since I'd worked for someone besides myself. He didn't see the red flags I did, impressed that my family owned a frame shop. So I played up my role to the Nth degree. For some reason, he assumed I knew more than I did, so I embellished it. A lot. More than a lot.

He had other applicants in the afternoon and would call me, he said.

I dashed home and celebrated with by toasting myself with a vodka-tonic, a double. At last, my hands quit shaking and my headache disappeared.

At three o'clock, on my third double, Roman called to say the job was mine. He asked me to come to the shop before five to pick up the manuals for at-home study. *Uh-oh... shit.* I switched to coffee, showered and waited until the last minute, but I was still loopy when I arrived. He said, "You look more relaxed already!" *Uh... yeah.*

My job included setting up the store for the opening... organizing the hardware and frame-it-yourself counters, a shitload of paperwork, stocking the shelves, labeling the molding, stuff like that.

The most important project was creating the samples for display. Both the choice of print and the framing design were at my discretion.

There would be forty or more samples needed to create an impressive shop. I poured through the hefty art-print order books, covering all genres, colors, and tastes. Nursery prints, above-the-mantle stuff, a Tennessee Vols print... the wider the variety, the better. I had a blast, and Roman approved all my choices.

I purposely designed the framing to be expensive and complicated. It would be up to me to bring them to fruition, a challenge for my skill level. Throughout the process, I enjoyed myself, got along well with Roman (only calling him Stuart six times, all when I was aggravated with him), and hired two cheerful girls for part-time backup.

I messed up the mat twice on the first sample... had to fix it by adding a third mat.

I messed up the next one, too. More and more money spent on supply costs.

On the third one, I messed up the frame and had to re-cut it from scratch.

With each of the following sample pieces, I made a series of stupid, costly mistakes.

Some mistakes were easier to hide than others; in the end, supply costs were double what they should have been. An expensive loss. And it didn't take long until Roman busted me. Now he knew I'd lied about my skills in the interview. And he knew I'd been trying to hide it. But the grand opening was in three days; there wasn't time to train another manager.

Opening day. The first order I took totaled $252.16! That was *huge!* Roman beamed and looked at me with a cocked brow. "Maybe you can just do the sales, Lela, and slowly train on the production."

"I think that's ideal, Roman. As you see, I am strong in sales and design, always have been. I just need more practice in the back room... that's all." *Saved!*

I sold twelve more customers that first day, with an average ticket of $150 or so. Roman danced around the shop at closing time, hugging me and telling me I was a genius. I felt like a million bucks... and simultaneously, I felt like a fraud. The ability to believe in myself disappeared, but I found relief in having done *something* with style.

Though it was only a ten-minute drive home, I stopped at a Mini-Mart and bought a paper-bag beer. It was nice and cold... and gone by the time I got home. I walked in to greet Murphy, feeling better but still anxious. Shaky. All I wanted was to zone out in front of the TV with a few drinks. I got my wish... but around ten o'clock, I became bored. Again, with the cranky DSL-connection grunts and groans, I signed onto the AOL chat room and found "George Washington."

<<<<<<<>>>>>>

"Hello, George Washington." I was leaning against his front door frame, wearing not much at all.

"Hello, Granny Liz." His eyes were wide set and wide open. He wore only a pair of jeans; the underneath was yet to be determined.

It was three o'clock in the morning, which is why I was so startled when my cell phone rang. I first thought to ignore it; the timing was horrible. But... the horrible timing is why I *should* answer; it could be an emergency. Quickly, I flipped the phone open to see the number. It was Stuart.

I slapped the phone closed and ran back to my car at breakneck speed. Like a rabbit, I hopped in the van and slammed the door. I screamed to nobody, "Oh, my God, I'm being watched! No way that's a coincidence!" I fumbled for my keys, my hands trembling, then jabbed the key into the ignition and backed out without looking behind me. I misjudged the distance and side-swiped George Washington's mailbox. It didn't faze me. I kept going.

My foot shook on the gas pedal, rat-a-tat, and my van jerked like a nerve. I varied between twenty miles per hour and sixty, getting home in less than three minutes. Tears ejected from my eyes, shooting straight forward and missing my cheeks. I ran to my B-4 door, dropping my keys. Finally inside, I ran to my bed, panting. My heart beat at four times the normal rate.

Oh, my God. What am I going to do? Is he in Rockville? Why? Only to spy on me? Or did he hire somebody? Who? Who does he know here? I couldn't think of anyone. No one. Even with my heart rate slowing, I was baffled. He had no friends in Rockville; we'd been each other's only friends. I, too, had lost my old ones except for Lola. And Damon.

Oh, Damon! My savior Damon... I need you!

THE HOTEL GANG

CHAPTER 34

"Is this your dog?" The man was rough-looking, tattooed, with brown leathered skin. His faded red cap featured a cracked logo: HOTEL RENOVATIONS, INC.

"Yes, that's Murphy. Is he bothering you?" My door was half-open; I expected to hear a camera click from Stuart's gumshoe at any moment. It was Sunday, but I assumed a private investigator's schedule would be 24/7.

"No, the dog... he was just hanging out with us. Hoping for his own beer, I think," the man chuckled. "Oh!" he extended his hand. "I'm Brady, next building over. C-3." I shook his hand and opened the door another inch. Murphy walked inside, home again and happy for the air conditioner.

The man, close to my age in his late thirties, rocked from one foot to the other, nervous. "Uh... well, I thought the dog might be yours because I saw the flap in your sliding-glass door and didn't want anybody to steal him. Cool dog. Fat as hell, but a cool dog."

"I let him come and go, even though I'm not supposed to. Apartment rules, right?" The man nodded. "But thanks for bringing him home." I smiled. We'd completed our business, I assumed, yet the man didn't leave.

"Hey, you never told me your name." A shy smile crossed his face.

"Lela." He had a niece named Lela, he said. Everybody knows a Lela; it was an unusual name in my youth, but not now, in the late nineties, there was a resurgence.

"Listen... uh... we're having a party on the patio over there. You wanna come?"

"Depends on what kind of party, Brady. My plan was to just hang out at home, stay out of the humidity today."

"A bunch of us... we're here just temporary, remodeling the Holiday Inn on Kirsky Road. A traveling team... we go everywhere."

He added more detail, and I got the picture. They were party-hearty good ol' boys who liked new faces in the crowd. "Anyway, it's hard to meet new people, ya know, and you seem nice, so come on over for a beer. Lines of coke inside, too, if you're interested."

"I'll stick with the beer, and thanks for the invite. Who knows? I may pop over there in a minute. I'm trying to stay close to home these days." He waved a boyish goodbye.

I laid back on the sofa, staring at the ceiling. Good ol' Bi-Polar depression had me down. Since Stuart's phone call at George Washington's door, I feared my depression would deepen, desperate in paranoia. Further, I couldn't shake my guilt about lying on my résumé and wasting materials at work. Roman was not on my fan list, and I wasn't used to that; I had always considered myself a loyal and conscientious employee like my Daddy had taught me to be.

"No, you're a screw-up," echoed in my mind, repeating through sleepless nights and lonely, depressed days. With a sigh, I settled in for a bout of dyed-in-the-wool clinical depression. *You need to find a new psychiatrist, Lela. Maybe change your meds.* But who wouldn't be depressed in my circumstances? *You brought this on yourself... because you're a screw-up.*

Too ashamed to call Lola and admit how wrong I'd been about Stuart. Too proud to hear Jennifer say, "I told you so." Too down to hear Damon's chirpy bullshit.

So I had another ham-and-cheese roll-up, my version of a sandwich without bread, and a cup of yogurt. My diet stunk because I didn't cook, didn't even care enough to zap a frozen meal. Yep, depressed.

Should you go to hang out with that Brady guy and his renovation crew? I wonder what they're like... he seemed nice enough, even a little shy. Can you stay out of trouble, Lela Fox? Pose for Stuart's cameras without exposing yourself? Maybe have a laugh or two, a contrast to the sighs you've mastered in the past week? I decided to not decide. I'd take a nap first.

Awakening at the height of the day's heat, I stuck my head out the door to check the humidity. The breeze had picked up, and it had turned out to be a nice day. I fed Murphy, who had dozed with me on the sofa, and changed clothes. Maybe the party was over, but I'll walk Murphy over there... see what's going on with them.

There was no need for a leash. No chance the dog would run from me; he was too fat to run. We sauntered down the back sidewalk, drawn to the sound of laughter from a patio in the next building.

Brady was front and center in the crowd, chugging a beer. "Lela!" he exploded the words. "Hey, everybody, this is Lela! Owner of the fat dog that hangs here. And there he is again, little porker..." He leaned down to call Murphy, and the dog trotted to him as fast as he could... which wasn't fast. "What's your pleasure, Lela? Miller Lite, Corona, or..."

He turned to an overweight man on his right. "What's that shit you drink, Danny?"

"It's not shit. It's Amstel Light. Hey, I can't help it you're a redneck and have no taste," the fat Danny answered... then he turned toward me. "You're welcome to an Amstel Light, Lela, anytime."

"I think I will, Danny." But it was Brady who clamored through the door; I assumed he was getting the beer. In the meantime, the partygoers introduced themselves. Eight men, about my age, and only three women - two butchy-looking, and one who looked like Barbie. Barbie with big boobs and red high heels with her denim shorts. She was the wife of the boss and the cook for all the guys. She tried to talk recipes with me and didn't respond to the brush-off I gave. Weirdo woman.

The beer was cold, and the group was in rare form – loud, raunchy jokes. The guys were funny and their laughter was contagious. Unexpectantly, I was having a good time. The two butch girls were interested in me; I could tell by their squinty eyes. But there were no sexual overtures from the guys. And I made it a point to send no sexual signals at all.

Not wanting to bum another beer from the same person, I opted for a Miller Light on the next round and a Corona on the third. Then Barbie walked out with a tray of Jello shots and the crowd cheered.

"I'll pass on the Jello shot," I said. "I swore off tequila years ago when I 'came to' in the shower with a man who was not my husband." The story got a laugh, and a rash of urges to have "just one." Someone called me an amateur and my radar antenna went up immediately. The phrase was a trigger. I shared the story of Lena Shelby calling me an amateur in eighth grade, accusing me of not knowing how much beer it took to get drunk. I'd responded by drinking as much as possible, as often as possible, for as long as possible. And my drinking career had lasted a full 26 years. Not long if you say it fast.

Brady jutted his chin forward. "So, Lela, if you're not an amateur, take a shot." After five more minutes of giving me shit, they let it drop. Five minutes after that, I gave in to the peer pressure that only existed in my mind by then. The first round barely made a dent in the quantity on Barbie's tray, so we all took another cup.

"Man, you made these strong, guys. I'm telling ya... tequila makes me crazy. And I've gotta work tomorrow morning."

"What the hell? Bottom's up!" the Hispanic guy said, then did a silly dance to accentuate the swallow of his next Jello cube. Showing great restraint, I stopped at four shots... but had six more beers. We partied until midnight and I stumbled home. Murphy had gone before me, walking through his dog-flap. I found him sleeping on the sofa, next to my phone.

Two missed calls, both from Stuart.

The thought of calling the police was heavy on my mind. But what would I say? "I'm being stalked and getting phone calls from Florida" wouldn't open an investigation; just make me look paranoid and stupid. The cops would think I was pure Looney-Tunes.

"And maybe you are, Lela," I spoke to the empty room. "Maybe you are."

ROMAN GOES ROGUE
CHAPTER 35

"Are you up for happy hour?" I asked. I noted an odd flash across Roman's face… terror, a grimace, and a sneaky grin simultaneously.

"Why not?" he said with exaggerated bravado, hiking up his pants. He slicked his hair back with shaking hands, causing a squinch in my brow. *What's up with that? Am I out of order to ask?*

"The restaurant next door has buy-one-get-one apps between four and six, so we could get the last half of the deal if we hurry. It's mostly fried stuff, though." Fried food didn't bother me much in those days. I found it useful in absorbing the excess of alcohol.

As if he heard my thoughts, Roman said. "Fried is good with a few beers."

We sat at the bar. A glass of wine for me, a beer for Roman. The bartender announced, "Dollar draft until six," so Roman ordered *two* beers. That tickled me; the penny pincher would drink warm beer to save eighty cents.

"We have 55 minutes before the end of happy hour, Roman. You don't have to order two at a time."

A devilish smile broadened his face, all teeth glowing in the sparkle of the bar's spotlights. "But I can have four beers if I order it this way."

I clicked his mug with my glass. "My kind of drinking man."

We talked shop, mostly. He told me of the franchise agreement and his upcoming balloon payment, due after the first quarter of opening. "We made the numbers, thanks to you." He said. One more click of mug-to-glass. He quizzed me, wanting to know my secret to sales.

"I don't have a technique, really. I just give the customer credit for *my* good decisions. Like... 'Let's try this color! Oh, my gosh. That's it! You did it!' Shit like that."

He shook his head. "I've tried to copy you, but it doesn't work. You're good, Lela. Talented."

My head swelled. First, he was right – I *was* good. And it felt fabulous to know he was pleased with my work. Job security, you know?

He downed his two beers before I finished my wine. "Damn, Roman! Few people can out drink me, but you're chuggin' like a college boy. Way to go!"

We had appetizers. More beer. More wine. I wondered why he didn't need to rush home to his wife, but I was enjoying myself, so I said nothing. Shop talk turned to personal talk. He came from Illinois and insinuated he had lost his ass in a business venture of some sort. Details were sketchy, but he talked about "reaching a bottom." Self-explanatory. He ordered more beer, and I wondered why he was so... weirdly thirsty about it. Obsessed.

We stayed for three drunk hours; six glasses of wine did me in, despite the food. Roman had drunk at least ten beers and slurred every word. He stumbled, nearly falling, on a trip to the bathroom then stumbled back and asked if I played pool. *Oh no, not again. I'm not going out and have Stuart call again.* Bravely, I told him what was going on: the surveillance, the phone calls, and my extreme paranoia.

"Well let's just stay here, then I'll take you home. Make sure you don't get accosted by the FBI man on your tail."

I chuckled. "Not FBI, Roman. Probably some sleazy, cut-rate investigator. But he's on target because he's caught me every time. Besides, you're not taking me home or anywhere else."

"You're right. I'm not. Still, being stalked... that must suck."

"You're the first person I've told. Honestly, I don't know what else to do but lie low, wait him out. The police won't do anything."

"But you should probably report it."

"Uh... reporting it may have repercussions worse than a phone call."

"Where did you find this guy? Scary."

With a laugh, I shook my head. "I'm a dumbass. Yep, I answered a classified ad."

"Wow. You seem smarter than that," he said before nodding to the bartender, gesturing for another.

"Uh... Roman, it's none of my business, but that's maybe your twelfth beer. How are you going to get home?"

"Not going home... staying with *you*." In the same motion, he leaned forward to kiss me.

I backed up and stood quickly. He fell forward, barely catching himself before cracking a tooth on my bar stool. Unfazed, he asked for a cigarette. Seeing him struggle to light it turned my stomach. He was sloppy drunk, too drunk to be funny.

He sat up and looked me straight in the eye. "So, here's the deal. I haven't had a drink in twelve years, so I had one drink for each year I've been sober. Those AA fuckers can kiss my ass!"

"Oh, my God!" I instantly felt responsible for a man's downfall. *This is your fault, Lela Fox, you lousy drunk.* "No, Roman. A relapse, a bad one. You've got to call your wife. She'll help you... or something."

"It's 'or something.' She'll leave me, no doubt. One little drink would do it, she said." He turned up the end of the beer, gulped it, and burped. Loud and proud. "I believe her." He took a deep draw on the cigarette. "FUCK HER!" he yelled loud enough to draw attention from the other patrons.

What have I done? I thought it was an innocent invitation. Worried and confused, I considered calling him a cab, calling his wife for him... I didn't know what to do, but I knew this was all my fault. "Oh, Roman, I'm so sorry. This is all because of me."

"Tell that to my sponsor!" He laughed hysterically.

"Let's get out of here." I signaled the bartender for the tab; he nodded and dashed to the other end of the bar. "This one's on me, Roman... in more ways than one. I'll take you to the shop, then get us some coffee. And some White Castle burgers, they seem to do the trick every time." He stubbed out the cigarette, attempted to blow smoke rings, which seemed to amuse him.

I needed him to be distracted and wondered how to get him back to the shop. He was falling-down drunk. As I signed my name on the tab, his head hit the table. Passed out cold.

The bartender smiled at me, realizing my predicament. Half-smiling, he said, "Bouncer comes in at nine." *Ten minutes, I can wait that long. And yes, another glass of wine would calm my nerves.*

<<<<<<<<>>>>>>>

"It's just three storefronts down," I said. "This is a tragedy. He said his wife would leave him if he had just one drink!"

"Well, it looks like he's had a lot more than one. He's a big fella." I tried to shake Roman awake, but he didn't respond.

"What if he's dead?"

"Then he'll be easier to carry." The muscle-bound bouncer put his hands under Roman's armpits and pulled him backward off the stool. His head lolled to the right; he was out cold.

"I'll run ahead and unlock the door, wait for you, Okay?"

"No problem; he's not as heavy as he looks. Soft around the middle."

I watched the bouncer drag Roman through the frame shop's front door and into the back, where he lowered him to the concrete floor. "Watch his head," I said. The bouncer looked at me and rolled his eyes.

"This dude is your boss?"

"Yes. And I'm in big trouble."

"Looks like he's the one in trouble." Yeah, for sure. He's in trouble. But I'm the one who got him that way.

I locked the door behind the bouncer and dashed to the back to write a note for Roman, in case he woke up before I got back with the coffee and burgers. I put a bottle of water on top of the note, thinking he might wake up thirsty, then I snuck out the back door and locked it behind me.

When I returned, Roman was gone. His car was still in the lot, but he was nowhere. The bottle of water was gone, leaving only the note... wet. Then the acrid odor hit me, wafting from the bathroom. Oh, my God! He had puked everywhere! My guilt took me to the supply closet for cleaning supplies. Gagging, I cleaned the puke, finding an intact shrimp. *Oh, God! Gross! Gross!*

Finished, I sat in the back room and drank the coffee, ate the burgers, feeling like I was in a trance. I had sobered up the moment he told me it was a relapse, but the greasy sliders eased my headache. Too bad they didn't ease my Guilt and Shame.

There was nothing to do but go home, hoping Roman had found a way home and a way to keep his marriage together. I felt like an instigator, a tormentor, a source of evil. It was my fault, leading him to doom. Now his life may never be the same and it was all my fault.

The next morning, a Saturday, I opened the store with no Roman in attendance. Noon came and went; he still hadn't shown up. I thought of calling his wife but feared she would blame me. The day passed. Roman never showed. There were few customers that day and at five o'clock, I closed the register and locked the door.

The store was closed on Sundays and I worried the entire day. There was no communication from Roman... no phone call, no email, nothing. I showed up for work on Monday to find that my key didn't open the back door. *Somebody changed the locks*. I drove around to the front, wanting to know the full story.

There was a hand-written sign taped to the door. STORE PERMANENTLY CLOSED. Underneath, "To pick up completed orders, call 800-876-9059." Barely breathing, I punched in the number. Three disharmonious beeps and a recording: "The number you have reached is not in service at this time."

THE MAILMAN

CHAPTER 36

Home. As I fed Murphy, the phone rang. *Dammit!* Yep, it was Stuart. Angry and against my better judgement, I answered. "What the hell are you doing to me, asshole? Stalker! FREAK! SONOFABITCH!" I screamed into the phone with my voice an octave higher than normal.

"Hey, baby..."

"Don't 'hey baby' me! Why do you keep calling me? Why are you having me watched? What the hell is WRONG with you?"

"Having you watched?" He laughed sanctimoniously; I felt he was treating me like a child. "I'm not 'having you watched!' Why would you even *think* so?"

"Timing is everything, Stuart. Don't try to get out of this one, okay? Asswipe, you can't fool me with your insanity. No!"

"What are you talking about, Lela?" A smug statement, not a question.

"Just shut up, dammit. Why did you call? What the hell do you want?"

"Lela, I'm serious. I'm glad you caught me with the crack now, even glad you called my mother. Trust me. Now I'm clean again. That was a relapse, but I can't go back to that life. I don't want to. I've turned over a new leaf.

"In two short months, suddenly you're cured? Riiiight..."

"It can happen. I've been going to NA meetings every day. Even got a sponsor. Uh... do you know what that means?"

"Don't want to know."

"A sponsor is like... a teacher. A mentor. Mine is Ralph, a cool guy who's been clean for twelve years. And he's been helping me. A lot. So why am I calling, you ask? For lots of reasons, Lela. First of all, I love you... miss you."

"Oh, give me a break!"

"No! Listen! First, I'm sorry. Lela, I was wrong. Dead wrong. And I won't do it again. This is a heartfelt apology we call making amends. I will never hurt you again, never act like that, never smoke crack. And I'll pay your credit card. Doing that was wrong, too."

"Give me one reason I should believe you, Turd Face." My grip on the phone had relaxed, but my hands still shook.

"It's true, honest to God. What else can I say?"

"There's not a damn thing you can say, Stuart. So why don't you practice that and quit calling me? You've said your apology. Now give up. Leave me alone."

"But I need to send a check for your credit card."

A pause. *Is he really going to pay me back? I wouldn't be giving my home address, just the PO box. Dare I give it to him?* Another pause as the buzz between my ears screamed at a high pitch. "Look, I have a Post Office box and I'll..."

"A Post Office box? Why?" he shrieked.

I shrieked back. "Because I don't want you to find me, you stupid fuck! I guess I need to change my phone number now, too. I didn't think about that 'til this exact moment."

"Please don't, Lela. Surely we can be *friends* at least! We've been through a lot together."

"Your definition of 'together' obviously differs from mine." I sat, realizing my knees were knocking together... my entire body was a ball of nervous tension. "Anyway, I'll give you my PO box, not that I expect a check. Oh, actually, it should be a money order..."

"Oh, okay. Don't worry. I'll send it, Lela. I swear!"

"Ha! So you *swear*?" The brain-buzz turned up a notch. *Could I forgive him if he gets clean and pays that bill? Is that possible? Can I talk myself out of hating him?* I was still in love with him, or the concept of being in love with him; there was no denying that. "Tell ya what, Stuart Weinstein... against my better judgement, I'll take the money. It's the right thing to do, for you. Isn't that what twelve-step programs tell you? Do the right thing?"

"Exactly. And that's what I plan to do."

"Do that, Stuart." It was a snotty, hateful comment on my part. "Sure, do right by me. That might raise you one little level in Hell."

He sighed. "Don't be mean, Lela."

"Whatever, Stuart! Here's my address."

"Hold on…" A pause and a grunt. "Okay, go."

I told him while feeling like I shouldn't. *But why wouldn't you accept the money he stole? You're not stupid, Lela.* The little bird in the back of my brain knew Mom wouldn't approve of this and I cringed.

"There's nothing more to say, so… goodbye, Stuart. Maybe you can call back when I receive your money order if it's not a counterfeit one." I said. I hit the END button hard enough to strain my finger.

Two days later, I swung by the Post Office to check my mail. Lo-and-behold, an envelope from Ace Transmissions. Inside, a money order for two-hundred bucks, payable to me. *Well, it's something. You can't get blood from a turnip.* Sigh.

Four days later, back to the Post Office, expecting another rejection letter from a potential employer, I received another money order. The third one had a Post-It Note attached: "You have rocketed me to the fourth dimension! Love, Stuart." The next week, another money order, this one for $250.00. *Well, at least he's regular, and increasing in amount.* During that time, there were no surprise phone calls when I ventured out to party. I soon forgot the paranoia of being watched.

There were no bites on the dozens of résumés I'd sent. With no job… no money to pay the rent; I had to take money out of my 401K, but I didn't tell Mom. Soon, I would need groceries and gas and knew I'd have to call my stockbroker again.

<<<<<<<>>>>>>>

The Sunday newspaper classified ads were thicker that day; more jobs than I'd seen in previous weeks. With a doctored coffee and a red Sharpie, I sat down to focus on the small print. I had already hit the frame shops in the area and two granted me an interview, but neither had the blind trust to hire me.

My job experience was advertising and making costume jewelry, not much to sell to a potential employer. Nothing new today. I popped a beer and took Murphy on a walk, in search of the hotel gang.

The guys had gathered on the same patio. I'd quit resisting the Jello shots, accepting Tequila craziness as part of my daily life. I sang "Here We Go Again," with each shot.

Today wouldn't be different from others; I'd be the same ol' drunk... same ol' delusional Lela. My routine was a yawn, followed by the blur of drunkenness and the crazy scream of doing stupid, drunk things.

It seemed everyone was moving on, settling down, growing old gracefully and happily. Except me.

My sister Jennifer had met a nice (but I thought boring) man named Rick and spent her time fly-fishing in the mountains and reading books by the fireplace. Lola still dated Mel Durren, helped on his horse farm and managed his household... but they didn't go out much anymore, she said. Cowboy Logan had divorced and now lived in Jay's opulent barn, staying close to home. My party crowd had calmed down permanently.

I was the only one still floundering, still staying out all night, giving in to the Great God of Tequila, the Queen of Smirnoff, Baron Von-Vodka.

Lela Fox was broke, drunk, and miserable... feeling like an utter failure and drinking those feelings away. It was my life.

And it sucked.

TELLING DADDY

CHAPTER 37

Three AM. Home from a drunken night with the Hotel Gang, including a lasagna dinner by chef Barbie, I cried and wailed, lamenting the state of my life. On a whim, I picked up the phone and called Stuart. He answered on the second ring, obviously awake himself.

"Hey," I said.

"What are you doing up at this hour?"

"Crying."

"Why?"

"I miss you."

"Really?"

"A lot."

"I'm happy to hear that." There was a long sigh. "Minus the crying, I'm doing the same thing. I mean... missing you."

"Everybody has a boyfriend but me. Everybody is all settled down... calm, boring, dull as a butter knife. You and I, Stuart... we could party-hearty, eat 'Love Pizza' and screw like wind-up toys. Until you went off the deep end, we had a good thing."

"Yeah, we did. Always had a good thing, from the beginning. But I *did* screw up, and I'm sorry it happened. I'm still waiting for you to forgive me."

Kleenex in hand, I blew my nose. "*You're* waiting? *I'm* waiting for *me* to forgive you."

"Think you can?"

"Dunno. Maybe. Eventually."

"And in the meantime?"

"Dunno. Drink, I guess. I haven't found a job yet. Lost the other one."

"Oh, wow. I didn't know. Do you need money? You know I can send more."

"Thanks for what you're sending – it's helping pay the bills. But I wish you would pay the whole balance like you said you would."

"Would that help you forgive me?"

Hmm... would it? "Sure, I guess. Hey, I gotta go. Too drunk to talk."

"Good night, then. But Lela, I want you to know something. I want you to believe it with all your heart."

"What?"

"I love you. Pure and simple. I've loved you for a long time and this bullshit hasn't changed it. Trust me, if you can. I want the best for you, sweetheart, and promise to never hurt you again. Do you understand?"

Tears fell, pounding against the leather of the sofa as they dripped. "I miss you, Stuart. Please, I want to see you."

"Then let's meet in between for a weekend, just a weekend. See what happens. Let's try Jacksonville, maybe."

"I'd like that."

"Consider it done. Jacksonville, this weekend. I'll call you when I've made the reservation. Is that okay?"

My voice was so weak, so pitiful. "Yeah, it's okay. Maybe I'll have a job by then."

"I'll bring money. How much is your rent? I'll pay it."

"Six hundred dollars! And I don't have it, not even close. I'm so screwed."

"No, you're not. Let me find us a nice hotel and we'll work everything out. Don't worry."

"Okay, baby. I believe you. I love you so much!" Drunk, but sincere, I loved him dearly.

He made kissy noises into the phone, as was our inside joke. I did the same.

<<<<<<<<>>>>>>>

On Friday, Mom and Daddy came to Rockville to visit. Jennifer's kids were in town; Bella and Lizzie came on the same weekend, not the usual arrangement. My parents were glowingly proud of this branch of grandchildren and scrambled to see them whenever possible. Bo was still an up-and-comer and a rare visitor to Rockville, I was sad to say.

Daddy hugged me long and hard; we hadn't seen each other in months. Since I'd been back in town, I'd only been to the farm once. It was boring there and I couldn't drink. Not one beer, nothing. I suspected they hid the liquor when I was due for a visit.

Lunch at Barkley's, famous for barbeque and ribs. I made sure I sat next to Daddy; the talk was of their life at the farm... the garden, the cows, their neighbors' goings-on, etcetera. Happiness exuded from his pores, more than usual.

"Why are you so happy, Daddy?"

"Because I'm with my baby girl. I'm sooooo happy you left Florida, Lela. We did nothing but worry while you were there. Now you're safe, where you're supposed to be, and that makes me happy, happy, happy." His sideways smile warmed my heart, and I dreaded what I would have to tell him.

"Uh, Dad... Stuart and I are meeting in Jacksonville this weekend. In fact, my suitcase is in the car. I'm leaving right after lunch." His face fell like a rock from space; if I hadn't been so ashamed, it would have been comical. "Daddy, I know you don't understand, but he's clean now, going to those NA meetings. I have to see if what we had can continue."

"Oh, Lela..." His head pointed to the floor. "Lela, Lela... you will put your mother in the grave with worry."

"I'm sorry, Daddy." Tears flowed down my cheeks; one rolled into my mouth and I tasted the salt. "But, Dad, I'm being cautious, like you'd want me to be. This is just to test the water."

"The water? Damn, Lela, don't you realize you're drowning in those waters!" It was not a question and Daddy's voice had risen two notches in volume. Mom caught my eye, furrowing her brow when she saw Daddy's face.

"I think I can trust him again."

"*Trust* him? How could you *possibly* trust him? What is it going to take to open your eyes, baby girl? He stole your money, told a string of lies, mistreated your family. Can't you see that?" His voice was calm, but I heard the anger behind it. Daddy doesn't forgive easily and couldn't understand why I was so quick to forgive... actually *desperate* to forgive.

"It's just a weekend, Daddy." That's all I could think to say. Deep down, I heard him loud and clear but felt he just didn't understand what Stuart had been before the shit hit the fan; he didn't know his heart.

I continued, "I guess I didn't tell you the frame shop closed. I lost my job."

He shrunk. Looking down at his lap, he said, "No, honey, I didn't know." It was as if I had pulled the plug on an inflatable raft.

"Yeah, it sucks." But I had no intention of telling Daddy all my troubles. Instead, I wanted it to seem like I had it all together.

Daddy threw the last rib on his plate and used the cloth napkin to wipe his greasy fingers. All the "normal activity" didn't hide the pain in his eyes; it was as if they turned from their usual blue to a dull gray in a matter of seconds.

"I owe him another chance, Dad."

"You owe him NOTHING!" Everybody at the table became instantly silent, I suppose shocked that Daddy would yell in public. Five long seconds later, my distressed father threw his napkin on the table, stood and left, saying nothing. He veered to the right, toward the exit.

With our group still silent and gaping, Mom stood and followed him.

My chin shook as I tried to hold back tears. Disappointing my father was 100 percent heartbreak. *But what can you do, Lela? Daddy doesn't understand! Daddy's not the one who loves your man! And Stuart is clean and sober now! He DOES deserve a second chance!* Even worse was the glare Mom shot my way as she squeezed through the end of the table to follow my father. *But you've let them both down, again. AGAIN! STOP IT!*

HALFWAY WEEKEND
CHAPTER 38

While driving to Jacksonville, my thoughts ran both hot and cold. *Is this stupid? What can he possibly say that would make me believe he's changed? Will he give me all the money to pay off my Visa? Why didn't I ask him to put the money for this weekend's motel toward the balance?* I cried about disappointing my Daddy, but it never occurred to me that I should listen to him.

Stuart was there when I arrived, of course; the halfway mark favored him by at least a hundred miles. *Why didn't you look on the map and figure that out beforehand, nitwit? One more example of Stuart taking advantage of you?*

A pause and a knock at Room 316. "Oh, boy!" he said from within the room. Then he threw the door open, reaching out for me. "My baby is here!" The hug was long and hard, standing in the hotel hallway. He pushed me back and looked me up and down. "You've lost weight, Lela. Are you sick?"

"No, man. Uh... can I come in?" Surprised I was still in the hall, I suppose, he ushered me inside. A dozen candles were lit, yellow roses stood haphazardly in the impromptu vase of the bathroom trashcan. Soft music played.

"Welcome back into Stuart's arms," he cooed, sitting on the bed and patting a spot, urging me to sit. A deep kiss as he slowly pushed me backward on the bed. An hour of foreplay passed without interest in keeping time... a cycle of slow, undulating rhythms and frantic, spiking crescendos. He undressed me slowly, lovingly, commenting on each "beautiful" part of me. It was an out-of-body experience for me; I was putty in his hands. We ended with a flash of sweat and passion, desperate for each other, and finally, reluctantly, we collapsed within the tangled sheets.

The lighting of the cigarette ritual complete, Stuart got up to mix us drinks. I assumed his would be ginger ale, and I squirmed to think about living with a non-drinker. Then I saw his bottle of Crown.

"Aren't you supposed to not drink, either? I thought NA would be the same as AA, in a way. Clean and sober, right?"

"Different addictions. No problem." I thought about it. *Maybe he's right. What do I know about it, really? I've never been an addict, never been to a twelve-step meeting.* Then my eyes popped wide – *yes, you HAVE been to a twelve-step meeting. One meeting. One bullshit meeting.*

I wondered if Stuart's meetings were bullshit, too, and wondered if he'd ever let me go with him. Stuart interrupted my thoughts. "Yeah, baby, we've still got it! You are some hot momma."

"I think it has something to do with one hot daddy."

"Oh yeah?" A Cheshire grin. "You like?"

"Absolutely, Rudy," I said.

"Why do you say that all the time?"

"Dumb thing, I guess. Rudy was the name of my first car."

This began a long conversation of our youth when the world was before us and nothing resembling "real life" interfered with our idealistic, rosy outlooks. He laughed and reminisced, sharing details about his early years... details he'd never shared with me.

I realized there was much about his life I didn't know, big gaps he didn't talk about, like Switzerland, his dad, and I'd never, ever heard him talk about being married to Janey or his son's first years. I asked these questions. He answered as briefly as possible, leaving me in the dark again. *There must be a reason. But maybe it's just human nature... what man wants to talk about painful times?*

An hour of nice conversation, tinkling laughter, intimacy. Things we hadn't shared since before the final trip to the Bahamas. A few drinks later, I said, "So tell me how you're staying clean, how it happened... about your sponsor and all that." Although I was loopy, the answers to these questions were key; they would determine whether we would stay together.

"It's a long story."

"I imagine."

"Okay, here goes. After you left... the day after, in fact, I went back to see 'the man.' You know what I mean, right?" I nodded. "Well, there were people in front of me and I was sitting in the car waiting for the last customer to leave." He seemed to hesitate.

"Go on," I urged.

"Though the edge of the windshield, I saw a shadow, like a man. In a helmet, crouched down and running. At first I thought it was a stick, but it was a rifle leading the way. He was running toward the house, at an angle, but pointed straight at the front door. Then I saw another man, and another, and another... coming from different directions, each running in spurts then hiding behind things. Like in the damn movies! There were about five men, maybe six, then more of them running to the back of the house."

Another hit from his cigarette. My heart rate was zooming.

"So I'm thinking... SWAT team, right? I was paranoid, anyway, high as a kite. I started the Lexus and pulled out, really slow. Just my running lights. The sound of my tires on the road was so loud, Lela, I thought they would turn and come for me. I about shit my pants, no kidding. Trying to keep my eyes straight ahead, I drove by his house. But I saw it all. Suddenly, all the men moved at the same time. Like 'boom!' A signal, I guess. I heard a crunch and people yelling. I assume that's when they kicked the door down. My leg was shaking so hard on the gas pedal I flooded the engine. Or something happened. The car coughed and died.

He paused, but I was in rapture, eager for the rest of the story. He continued, "So there I sat, in the middle of the road in the middle of a bust. Everything in the rearview mirror now. A cop car pulled in, parked in the man's yard. Another came toward me. Sirens, flashing lights, and I was in the middle of the road! But my car wouldn't start, and the cop had to swerve to get around me. He looked right at me when he passed... a rock-hard jaw, piercing eyes. Mean as hell, you could tell. I freaked out, Lela. I didn't know I screamed until I heard the echo in the car."

Another pause. Another hit from the cigarette, and then he reached to stub it out in the ashtray. "So you were scared, huh? Scared straight, like they say?"

"There's more. I tried to start the car again. Nope. Another cop turned the corner and came right at me. Fast. I was 'in the way' again, or so I thought. But the car stopped right beside me. A woman cop, fat, a butch-girl... know what I mean?" I nodded.

"Her car was close to mine – almost touching, way too close to open the door. She motioned for me to lower the window and said, 'Get the hell out of here, sir.' Oh, my God... her voice. All business. I told her my car wouldn't start, and she glared like she thought I was lying. I said 'Seriously, it's flooded.' Her eyebrows came together in one hairy line and she said, 'If you get out of the car, you'll be shot, do you understand me?' I about shit."

"Damn! So far, you're lucky. But get to the end!"

"So I saw the, uh, customer in front of me coming out in cuffs. Then my friend, cuffed. Cops were crawling all in the front yard. I guess there were five cars there by that time, all with the lights swirling. It was frantic as hell, everybody shouting. The cop's hand on the top of the guy's head, pushing into the cop car. I mean, the guy who just happened to be in line before me! Lela, that could have been *me!*"

"Easily."

"So you were scared straight? Isn't that the phrase?" He nodded. "So what happened with the car? Did you get it started?"

"I don't know how long I sat there watching. But I knew the only thing that would make the car start was time. So I said to myself over and over 'wait, wait, wait' but the urge to run was overwhelming. You think I fidget normally? Ha! I was a mess. And I knew if I was still there when they finished the bust, I'd be next."

He sighed, lit another cigarette. "This story is hard to tell. Sorry. I thought I'd never get out of there."

"And?"

"And I never went back to Fort Lauderdale again." He chuckled. "And they lived happily ever after."

"That's the end of the story? My sphincter is a decimal point for an ending like that?" I re-thought my comment. "No, I take it back... that's the best ending *ever*. But answer me this: you quit crack only because you lost your connection?"

"That's part of it. But mostly, it scared me straight."

I lit a cigarette of my own, silent for a while as I sipped my drink. "Well... maybe I believe that and maybe not. I'm assuming you know more than one person to buy from, right?"

"Dozens I've met over the years."

"Dozens? For God's sake! How long have you been smoking crack, you ass?"

"Let's just say it's not the first time I've quit."

"Oh, my God, Stuart! You've *lied* to me, about so many things... and for so long! Why should I believe you now?" He put his hands up and opened his mouth to speak. I interrupted, "Hell no. Sins of omission are still sins." With a shrug, he closed his mouth. I continued, "So who's to say you don't start again? Because starting again would ruin everything. What's changed, Stuart? At the core of you... what changed?"

He stared at the ceiling, pondering his answer. "It was like... something touched me, Lela. Something outside of myself. The next morning, I called my old, old sponsor. Met him at an NA meeting that night. Found a few meetings in Wellington, and a club in West Palm. I've been to a meeting almost every night since you left."

Do I believe that? Do I? The story sounds plausible. And this "act" can't be an act when he's sweating just telling the story. An event that makes you shit your pants, thinking you're busted big time... that would make a person change.

"Okay, say I believe that, and believe you've changed... the big question is – why did you have me followed?"

"I didn't!"

"That's a lie."

"Lela, dammit!" He froze, looked at me. Finally, a shrug.

"I knew it! You were fucking *spying* on me! Do you realize how spooky that is? Do you realize what that did to ME? Did you think of THAT?"

"I just didn't want you to get away from me. Didn't want you to move on, forget about me. I fired him, anyway. No more calls, right?"

"Well, I haven't been out in the middle of the night lately."

A smile. "Good! I need you to be mine. Will you, please?"

<<<<<<<>>>>>>

On the way back to Rockville, I realized I had forgotten to ask for the money to pay my Visa balance. *I wonder why he didn't offer it?*

A FLORIDA SURPRISE

CHAPTER 39

Another cross-country move, another day of re-hanging, re-stocking cabinets, re-stocking groceries. I hadn't prepared for the second move; I'd left my Rockville bank accounts opened, left my safety-deposit box, didn't even say goodbye to Damon Toomey or the Hotel Gang. I just left, without a lot of hoopla.

Stuart was at a meeting when I arrived, according to the note he left, and a no-show when the moving truck arrived. When the movers left, I began unpacking. Things were somehow different than when I moved in the first time. I'd grown up, maybe? No, I just wasn't manic this time. I'd been taking my medicine religiously and felt stable and smart. *Just right. That's what this is, Lela... just right. Like The Three Bears rocking chair... this one is JUST RIGHT. I'm supposed to be here.*

That was the night I met his sponsor, Ralph. Rough as a cob. Beached hair to his waist, left wild, unbrushed, and as greasy as his skin. Ralph's beard was monstrous and bleached lighter than his hair, mostly frizz and fluff, and I couldn't take my eyes off the spot where it connected to his pale bottom lip.

He wore a too-small straw Fedora and a heavy silver chain to his wallet smashed in the pocket of his Levi's. A biker, complete with a hard-ass persona.

Here's how it happened.

Ralph zoomed into the apartment parking lot riding the loudest Harley I'd ever heard. He knocked but used a key to open the door. No pause, no greetings, no glance into the living room. He walked straight to the fridge and sniffed his way through containers of leftovers. I was too shocked to say anything; I didn't even know he was coming and he obviously hadn't seen me yet.

Ralph found his meal choice, popped the bowl in the microwave, grabbed a beer, popped it, and threw his head back for a deep swig.

With his head back, he saw me. "Oh! Hi! You must be Lela." Teeth were missing, but the grin was wide. Too wide, like a clown's grin. Ralph looked high, honestly, and he fidgeted just like Stuart. "Wouldn't trust him as far as I could throw him," I thought. Immediate dislike.

He looked around the apartment for the first time. "Whoa! There's a lot of shit in here! This all your stuff or something?" I nodded and waited for him to come up for air as he ate the leftover spaghetti. Red sauce stained his lips and droplets dribbled in his beard.

"I hear you guys are getting married, so congratulations! Stuart deserves to have you back, man. He's worked hard to stay clean and sober. He's even sober-minded, know what I mean?" He chuckled and shook his head. "Plus, he keeps me fed."

"Uh... why do you have a key to my apartment?"

"Oh... you don't like that? I guess not. I'll talk to Stuart about it."

"Well, he won't be home for a while. Said he was meeting you at a meeting, in fact."

There was a momentary flash of fear and hesitation before he spoke. "Oh, I decided to eat first. Then time got away from me. Thought I'd just meet him here."

"You ate first and now you're eating again?"

"Uh... yeah. I didn't know Stuart could make spaghetti this good."

"I made the spaghetti, Ralph."

"Oh, cool. I love a woman who cooks."

I groaned out loud. Ralph said, "Oh, I guess I shouldn't have said that." I ignored him.

Slowly, carefully, I asked, "So are you, like, are you... living here or something?"

"I stay sometimes. Stuart rented an extra bed – did you see it?" I had seen it, of course, and I planned to ask Stuart why the hell it was there. The movers put Bo's bunk bed in there anyway; there was a one-way path in and out of the room now.

"Gonna crash here tonight, too, uh, if that's okay with you. I live in Fort Lauderdale and it's a long way to drive."

"Fort Lauderdale? Why?"

He laughed. "Why? I have a job there most of the time. Construction. Can't work every day because of the weather. And because of my damn shoulder." He rotated his shoulder, holding it with his left hand. "Rotator cuff, I think."

"Sounds like you need a doctor."

Another cackling laugh. "Who can afford a *doctor*? He scooped the last of the spaghetti sauce into his mouth like a baby bird. *Gross!* "So, let me see your ring. Have you guys set a date yet?" I showed him my engagement ring, purchased at a pawn shop – the first time I had entered such an establishment. But it was on the safe side of town in Rockville, on a weekend Stuart flew up to "visit his TV."

"Nice! A'course Stuart has the bucks. And he's generous with 'em." I wondered how he knew that; how much money Stuart had given this loser. And why Stuart was "generous" but hadn't paid off my credit card.

At rabbit pace, Ralph jumped from the sofa and dashed back into the kitchen. He semi-rinsed his bowl and threw it in the sink. The spoon clattered on the stainless steel. In the same movement, he opened the cabinet and grabbed a bag of chips, opening it as he hurried back to the sofa. He crunched the chips like a child, crumbs flying.

I sighed. *Shit. A roommate? Are you kidding me? And why didn't Stuart tell me this? I do not, do NOT, want him here. And he's not the sponsor-type, anyway. Definitely not the picture Stuart painted. He looked like a druggie, wild in the eyes and jumpy. And how RUDE that he jumps in here and make himself at home. MY home!*

My sigh was audible. "Well, I guess I'll wait for Stuart in the bedroom. Just... make yourself at home, I guess."

"Oh, I certainly will! Glad you're comfortable with me here." *Why did I say that when I didn't mean it? Damn Southern manners that Mom taught. Too nice for my own good.*

<<<<<<<>>>>>>

"Stuart! Why in the hell didn't you tell me this Ralph guy had practically moved in!? I don't want him here, not at all. This is *our* place, *our* life. He gives me the creeps, anyway. And are you sure he's not high?"

Stuart pushed my curls back with his stubby fingers. "Oh baby, it's okay. Ralph's different, but he's helping me, honey. He talks sense. He's been clean for a while. A few relapses, but this time he's solid, taking me through the steps. Can you just chill for a while? Until we get married, anyway?"

"Then we're getting married ASAP! I don't want him here! Get that damn key back!"

"I've been thinking about our wedding, too. A good idea. You and I are going to dinner with Mother and Elijah tomorrow, by the way. And to this incredible Chinese restaurant. I've already talked to them about renting the back room."

"A Chinese restaurant? Why do you want the back room? For an NA meeting?"

"No, Dumb Butt, for our wedding!"

"You want to get married in a Chinese restaurant? What the hell?" My eyes bugged out in surprise, but there was a laugh underneath. *Wouldn't that be a hoot!*

"It's a five-star Chinese restaurant. We used to go there as a family. And the room is a perfect size. I've already talked to Mom, and she's paying."

"What!? Why are you planning this wedding without me?" Incensed and frantic, I thought I must be hearing things.

"Because it would take you a lifetime to get down to business, Lela. Honestly. You can't tell me you're Johnny-on-the-spot... about anything! That's why you can't work, Lela. I mean, nothing personal, but your shit is *not* together, dear. And I'm an organizer. I get things done, make decisions, delegate. It's my special talent."

I had to agree; Stuart was a top-notch organizer. But it was hard to hear that I was inefficient and getting worse. By the third drink, my day was lost. Used to be, I could drink all day *and* get things done, but no more. I slept late and by four o'clock or so, the day was done. Then the evening drinking began, and nothing was ever accomplished at night, either.

Stuart interrupted my thoughts. "Okay, baby. I'm taking charge. Is that cool?"

"Just discuss things with me before you finalize decisions, please. I have my own ideas, ya know."

"I suppose. So, I'm calling them now. The restaurant. The China Pearl. See what dates they have open. I'll book the first-available."

"But I don't even have a dress!"

"You can shop tomorrow if you time it right. Mother will go with you. Pay for the dress, too." I shrugged. *Yeah, I could do that. I guess.*

With a sigh, I sauntered to the kitchen to mix another drink, happy to see that Ralph had gone to "his" room. I mumbled under my breath. *Face it, Lela. What's the chance Stuart will even talk to this unwanted roommate or get that key back? How can he be so "taken" with a loser like that? And, shit... recovering addicts shouldn't be drinking so much!* With a sigh, I threw a lime slice in my vodka and sauntered back to the sofa, just as Stuart came out of the bedroom.

He spoke before I could ask my burning question about his drinking. "January fourth. That's our wedding day."

"That only gives me a month to get ready!"

"Piece of cake, baby. There's not that much to do. We can *call* to invite the guests... no need for a mailed invitation."

"But–"

"But nothing! Remember, I'm in charge. Never fear! Stuart is here!"

"My Daddy used to say that!" Stuart smiled a silly one, bringing warmth to my heart for both of them. I knew Daddy wouldn't approve of us getting married; he'd hardly spoken to me since the weekend I met Stuart in Jacksonville. *Don't go there, Lela. Don't get yourself upset.* I shook the thoughts from my head. "So Stuart, how was your meeting?"

"Good. Lots of people there."

I picked up a folded, stained and dog-eared piece of paper from the side table as Stuart rustled up something to eat in the kitchen. "Where's the leftover spaghetti?"

"Ralph ate it."

"Shit!"

I unfolded the paper. The heading at the top: COURT ORDERED 12-STEP MEETING ATTENDANCE. Underneath, there were boxes of scribbled dates and signatures. *Court ordered? What the hell?*

"Stuart?"

"Yes, dear."

"Why does this say 'court ordered?'"

There it was... a flash of panic on his face. Wide eyes, open mouth, and a gasp of air. "Oh, that's just an old thing, years ago."

"Then why is it on the side table here? Looks like it just came out of your pocket."

"I have no idea."

"That's it? You have no idea? You think I'm going to buy that?" He picked up the remote and changed the channel. "A hockey game? You don't watch hockey!"

"Sure I do." He said nothing else. Slowly and carefully, I folded the paper up again, walked to the bedroom, and put it under the mattress on my side. I don't know why, but I didn't want him to have it anymore. If it was truly old like he said, what would it matter?

ARRANGEMENTS

CHAPTER 40

"Wow! This *is* a nice place, Stuart! But, still..." I continued to mumble through uncertainty. Finally, I threw up my hands. "I mean, it's a Chinese restaurant! How many people do you know who got married in a Chinese restaurant?"

He chuckled. "A story for the grandchildren. And just look at this perfect room! This is way-upscale Oriental décor, baby, and twenty carved tables. I like it. Let's do it!"

"I just always imagined a dance floor, a dee-jay, ya know?"

"We're too old for that, don't you think? And we have more class than that."

"We do?"

Stuart laughed. "Yes, we do."

That night, Ralph stayed away and Stuart didn't go to a meeting for the third night in a row. The meeting-skipping bothered me, but he said there was too much to do in wedding preparations. "I can stay clean without meetings, anyway. They help, but there's no reason for seven days a week."

"But it's so soon in your... uh, new life. I thought you were supposed to go every day."

"Don't worry, Lela. You don't know a thing about it."

"When do I get to go to a meeting with you?" I'd asked five times and his answer had always been something about a closed meeting, which I didn't understand. *Is NA some kind of secret society? With a secret handshake and shit? And how do I know he's actually going?*

<<<<<<<<>>>>>>>

Back home, we both sat down for phone calls... phone invitations to a January fourth wedding. Mom was eerily silent when I told her the news. I knew she wouldn't jump for joy; that's why I hadn't told her when we became engaged, but I didn't expect the silence she gave, and I was miffed. Daddy didn't respond to the news, either. Hurt and sad to the core of my bones, I wiped a bucketful of tears before making the other calls.

I called Bo's dad who answered on the first ring. He wasn't happy that Bo would have to fly alone to Rockville where he would meet Mom and Dad for the rest of the ride. "He's old enough, Andy! And you know how airlines treat minors! They're accompanied every step of the way, can't let them out of sight. Seriously... relax!" More mumbling and whining, but he finally agreed when I reminded him that the flight to Rockville is less than an hour long. "Unless you want to drive him there... meet up with my friends." He didn't like that idea at all.

I went on, "Besides, he'll be flying down here alone several times this year to see me. He's seventeen! Taller than you, and probably more responsible." I guess I had to get that little jab in, just to keep myself in power.

I called Karen, who voiced concern. "Lela, are you sure you want to do this? What if he goes back to drugs and leaves you stranded down there? I worry so much about you, sweet sister. Maybe I should shut up and just say 'congratulations,' but, instead, I'm crying." I had no answer, so my defense was anger.

"Then don't come – either of you. Bitch! Thanks for your well-wishes!" I pulled the phone away, ready to slap it closed for a dramatic hang-up.

"NO, LELA, WAIT! I don't mean it like that! Of *course* I will come to your wedding! See you walk down the aisle like the beautiful bride you will be. I just had to tell you how I feel."

"Well, I didn't tell you how I felt about John before you married him!"

"But you love John and told me so! If you had told me otherwise, I might have thought twice about marrying him, dingbat!"

"Oh really?" I snapped, "My opinion is important to you or something? I'm just the dumb little sister." Such a smartass tone; my goal was to shame her.

"Not so dumb most of the time. I'm just not sure this is the smartest decision you've ever made."

"Well, it's happening. We're covering plane tickets for everybody, so you really have no excuse." By the time we hung up, we bantered like our old selves. Karen was cool with it, I thought.

Jennifer wasn't home and didn't answer her cell. I left a message on both phones.

Lola seemed 100 percent happy to hear from me. We talked for an hour, until I begged to go, saying "I have a dozen more people to call."

But in the call to Lola, I discovered a problem. January fourth was a big day, she said. Tennessee football! "If we keep winning, and we're supposed to, we'll be SEC Champions and in the Fiesta Bowl, the national championship game!" I had no idea. For the first time in decades, I'd lost touch with my alma mater team and the rabid fans of Tennessee. Lola laughed but her tone was serious: "Lela, I'll kill you if we win and you've made me miss that game! Why not just postpone your wedding?"

As we discussed the details, the Chinese restaurant, and that Stuart's mother would pay for my dress, she snuck in a few comments to hint of her disapproval. As I could easily do, I blew her off. Selective hearing.

I called Caroline, then all my party friends: Brenda, Debbie, Tina, Baron, and Blitz, in that order. Each repeated the conflict with the football game and acted a bit strange. "Isn't he the *evil* ex-boyfriend?" they asked. Blitz, in particular, objected and said enough to piss me off. I didn't attack him as I had Karen, but when I told him it was a free plane ticket and free food for the entire weekend, he recanted.

The most difficult call was to Damon. I knew he disapproved of Stuart... rather, me and Stuart as a couple. On the phone, he said, "I have a bad, bad feeling about this, Lela." I called him paranoid and untrusting, barreling guilt into his gut. Damon knew most of the "first-time-in-Florida story," including the credit card balance, so I told him Stuart had paid it off. A bald-faced lie, but he didn't seem impressed, anyway.

It never occurred to me that Damon would refuse to come to my wedding, but he did. "On principle," he said. I cried, deeply hurt. Then hurt turned to anger and, a hand on my heart, I swore I'd never speak to him again.

The calls made, Stuart and I joined again in the living room. Turned out, many people had warned him, too. *What's up with these people? Don't they know what love is?*

With the guest list complete. Stuart called Delta Airlines and booked nineteen flights from a half-dozen departure points. I laid beside him on the bed, smoking a joint (which he refused, quoting his NA book: "No mood or mind-altering substance, Lela.")

The booking process took a long time, and I had to jump up to refresh our drinks twice. *Wait a minute... alcohol is a mood-altering substance. Why wouldn't that count?* I'd ask Stuart after he hung up with Delta, I decided... immediately after. Then I returned to the sofa feeling sad. Scared. Unsure of my soon-to-be. At last I heard, "Okay, don't say the total or I'll have a heart attack. Hold on and I'll get my credit card."

That's when I left, not wanting to hear the total either.

<<<<<<<<>>>>>>>

The Justice of the Peace Stuart had booked called the day before the wedding to cancel. I freaked out but Stuart simply picked up the phone and starting dialing. Within the hour, another JOP was booked. A black man, he said. "I hope that's okay with your bigot parents." I didn't bother to reply to that smartass comment.

My dress needed a third round of alterations in as many weeks. It seems I was dropping weight like pennies from a pocket. Details were happening all around me as I sat with a drink in my hand. Like a lost puppy, I sniffed my way down six different paths, unable to follow any scent to the end. I knew I was lost... and my solution was to keep drinking and keep crying. *Lela cries – what a surprise. You know why Daddy calls you "Tear Bucket Jim."*

For guest accommodations, Stuart leased four furnished apartments in our building for the weekend. They called them "corporate apartments," he explained. I objected at first, thinking it must be horribly expensive, but he shushed me. "I bargained for a good weekend rate, babe. Besides, this is on my tab."

"No, because it's money that could be paid toward my Visa balance."

"*Please* quit worrying about it, sweetness. I can pay the whole damn thing with another trust fund payment in mid-February." He patted my head like I was a damn puppy and continued his assurances, "Trust me... trust the process."

Pouting wouldn't solve the problem or make him pay faster, so I'd learned to say nothing.

It was a given that my girlfriend's three-bedroom setup would be the party room, but Friday night dinner would be in our apartment. I had worked all week to clean the house, but I only managed to straighten the living areas. I kept getting drunk too early, I complained.

Friday arrived. Before Stuart left for work, we set up the rented tables and chairs for a casual dinner and I took off for the airport to pick up my friends and family.

Seeing Bo... a shock! It had been almost six months since I'd seen him and I marveled at his grown-up looks. It seemed he'd grown several inches taller and a foot wider across his shoulders. Bo and Daddy standing side by side was like looking at the same body. Such upper body strength! Same thick neck, broad shoulders, and biceps that looked like strong-man bodies in magazines.

(Unfortunately, I had inherited the same body type, setting me apart as a "big girl" even though my 5'6" frame weighed a mere 120 pounds. *And dropping... maybe 110 pounds by now, Lela.*)

I hugged Bo as hard as he would allow, and my heart swelled with pride. But something was amiss; he seemed shy, unable to look me in the eye. My heart shrunk more than it had swelled when first seeing him. "Are you okay, buddy?" I asked. His reply was a shrug and a *hrummph*.

The same flight carried my family and friends from Rockville. As if to match my own buzz, the friends had been drinking and all fooled around in a drunk's boisterous style. I saw Mom looking curiously at Blitz, who was loud and somewhat belligerent by nature, but he'd always been the one who protected me, physically and emotionally.

Seeing my friends drunk and having fun made me wish I'd stayed in Rockville for a minute... then I thought of Stuart's smile, our vivacious lovemaking, our long talks sitting on the shore... and I knew my choice had been the correct one.

A sober Karen wore shorts, her pasty-white legs glowing in the yellow light of the concourse. And her sweet hubby John, always gregarious and friendly, picked me up in a hug of congratulations.

"Where's Jennifer?" I asked. No one spoke. "Did she miss the flight?" Again, nobody said a word, looking sheepishly at their shoes. "Is she coming?"

Silence. I felt my stomach drop to my knees and my throat tighten in diameter. Karen broke the silence. With tears streaming down her face, she said, "She won't come... because she's a bitch!"

Mom interjected. "Karen! Language!"

Still teary, Karen continued, "She says she's not coming out of principal. She thinks you shouldn't marry him. I call that selfish and bitchy, I don't care what Mom says!"

I closed my eyes, feeling hurt at the bottom of my gut. *My own sister isn't coming? She's that high and mighty? What the fuck?*

Mom, seeing my reaction, reached to hug me, patting my cheek as one would console a child. "It's okay, Lela. Your sister loves you and you two will work it out later. I have her ticket so maybe you can get a refund or something. But shush my little one. It will all be okay." I leaned against her hard, needing her assurance.

"Am I the one being stupid, Mom, or is it Jennifer?"

Mom gently touched my shoulders and eased me backward. A straight look in the eye. "You're both hard-headed, Lela. You know that. Now wipe your tears and keep a stiff upper lip. We can talk later." The tissue she handed me sopped up tears and came away with mascara blobs.

"Did I get it all?" I asked her, referring to the mascara.

"You look beautiful."

Deep breath. Carry on. Fuck Jennifer.

Back at the apartment complex, I arranged everybody in their assigned apartments and dashed home to get ready for the barbeque dinner we'd ordered in. They called the deal "With One Cow, He Fed a Multitude," which cracked me up.

After dinner, Bo and I took a walk as I smoked a cigarette. He seemed nervous and out of place; I had never seen him act so shy, even if he *was* the only youngster. "Are you okay, son?" I asked again.

"Yeah, it's just weird. All these people, your friends. Does everybody get drunk like that?" *Oh, I'm forcing him into adult situations! What are you doing, dumb Lela?*

"How can I make it better for you, honey?" He kicked at the sand in the landscaping and shrugged.

"I just wish you would come home, Mom. Quit acting young and dumb like this." *Young and dumb? What?*

"What do you mean, son?"

"It's like I'm more grown up than you are sometimes. And, I mean, this is the third time you've been married. My dad says that's ridiculous. A 'three-time loser' and I don't even know what that means!"

"Your dad shouldn't have said that. Sometimes it takes a few strikes to get a hit... you know that, right?" He *hmmph*'ed in agreement. "Stuart and I can give you a lot, Bo. It's an opportunity... you can move here and play baseball at Florida State like you've always wanted."

Another shrug from Bo, who still wouldn't look me in the eye. "And if you don't get a scholarship, Stuart can pay college. A free ride, buddy! Half of the point of my being here is an opportunity for you."

"Don't get married because of me!" He snapped the words, challenging me with a glare in his eye.

"Whoa! Calm down, son. I think of you first in a lot of things."

"Then just leave this... whatever it is... and come home. Quit drinking."

"Quit drinking? What makes you think I should do that?"

He started with a chuckle, then a guffaw, then threw his head back to laugh at the sky. "Isn't it obvious, Mom?"

"Uh, no. I'm not sure. But stop laughing!"

"Right. You don't know what I'm talking about. That's the problem." With no comeback for that, I shut my mouth. I refused to acknowledge that Bo knew I drank too much or was an alcoholic– *oh shit, do I have to even THINK that out loud?*

Embarrassed, I mumbled a non-response. Bo looked at me and sighed. "Just forget it, Mom. Let's just get this over with so I can go home. Right now, I'm going to bed. I'm going... to be with Nonnie and G-Daddy. I don't want to be with drunk people."

"Drunk? No, son, they're not drunk, they're just having fun, and a few drinks are part of that. It's no big deal."

"Well, *you* are drunk and it *is* a big deal." I stopped in my tracks and watched him walk away, down the sidewalk and into their appointed apartment. Tears burned my eyes and my heart sunk to my feet.

Oh, God! I had disappointed my son. Again. And it sounded like it was more than disappointment... like I had disgusted him. *He says he's more grown-up than you are! Dammit, you! What kind of Mom ARE you? Is that why you left him behind with his dad and Ella? Is he right in saying what he said?*

Mom, Dad, and Bo stepped out to the sidewalk. "We're going to bed, Lela."

"But it's not even dark!"

"No matter. See you on your wedding day! Then Dad saluted me. Mom waved in a small, barely perceptible gesture. Bo turned on his heel and disappeared into the shadow of the apartment.

'TIL DEATH DO US PART
CHAPTER 41

The room boomed with volume. Just as most people were going for the second round of barbeque, Stuart's brain-damaged sister arrived. She waltzed in with her "life coach" around nine o'clock. The noise level dove to zero; you could have heard a mouse squeak. Like me, we were all shocked by her appearance – she weighed three hundred pounds, at least. The man who took care of her was equally huge. I wondered if they slept together and stifled a giggle at the vision of a mattress flattened into a thin pancake.

Carla's eye area was stretched, typical in a Down Syndrome patient, but it was more than that... instability was evident. Her eyes darted around the room as she gnawed on her fingernails, or maybe her fingertips. Stuart stood to greet them, then introduced them in a booming voice. "Everybody, this is my sister Carla, from Boston. And her friend Joey." All in the room raised a glass.

Stuart scrambled to find a place for Carla, not apologizing when he asked Blitz to move from the sofa. Carla's gargantuan thighs moved in steps toward her appointed seat with great effort. The sound of her pants, polyester rubbing on polyester, filled the room. It was scary, actually, waiting for the friction to set her thighs on fire. Stuart hadn't warned me about her weight and it took a while for my mouth to close. Only embarrassment snapped it shut, and I rose for a personal greeting.

"Hi, Carla. I'm so happy to meet you. Heard a lot about you, of course. I'm so glad you could make it for the wedding." She seemed to look at a spot above my head as I spoke to her and didn't reply, her eyes still darting here and there. Giggles escaped her as the group greeted her one at a time. When it was Ralph's turn, he stood and sang his name, in a damn-good baritone, shocking everyone.

Her friend Joey, perhaps to make up for Carla's social awkwardness, said to the group, "It's nice to meet each one of you."

"Where's Mother?" Carla asked three times in a row, fidgeting and searching the room for Stuart's eyes. Stuart stepped out from the crowd and waved, catching her attention.

"Carla, Mother and Elijah aren't coming tonight. They will pick you up early in the morning. I've told you that twice now, Carla."

Joey touched Carla's shoulder. "Remember what I said, Carla? We're staying down the hall tonight, in a room like yours at home." She nodded, but her face was puckered with confusion.

Stuart walked toward Joey. "Let me show you to your room now."

"YES, NOW!" shouted Carla, now visibly shaken. "Away from scary people! And I have to pee!" She started to cry, then wail, then scream with terror.

Lola looked at me with pity and I glared back, daring her to feel sorry for me. *It's my wedding weekend, dammit!* Then she saved the day. "Let's go to our room with another bottle of champagne! Everybody!"

I hopped to my feet, "I'm leaving the clean-up to Stuart, but let's take some leftovers." "Come on, Karen! The party isn't over yet."

<<<<<<<<>>>>>>>

Karen and John had stayed at our place in the guest room. We joked about the bunk bed, but that was the only choice.

In the morning, leaving the men to sleep late, Karen and I sat together on the sofa drinking coffee. I resisted adding my usual splash of vodka, knowing Karen wouldn't approve, but she had me laughing so hard, I forgot my need for it. The two of us drank a full pot before John and Stuart wondered into the living room, Stuart bitching about how loud we'd been.

Stuart's pissy attitude worsened when he realized all the coffee was gone. "And all you and Karen do is laugh. Laugh, laugh, laugh. At first, it was endearing, then it really started to piss me off."

"Don't be an ass on our wedding day, Stuart." He rolled his eyes, filling the coffeemaker with water. John was the ultimate friendly houseguest, teasing about us seeing each other before the wedding. "Fuck the tradition," I said, "It's not exactly practical, anyway. Not here, doing it our way."

"Your way is a Chinese restaurant, Lela!" John said, still laughing.

Stuart interrupted the fun, returning to the living room dressed. "I'll be back from Mother's around three. Try to stay sober on your wedding day, okay?" I snapped my head to glare at him, but he flashed the I'm-just-kidding-and-I-love-you smile.

Stuart dashed to the afternoon luncheon at his mother's McMansion, for the Weinstein side of the family only. I found her non-invitations for the Fox family rude as hell; isn't the blending of two families half the point of a wedding?

Karen and John followed me to the girl's party apartment and I can say it was the best time I've ever had sober... then again, neither having a good time nor being sober had happened in a long time.

I'll be a married woman in seven hours! The thought both excited me and sent chills of fear down my spine. *Oh, God! What if my dress doesn't fit? What if the Justice of the Peace doesn't show? What if the tape player runs out of batteries? What if a last-minute zit appears on my chin? What if I fall and chip my tooth? Oh, God!* Sudden and all-encompassing anxiety.

My hands and body shook and no amount of self-talk would stop it. I slipped around the table to whisper in Karen's ear; she listened as a smile spread on her face.

She wiped the barbeque sauce from her lip and announced to the crowd, "It seems the blushing bride is having a case of last-minute jitters. She says it may take her the full seven hours to get ready." Everybody laughed. "But y'all stay and I'll take her rattled nerves home to make sure the dress still fits... and what else, Lela?"

I couldn't speak; I think that was her point. "Yes, and to fight the dragons that bring devasting catastrophes." Everybody ooh'ed and aah'ed as if they thought my jittery nerves were a good thing, sweet and romantic.

Relief. Karen was the one to calm me and keep me laughing. Her irreverent humor put my fears in perspective... always had. Lola put a flute of champagne in each of my hands "for the road," she said. But "the road" was two doors down. I drained the flute in one gulp before entering the foyer, extending Karen's flute toward her. "No, Lela... nothing alcoholic so early in the day!"

Happy to hear that, I downed hers in one gulp, too. *Aaah.* An instant fix for the worst of my frazzled nerves.

<<<<<<<<<>>>>>>

I had several drinks in the restaurant bar before the wedding. My friends had gathered around the pitifully small TV to watch the pre-game show of the Fiesta Bowl. "Go Big Orange!" they sang. Then my girlfriends, Mom, and Karen gathered around me, parading me to the restroom for the final check on looks.

Barking orders, I called Stuart and demanded he call everybody to confirm the details, including the florist. Good thing, because they had a question: "The address must be wrong. It's a Chinese restaurant!"

At the last minute, I had Karen call the photographer and reiterate the photos I wanted because some had changed without Jennifer in attendance. *Dammit, Jennifer! You and Damon both! It's like you don't trust me to make my own decisions! And, to make your point, you hurt my heart. On purpose! Is that fair? Is that friendship?! You don't think I should marry him? What other choice do I have? I can't get a job... and I need somebody to take care of me!*

Karen and I stood before the oversized mirror in the bathroom, five minutes before liftoff. All the guests were seated and waiting for the bride. Karen inspected my face and makeup. "You need a little more lip gloss, the shiny kind." I reached out, expecting the *slap* of lip gloss in my hand.

She looked at me, confused. "Oh! I don't *have* any... it's just that you need it." After the shock, I bent over in laughter and we spent five minutes cackling. "Come on! You're late!

We tiptoed to the banquet room's entrance and Karen slipped in. The "Wedding March" CD was cued up and Bo was ready to hit PLAY at my signal. This time, I would walk down the aisle alone. Nobody needs to give me away again, I reasoned; I'd been given away twice.

Deep breath, standing ten feet from the entrance. At the far end of the room, I saw Stuart towering beside a black man. But was it a man? A man, as small as a child! The Justice of the Peace was a midget!

At first, the noise from my mouth was a snicker, then a laugh, then a snort which caused another loud laugh. All the way down the aisle, all the way through the ceremony, I laughed through the vows and the "I Do" promise.

Stuart got tickled at my laughter and chuckled along with me, a few times bursting into a hearty, sincere laugh. With "You may kiss the bride," I opened my mouth wide and laughed like a hyena. The kiss didn't connect; we laughed with our teeth together as the black midget pronounced us husband and wife.

The audience was nervous, only guessing what we were laughing about. They'd had twenty minutes to get their own laughs at the insanity of it all before the doors slid open for me. Carla laughed as loud as I did, clapping her hands and swinging her legs. Joey tried to stop her, but she shouted repeatedly, "Funny! Itty-bitty black man! Carla laugh!"

But the laughing ceremony was a tragedy, in a way, because I'd laughed myself sober. The solution was to slip to the bar and drink with animal greed... double vodka-grapefruit, three of them in quick succession. Then I felt normal again. Everybody was laughing and having a good time, but a look of horror crossed Mom's face when a Weinstein family friend let loose with a punch line that included the F-word. *Yep, that will give your mother the vapors.*

Blitz and Baron disappeared now and then, which was a puzzle to me. Then they burst in, jubilant. "Hail Mary pass! Tennessee wins!" The room cheered, even Elijah and Daphne looked happy. They, too, knew Tennessee was playing for the national championship that night. "It's a good omen for the marriage!" Blitz shouted.

"Lela and Stuart, national champions! A toast!" My crazy friend Brenda was feeling no pain but managed to pull off a toast with a Tennessee tongue twister.

Stuart whispered in my ear. "Another reason to think this is the best day of your life!" I turned, shaking my head.

"Wait... what about the best day of *your* life? You *despise* Tennessee football, teasing me about it all the time!"

"Today, I cheer." We locked arms and drank, gazing at each other for ten full seconds. Then Stuart's eyes became glassy with tears. I thought I'd found nirvana.

VISITATION DAY
CHAPTER 42

After a thirty-day job at a horrifying place called Hair One (suppliers of human hair for clients like Hair Club for Men), my "job" became endless days at the spa. Weekly facials, waxes, manicures, pedicures... the works. I felt as beautiful that spring as I'd ever felt, with a nice tan from walks on the beach. Also, Stuart booked a weekly couples' massage and I discovered the joy of hot rock treatments. At all times, I was as pampered as I was drunk.

By then, Stuart had been clean long enough to pass the court's drug test; he hadn't seen his son in almost a year. Serious as hell, he called to make an appointment at the lab. Since returning to Florida, Stuart had acted as his own lawyer in the custody battle, saying that paying the Rockville bankruptcy lawyer was enough to pay in attorney fees.

But he knew the laws; he knew his shit, proven in many "speeches" about family law. I thought he knew all there was to know, but never asked why he was so determined to screw with her. Stuart's plans were dastardly; he was hell-bent to destroy her.

Each phone call to Janey ended in a screaming match which upset him for days; they upset the hell out of me, too. I couldn't keep up with the blow-by-blow and ended up confused and anxious... and afraid of Stuart's anger afterward. He seemed to seethe with hate for her. Abnormal hate. Spooky hate.

When the lab called with the drug test results, he raced to Ft. Lauderdale for a copy and faxed it to Janey's lawyer. In the next night's phone call, she had no choice but to agree to a visit, scheduled for the upcoming Saturday.

He didn't tell her I would be there, too.

<<<<<<<>>>>>>

Jeremy, now six years old and failing first grade, looked like a feeble, stressed-out man in a child's body. His pale face showed fear and mistrust; the purple veins in his neck stood out far enough to see the beat of his heart. And his eyes, which used to be blue, Stuart said, darted left and right yet he wouldn't look either of us in the eye, especially Stuart. He seemed more comfortable with me, so I took advantage.

"What do you want to do today, Jeremy? Do you want a Happy Meal?" I asked.

"I don't like this. It's dangerous for me," he muttered. Yep, his mother had done a number on him. Poor kid.

Stuart was more hyper, more fidgety, than normal. I felt sorry for *him*, too, but kept my focus on Jeremy. "A Happy Meal is a great start to a day in the park, right?" I was driving, so Stuart tried to look at him in his backseat booster, but he only shot a quick glance at Stuart's face and turned to look out of the window. Stuart gave up and spoke for him. "To the closest McDonald's, Lela! There's one on the corner about two blocks down." I pulled into the parking lot.

"A playground!" It was the first normal-kid phrase he'd said.

"Can we go down that big slide together?" Stuart was reaching for anything to connect with the kid.

"You're too big. Mom says you're fat."

A chuckle. "Well, I'm not too big for the slide! Let's play!"

Jeremy nodded, almost imperceptibly.

We ate first, forcing Jeremy to wait for playground fun, a mistake on my part. About twelve other kids close to Jeremy's age raced around the play area, shrieking in joy. Parents sat at the tables lining the area, mostly women in tennis dresses and oversized sunglasses.

Jeremy ate little, never taking his eyes off the kids. "Please, Lela, can I go?" Poor kid wouldn't even ask his father. I nodded. We took the rest of his Happy Meal to the play area. He flung his shoes at me and climbed backward up the tube slide.

"Stuart, he's going the wrong way! He's not supposed to do that!" I saw a bigger kid heave himself down from the top, gliding down the tube toward Jeremy. "Go get him!" But Stuart stayed still, saying nothing, just jiggling his foot.

The inevitable collision happened halfway up, inside the tube. Suddenly Jeremy appeared, flying through the air with the larger boy's legs wrapped around his neck. A high-pitched scream erupted from small Jeremy and an eerie, low laugh from the big boy's throat. They landed in a heap on the sand bottom of the pit. Still, Stuart didn't move. Instinctively, I rushed to help Jeremy get up, but he was on his feet and running toward our table before I could take but a few steps.

He ran to Stuart, screaming. "You're a bad daddy! You let me fall! Just like Mommy said!" The other parent's heads snapped to look at the red-faced little boy who screamed at full volume and smacked at Stuart's legs. "You're dangerous b'cause you don't watch out for me! You are a bad daddy. Bad, bad, bad!" Exhausted, he sunk to the concrete and wailed. "Mommy! I want my Mommy!" He jerked his body in every direction, kicked his feet, and swatted the air as if surrounded by bees.

Stunned, Stuart looked at me. *What the hell do I do now? How do I comfort a kid with elbows aiming for my Adam's apple?* The sadness of the scenario had silenced me... and embarrassed me. The sixty seconds we waited for Jeremy to calm felt like a lifetime. Stuart said, "You handle it." I nodded, ready to take charge. But my heart went out to Stuart. *How sad this must be for him... to be totally rejected!*

I sat on the concrete and spoke in a whisper. "Let's put on your shoes, Jeremy, then we can leave, okay?" His bottom lip stuck out four inches, it seemed. Tears stained the concrete and flowed down his cheeks. With soothing sounds and mother-hen clucks, I put his Thomas the Train shoes on his little feet.

The tears didn't stop in the car. Stuart took the wheel, looking despondent. I sensed he didn't know what to do or say, so again, I took the lead. "Hey, kiddo, do you want to go to the park?"

Jeremy screamed, "NO!"

"Then what would you like to do? We can have a fun day! What about the drive-through zoo? You can see giraffes and zebras. Sometimes the animals come right up to the car!"

"Really?" *Great!* I had hit a nerve.

"To West Palm, Daddy Weinstein!"

Stuart spoke up. "And you can see our apartment... ride your bicycle. It's in the back, you know?"

"I saw you put it in. It almost didn't fit!" He laughed. *He laughed!* And I laughed, too, because he had mispronounced the phrase as "fidn't dit." I wondered if it was dyslexia, but either way, I found it sweet.

I shot a look at Stuart, who returned the smile and reached to pat my leg. He mouthed "Thank you," and I nodded in return. We would have a thirty-minute drive to the zoo. *Maybe, just maybe, I can get the kid talking.*

"So, you like Thomas the Train, like your shoes?"

"No, these shoes were just cheap at the used-clothes store. Mom says Daddy doesn't pay enough money to get fun shoes." *Great.* I saw Stuart's face drop.

"Sure I do," he piped up from the front.

"OH NO YOU DON'T!" Jeremy screamed. Tears welled in his eyes.

"Let's talk about something else, okay? What's your favorite animal? We may see it at the zoo!"

"I guess a rhinoceros," he said, but terribly mispronounced, as a six-year-old would say it.

Stuart found a way to get to him, maybe. "I call them rhinos because rhinoceros is so hard to say."

"Yeah," was Jeremy's simple statement. Again, he turned to look out of the window as we zoomed down the Turnpike.

"Me, I like *giraffes* the most," I said. "I wish I was that tall. I'd eat leaves from the tippy-top of the trees."

"They have spots. And you know what?"

"What?"

"Zebras have stripes! And I have a teensy-weensy zebra in my room!" At last, excitement from the kid who was so obviously troubled. His fear had abated, it seemed, as he continued to talk about which tiny animals he had in his room, providing their names and color scheme.

"You have a lot of stuffed animals then, huh?" Stuart was trying again.

But Jeremy wasn't having it. As he had done each time his father spoke, he gave a one-word answer in a sad voice and turned to look out of the window. *It's all on you, Lela. Help the kid. Help Stuart.*

I hadn't had a drink beyond the shot in my coffee that morning and asked Stuart to stop by the 7-Eleven for a tall boy. "Do you want a juice box, or a candy bar, Jeremy?" Stuart asked as he pulled into the store's lot.

"Mommy said not to take candy from strangers."

"But I'm not a stranger! I'm your Daddy!"

"No, you're not! Quit saying that!" I closed my eyes, hurting for Stuart.

I whispered to my new husband, "Sorry, baby, I know this must sting," It was an attempt to make him feel better, but his jaw clenched and his eyes stared straight ahead.

"You're the one going inside, so *you* ask him if he wants anything," Stuart snapped.

"Jeremy... how about a candy bar, or a juice box or something?"

"Apple juice." It was a statement, said with no inflection or emotion.

I looked at Stuart and shrugged. He rolled his eyes. "You want one?" I asked.

"Twenty of them."

"Seriously... tall-boy in a bag?"

"I'd better not. And you probably shouldn't either."

"But... um, can't I just..." I blew an exasperated breath. "None all day? Are you *kidding* me?"

Stuart stared. I didn't flinch. Then he sighed through the comment, "What the hell? Go ahead."

Inside, I bought a large apple juice and two beers in individual bags. Maybe Stuart would change his mind, or maybe I'd drink the second while driving through the zoo. I hopped back in the car to find Jeremy in tears. I didn't bother to ask what had happened. My heart went out to Stuart. *What a terrible day with a kid he's been fighting for!* Crazy Janey had poisoned him against Stuart in an unwinnable war. I sighed.

At the drive-through zoo, Jeremy's eyes beamed with amazement at the animals roaming free. First up were three rhinos, fairly close to the driving path. I let him unbuckle the seat belt and stand on the floorboard, but he refused to lower the window, or even to put his face too close to the glass.

Around the next bend, a giraffe approached the car and Stuart lowered his window. I braced for a melt-down, but he just opened it a crack. The animal stuck his nose in the space and suddenly a giant, rough-textured tongue skimmed Stuart's cheek.

Jeremy squealed, half delighted and half scared. But no tears, no accusations of his dad putting him in danger. We were free to stop and gawk at our whim but the kid was in a hurry for whatever reason, whining "We already *saw* zebras! Back *there!" Will this kid ever relax? Will he turn into a kid at some point?*

We stopped to let a line of ostriches pass the road. The ostrich at the end of the line, the largest one, suddenly veered and *bounded* directly at Jeremy's window, aiming a hard peck in the center and exactly where Jeremy's nose pressed against the glass. The guttural scream that came next was from the bottom of Jeremy's toes, followed by a gasp so restricted I thought he had already choked to death.

By then he'd rolled down the window several inches, and the ostrich continued pecking, squawking and sticking his beak through the opening. Jeremy screamed "NO! NO! NO!" and exploded to the opposite side of the van. Two heartbeats later, he scrambled over the seat and into the cargo area. His screamed echoed in the small space and my head pounded with the full gamut of emotions.

He was right to be scared of the ostrich... it had been an *attack*, meant to maim. Stuart rolled up the window, but the ostrich continued the assault. My scream trumped Jeremy's, "Get the hell out of here! Go!" I was scared, too, but realized we now had a very, very bad situation at hand.

I crawled over the seats to where Jeremy lay in a fetal position, his thumb in his mouth between sobs. He had shit his pants. I leaned close to his face and spoke softly, "It's okay, Jeremy. He's gone now."

As I reached to rub his back, Jeremy took a swing that hit home on my left eyebrow. He screamed, "Leave me the fuck alone!"

It took an hour to calm him down and talk him into going to our place to change clothes, which the paranoid Janey had provided in a bag along with all possible needs. "You'll like being at our house, Jeremy... it's on a lake with ducks!"

"No ducks. They have sick disease."

"Well, then you can see our dogs, Rock-Bob and Mur–"

"Dogs bite people and make them die. They bite their face off."

With no way to win the battle, I just sat with him in silence. Eventually, Stuart drove to the Publix parking lot, bought a newspaper, and we sat in the van for an hour. I saw Stuart's fake smile in the rearview mirror, a smile *meant* to be fake... with a touch of evil underneath. It scared me.

"Okay, Stuart. Go to Dunkin' Donuts first, then we're going home."

"But I'm not supposed to eat that! Mommy said no!"

I paused with my jaw purposely cocked. "You know what, Jeremy? I don't *care* what your mommy said. We're getting donuts and I'm washing your clothes. Got it?" I wasn't mad; I just stated facts, cool and calm. "You're meeting the dogs and the ducks and you'll like all of it. And you're going to ride your bike with your dad and not be afraid. Do you understand?"

Only then did Jeremy relax... as if he had wanted somebody to take charge all along.

When his clothes were in the dryer, he went with Stuart to get his bike from the back of the van. My sphincter relaxed for the first time that day. I found a six-pack of tall cans in the fridge – they must have been Ralph's. I popped one and refreshing fizz-drops washed my fingers. *Aaah!* I'd only had the two beers from the 7-Eleven and I'd been upset enough to drink a case by myself. Just in case Jeremy came in, I slipped the can in my leftover paper bag.

Two seconds later, Jeremy ran in the door, wailing. "Daddy put a rock in the road! He made me have a wreck and I'm bleeeeeeding!" *Okay now, this is getting ridiculous! He's a 24/7 problem!*

I sighed. *Okay Lela, play Mommy. It will be over in just a few hours.* Armed with a clean washcloth and a bandage, I sat him on the breakfast bar. "I'll fix you up, big guy. Good as new..."

"Is that beer?"

"Is *what* beer?"

"In the bag."

"No."

"Oh," said flatly, like a kid. Then, "OOOUCHH!" reacting to my gentle touch on the boo-boo. *When will this day end?*

The front door opened. Stuart. "Okay, Jeremy, let's go! Don't want to be late back to your mom's house."

<<<<<<<>>>>>>

While Stuart distracted him, I threw another beer in my purse and we gathered his still-wet clothes for the trip back. According to Jeremy, Stuart drove too fast, passed too many cars, and didn't keep his eyes on the road. It was worse than being judged by a driving instructor. But I felt sorry for the bundle of nerves within that skinny six-year-old body. He couldn't be real. *He can't trust anybody... he can't love anybody. How sad. What a fruitcake this Janey bitch must be.*

We pulled into their apartment complex, hoping to park a bit to the side so Janey wouldn't see me. Too late; she was waiting at the end of the sidewalk. I supposed she saw me duck into the floorboard... then saw me as I sat up straight, beer-bold. *Fuck her!* I refused to hide from the bitchy Brit and I wasn't afraid of her like Stuart was.

Janey smoked a cigarette and glared at Stuart as he helped Jeremy out of the van. The kid ran straight to his mom, landing full force against her upper body. They fell back in a pile. "Mommy! I had a good time! I want to go again!"

The look of amazement on Janey's pompous British face was priceless. "Did Daddy protect you from danger? Did he feed you yummy food? Did Daddy have a drinkie-poo?" Her eyes leveled with Stuart's.

Jeremy's exuberance showed that he might have a personality after all. "Chicken nuggets and donuts. With sprinkles! And we went to the zoo, but the bird poked me and Daddy made me get a bike wreck... and a hurt at McDonald's."

"You got hurt? What happened?"

"Daddy did it but Lela made it better."

"Who is Lela?" she asked, alarmed. She swiveled her head, hoping for a better look at me in the passenger seat.

"Lela is a nice lady. Daddy's friend."

"Stuart," she snapped. "There was to be no 'friend' today."

Stuart spoke loudly, calm and controlled. "Lela is my wife. She's the one that helped Jeremy relax in the end... after he quit spitting poison at me. The poison you've pushed down his throat!"

"What the hell are you talking about?"

"Look, Janey, I'm a nice guy. I love this boy, but you've badmouthed me for so long, told him I was a bad person or whatever... I am fighting that 100 percent of the time! And it makes it impossible to build a relationship with him! Janey, you did it and you did it on purpose!"

"Yes, I did." Such a clipped, bitchy tone. "Because I don't *want* you to have a relationship with Jeremy. And you're *not* a nice guy, as you say! So quit pretending. And tell me about Lela. If she's taking care of my son, I want to meet her."

"She's asleep in the car."

"Then wake her up! I deserve to know who my Jeremy has spent his day with!"

There was a pause, a long one. "No." Stuart's simple statement.

Jeremy spoke with the same mistrustful and careful voice he used at the beginning of the day. "Beer in paper bags. Bunches of them – BIG! Lela likes beer."

I heard it loud and clear and shrunk into the seat. *Oh, God. Did he notice everything? How would he know that was beer unless he'd seen his damn mother drink it out of a bag?*

Crazy Janey said nothing, looking at Stuart with a smirk. Seconds later, her chest heaved with a chuckle. "Oh, Stewie... you'll get your due. You'll never see this child again." Stuart didn't bat an eye, staring Janey down with eyes of steel. As Jeremy squirmed in his mother's lap like a toddler, he said, "Bye, Daddy!"

"See you soon, son."

Jeremy shook his finger at Stuart as a parent would, "But next time no birds and no beer!"

"And no Lela," Janey added.

As if the earth froze and all sounds disappeared, Stuart glared at Janey with steely, squinting eyes. A time warp. His knuckles whitened as he balled his fists and his jaw clenched square. *Oh, my God! He's going to kill her!* I touched the handle to open the door but stopped myself. *How can you stop him from murdering her? In front of the kid!*

Never breaking eye contact with Janey, Stuart nodded a half-dozen times with a satirical and exaggerated pucker of his lips, then ceremoniously placed put Ray-Bans on his face. "I'll have the child, Janey, or they'll be hell to pay."

The comment was so soft-spoken and mannerly, said with no inflection or emotion, like a robotic voice. The opposite of the frantic, fidgety way Stuart spoke on any other day.

He walked to the van in silence and he didn't speak on the way home, no matter how much I urged him to process his feelings. All he did was gnaw his fingertips; he wouldn't accept my apology or answer my many questions about what 'hell to pay' might mean.

Home. He got out of the van and hopped in the Lexus. I asked, "You're not coming in?"

"Nope. Going out."

"Where?"

"To a meeting."

"Good idea."

"Don't wait up."

"What? It's early!" I was instantly frantic. As his taillights disappeared around the corner, I wondered if I'd ever see him again.

TAMPAX BOX
CHAPTER 43

The following four-or-so months were a blur, to be honest. I stayed buzzed and have little recollection of the specifics. Unable to even "go with the flow" anymore, I followed Stuart's flow... anything to avoid making decisions or being responsible. Hell, just being "aware" was a stretch.

At some point, we moved to a rental house with a grapefruit tree in the backyard. I don't know what season it was during this blur period, but I never ran out of grapefruit-mixer inventory and I picked a gargantuan basketful each morning.

I bought a super-duper electric juicer for the kitchen counter and kept it in continual use. Vodka-grapefruit, light on the ice... my 24/7 friend. When a new study proved that too much grapefruit can make Bi-Polar meds less effective, my psychiatrist strongly suggested I cut it out completely. And when I refused, she fired me as a patient.

Soon, I ran out of psych meds and came to feel more and more crazy, then feelings of abandonment and helplessness sent me reeling. With Stuart's suggestion, I found a talk therapist... who fired me for coming to an appointment drunk. The new bartender at The Limelight cut me off three or four times. Most every morning, I woke with unexplained bruises and cuts. Days went by with no memory of what happened.

Things were getting bad. I knew it; I cried about it. But I couldn't change it.

I lived in a vacuum, no longer able to function in the world, but I'd insulated myself well from hitting a bottom. Stuart had been a financial enabler for a while and slowly took control of all aspects of our life as my abilities died; he did the cooking, the organizing, the shopping, the financial management... everything but the laundry.

Eventually, I couldn't accomplish the one job deemed mine. "It's a simple load of laundry, Lela! What's so hard?"

"I've gotta get the timing just right, babe, or start all over! You don't want wrinkled shirts, do you?"

I saw his eyes roll, bringing fear because I knew he'd caught me being... useless. Yep, useless was the word. My heart fell in the realization I'd sunk so low. In my last attempt to save face, I mumbled, "Laundry is an art, so quit giving me shit."

"You're full of bullshit!" I remember that phrase, and another that stung deep in what was left of my pride: Stuart told me, flat-out, "You're worthless." I knew it was an accurate assessment and ran to the bedroom for a long crying jag. But I blamed him, and the resentment boiled to anger over several drunken days.

Finally, it exploded, and I raged, attacking Stuart... my hands around his swollen neck.

I couldn't hold onto his neck when he thrashed around, and I remember thinking he might hit me hard enough to hurt. My thought was peaceful; *he'll kill me and I deserve it...* and the image of a funeral procession played in my mind as a calm and expected event. What a fucked-up thought, right?

Being considered worthless was the end, I thought. Clinging to a few raveling threads of self-respect, it didn't take much to blow me down; I was a helpless, insecure, drunken target... with an inflated ego and a false sense of power.

The problem, I decided, was not having a job. And I needed a challenging job, not a mindless one... something to put my mind back in gear. A different type of writing, perhaps.

And I found the perfect job, I thought.

Milford Furnishings paid well. They manufactured high-end, solid wood, assemble-it-yourself furniture – a new concept at the time. They sold the furniture online only, a daring new approach in 1999. And to set themselves apart from the cheap, imported stuff, a big selling point was the quality of assembly instructions – written by a trained, English-speaking writer. I would be the writer of those instructions.

But first I had to figure out how to assemble the furniture.

The first day, while assembling the bookcase I was to write about, I hurt myself twice, deep gouges on my wrists with the screwdriver. Later, two huge scrapes on my knuckles using the provided Allen wrenches.

I kept going, joking about it with my new coworkers... but none responded with laughter. In fact, they didn't seem to like me much at all and I found that suspicious. I'd always been a well-liked person... the life of the party kind of girl. *So why didn't they like me?*

In the assembly area, I screwed up often. In fact, more often than not. Each time I got confused or frustrated, I stormed back to my office to throw back a mini bottle of vodka. By then, I was buying those bottles two cases at a time at a liquor store where the employees knew me by name. I thought the familiarity was the ultimate in customer service.

At work, I kept the bottles in a file drawer of my desk, stacked two-high in a value-size box of Tampax. I noticed the bottles disappeared quickly, but I didn't think the vodka had caused the struggle with assembly. I hadn't fucked up *completely*, only a little bit. Only once an hour or so.

After four days, I thought I understood why the other writers didn't like me; I couldn't wrap my mind around the core concept of Milford assembly. I just couldn't figure it out. *I guess they don't want to be friends with the resident fuck-up.*

I improved, but mostly I was drunk. Nobody knew; my secret was safe for the time being.

Then it was time for my thirty-day review. When I sat before my manager, I beamed with confidence, expecting a glowing recommendation and the highest level of a promised raise. *After all, that's just how things go for Lela Fox... always a standout, always a favorite.* Turns out, the review was admonishment, a "talking-to," a "do-better-or-else" warning. The sonofabitch said I was too slow, with the tools *and* the writing.

I didn't handle the criticism well during that self-focused period of my life, as you might imagine, and I jumped down his throat in defending myself. I felt like I'd been slapped.

He smirked through my string of complaints about how wrong he was, saying nothing. At last, I realized: *You can't change his mind, Lela... try another tactic.* With a sigh, I swallowed hard and pretended he may be right... which led to an explanation and suggestion. "Sir, maybe I have a deficit in spatial relations. I've heard that some people just do, right? But there's an easy solution! Why not move me to another department? Where my talents can be better exploited."

"Exploited? *Excuse me?*"

I began babbling immediately, trying to fix what I'd said. "No! I mean *exercised!* Where my talents can better help Milford Furnishings!"

"And to what department could you be of better help to the company, Lela?" I ignored his smartass tone, believing my idea was a win-win for all. *Fuck him, anyway.*

"I'm a trained copywriter, sir, with years of experience. So just move me to the copy department!" I knew that Milford copywriters wrote descriptions for the catalog itself (which were cutesy stories, not just specifications). I sat forward with confidence; sure I'd proposed genius.

But the sonofabitch laughed at me, threw his head back and laughed. What I didn't know: copywriters earned three times my pay grade. It would have been a three-step-up promotion. I received the balance of the lecture and went back to work with my head down. He'd give me another week to "straighten things out," he said.

I'd never been fired when I was truly trying, and I was in a panic. That "worthless" word is starting to be the truth! I can't let that happen!

The second time he called me to his office, I left with my tail between my legs after pleading for a two-week probation period. The rest of the day, I cried and hit the vodka harder than usual. Another injury ensued, and I got blood on my nice white pants. Thinking the injury may be a "disability" and a way to save my job, I rushed to the manager's office with blood still flowing, to show him the type of injuries that were slowing me down. I showed the scars of former injuries, too.

He sent me to the company nurse and when I returned to the assembly room, he fired me. In front of my coworkers.

The sonofabitch watched as I emptied my desk; I guess to make sure I didn't steal company secrets or the damn stapler. I gloated when transferring the Tampax box to the packing box, hoping to embarrass him. But the slick blue box slipped from my hand.

A few Tampax rolled out, but the vodka bottles clanged against the tile floor and one broke, creating an odorous puddle around his shoes. I refused to be embarrassed but as I gathered the bottles, I glanced up at him from a stooped position.

"Well, that explains a lot," he said.

I couldn't think of a thing to say, so I chose the worst-possible comment. I crawled to an errant bottle and thrust it upwards to him. "Want one?"

My theory: I joked about the bottle of booze rolling on the floor because it was the opposite of a joke. In reality, I wasn't amused at all; I was disgusted, disgusted with myself.

Drinking at work was one thing, but being *prepared* for it was appalling. Having an inventory of booze made it pitiful and desperate... not something an innocent person like me would do.

I snapped into protective mode and distanced myself from the Shame by denying anything shameful had occurred.

Thoughts like, "I would have quit that dumb job soon, anyway," and, "That motherfucker set me up," combined with the insistence I'd been treated unfairly from the start. All this to justify my righteousness.

As ridiculous as it sounds, the denial served me well; it kept me thinking I could hold down a job and do the right thing if given the right circumstances.

The test of that theory came soon.

STEP-IN STEPMOTHER

CHAPTER 44

Determined to find another job after the disaster at Milford Furnishings, I spent hours flipping through screens on Monster.com and refreshing my résumé.

On a Tuesday afternoon, after a week of unemployment and failed searches, Stuart called in a panic. "Janey had a wreck and got a DUI. I've got temporary custody of Jeremy. Full-time! Can you handle it?"

I panicked. *Handle it? Hell, no!* "Me? But I'm the one who drinks big beer, right? She'll throw a fit, Stuart!"

"She has no choice. Child Protective Services called me." Shock brought my silence. He continued, "I can't get away from the shop right now. You need to go get him."

"Me? Oh shit, Stuart. I don't know! How? Where? I don't know what's going on!" Instantly overwhelmed and frantic, I denied the truth of what was happening.

"The social worker is at Janey's house, waiting for *me*. I'll call and tell her you're coming instead."

"Stuart! Wait! I can't! I don't know how! I'm afraid of her! She hates me!" I probably had a few more exclamations I don't remember because my fear had shot like a missile, aimed for the stratosphere.

"Put on your big-girl panties, Lela, and go. Take a big suitcase for his stuff.

And in the meantime, I'll get school info. I want him in school tomorrow. I'll do anything and everything to impress that social worker. Baby, we may get full-time custody from this!"

Oh, God. To say I had a sinking feeling is an understatement. Barely functional, it was doubtful that I could take care of myself much longer, and I knew I wasn't able to add the responsibility of a six-year-old.

With wide eyes and shaking hands, I mixed an extra-tall drink, got dressed, and drove to Fort Lauderdale for a showdown.

On the way down the Turnpike, I dropped a lit cigarette in the van's floorboard and had to pull over to get it. The "trauma" of the burn hole in the carpet put me over the edge; I parked in the easement and sobbed for twenty minutes. Soon, the burn hole would be the very least of my problems.

<<<<<<<<>>>>>>>

Janey's leg was in a cast to the mid-thigh, propped on the coffee table with a pillow underneath. Her pale complexion emphasized the contrast with a purple/yellow and black eye, plus random bloody scratches. She looked like she'd been in a bar fight and her behavior convinced me she was still fighting it.

"Ellen," she screamed, addressing the social worker, "This bitch is a drunk! She's an unfit supervisor of my child! Stupid enough to marry the ex-father ex-husband sonofabitch, who is nothing but a worm... a greasy worm and unfit father, a lover of prostitutes, a drug addict, a Godless reprobate!" Blah, blah, blah.

I smiled at Jeremy and, surprisingly, he smiled back. "Come on, let's get out of here." He ran to me, hugging my leg. He insisted he was already packed, but I dragged him to his bedroom as he clung to my leg. I randomly grabbed clothes and toys, then put his "already packed" Ninja Turtles suitcase inside Stuart's oversized one.

I hobbled back to the living room as Crazy Janey continued to scream, now even louder. The poor kid's mother didn't even kiss him goodbye, too busy screaming about how bad of a life he'd have while living with Stuart and me.

Securing Jeremy in the car seat, I sat on the floorboard of the van and tried to calm him. Within five minutes, he'd told me the whole DUI story in detail. He'd been in the car at the time of the wreck. The car "went around in circles" and came to rest "in a field." Then a policeman pulled behind them but, evidently, his mom didn't see the cop. Jeremy said she was crying and throwing liquor bottles from the window. "Four of them," he said.

When the cop came to the driver's side, Jeremy crawled on his mother's lap to tell him another bottle was under the backseat.

They arrested Janey, and a cop accompanied her on the ambulance ride. Jeremy had spent the night with "some mean lady who smelled bad," and talked to his grandmother on the phone for what he said was two hours. The social worker retrieved him in the morning, calling Stuart as soon as Janey was home from the hospital.

The poor kid was traumatized, but he was opening up to me. My heart hurt for him, and I did what any mother would do: I reached to hug him. He screamed anew, saying I was trying to choke him. *What have I gotten myself into, dammit?*

By the time we arrived in West Palm Beach, Jeremy had calmed down so we drove to Stuart's shop. My husband beamed with pride when he paraded Jeremy through the menagerie of mechanics for introductions, but Jeremy showed his fear with a combination of whines and wails. His lips pale and quivering, tears ran down his cheeks and bounced off the stuffed zebra he clutched to his chest. Named "Zeeber" by Jeremy, the animal was well-worn, mostly gray, and missing one pink-lined ear.

Back in the office and back to business with me, Stuart spouted details about Jeremy's assigned school. "Take him there now. The principal is expecting you." The buzz of fear building between my ears hit a crescendo. Stuart seemed to see my breakdown coming. "No, no, Lela. Not now. Keep it calm and positive. That's your job."

"But–"

"But nothing!" His tone was serious and matter-of-fact. "Don't let me down, Lela. We're now parents, responsible, calm parents. Do you understand?" With this lecture, the buzz in my head gained volume again, but I'd been admonished, like a child with his hand slapped, and I willed myself to find a responsible outlook. *Breathe, Lela. In through your nose, out through your mouth. Again. And again. Don't let him see you sweat.*

On the way to Wellington Elementary School, I chirped, "It's a good school, Jeremy. They have the best teachers and the kids have the most fun there.

You'll like it."

"No! I hate school! I hate being here! I need to go to my room." He enunciated perfectly, speaking in staccato, and I sensed "going to his room" was what calmed him at home. Poor kid.

The school was just around the corner from our house, a big one with the most expansive playground I'd seen at a primary level. He looked at his lap, at the floorboard, anywhere but at the school or at me. "We're going in now... to meet the principal and find your room for tomorrow, okay?"

No comment. I literally dragged him by the arm along a narrow sidewalk as he wailed and shouted that I'd broken his shoulder. I hated to be so forceful but the one time I let go of his arm, he dashed back to the parking lot and tried to hide in a copse of pine trees. So I dragged him again. And I suppose he got the next idea from a TV show; between shrill screams, he shouted "She's a kidnapper! Somebody help me!"

Tears and wails continued into the office waiting area and throughout the interview with the uppity principal, Mr. Stern... aptly named. The staff didn't react to his screaming or express concern for Jeremy's special needs, neither the obvious trauma nor lifelong ADHD diagnosis.

Mr. Stern and the rock-faced nurse and secretary showed no empathy and offered no special accommodations for Jeremy; their attitude appalled me, knowing softer-hearted Tennessee souls would have bent over backward for a first-grader in such obvious distress.

Not going to happen at Wellington Elementary, not today or any day. All business.

He still hadn't settled down when we returned to the van to leave, pissed he had to start school the next day. "I *hate* this school! I *hate* that man! I *hate* everything! Just take me *hoooome! Pleeeeeease!*"

He didn't mean home to "our house," but to Janey's. I hated to explain the adult situation to an upset child, but we hadn't discussed the *why* of the change and I felt compelled to calm him. "Jeremy, hon, your home will be with us for a while," I spoke slowly, "Because your mom can't take care of you with a broken leg, right? She can't even drive you to school or fix your dinner."

"No!" More screams. Then his tears flowed freely, and he spoke with trembling lips. "Mommy can't take care of me when she has whiskey. And she told me she has to have it all the time! So I can't be with Mommy ever, ever again!" He wailed, and it broke my heart to know the kid actually knew the truth. The ugly, horrible truth.

Again, I sat in the floorboard for a one-on-one, searching for words that may calm him. The other half of the problem was my own anxiety. I needed a drink; I needed a miracle.

As a last resort, I closed my eyes and called on the God who once talked to me on the beach. No answer, no harp music, no peace. The absence of relief made my need for it worse, and I cried, which upset Jeremy more.

I dried my tears, chiding myself. "Here's an idea: what about a Happy Meal?" Food was all I could think of when my hugs and purrs of assurance didn't help. "How about a McNugget eating contest? Who can eat the most and who can eat the fastest?"

My eyebrows rose, suggesting a silly but serious challenge. Finally, a smile spread on his face. "I can beat you," he sang in a teasing tone, and another silly face from me brought a giggle. A giggle! *Thank you, God or whoever you are, please keep him laughing because I can't handle the pain that lives inside this child.*

<<<<<<<<>>>>>>>

He ate four nuggets, "winning" three of the races. But still turbulent in mood, he turned nasty again and threw a fit because I had "let him win." I sighed. *This sucks, but at least he quit calling me a kidnapper.*

We dashed to Target for school supplies and sheets, and a thousand other things we suddenly needed with a kid, but when the cashier ran my credit card, it was declined.

Shock. Confusion. When I asked her to run it through again, it was again declined.

You haven't used that card in a long time, Lela. How could it be declined? It's not over the limit... the balance is going down, no matter how slowly. And it's not past due... I've seen Stuart writing checks to Visa, and I put the last payment in the mailbox myself.

Saving my emotional breakdown for later, I pushed the shopping cart aside and drove to Stuart's shop. As expected, he had a stack of hundred-dollar-bills in his wallet. Jeremy and I dashed back to Target, to Subway for a take-home dinner, then swung into the driveway just as Stuart pulled beside me.

A black woman exited the passenger side of Stuart's Lexus, struggling with a heavy black suitcase.

A YONA OF MY OWN
CHAPTER 45

Who is this woman? What's up with the suitcase? Is she another of Stuart's NA friends, planning to move in like Ralph did? What the hell?

Jeremy stared at the jet-black woman with his jaw slack and his eyes wide in surprise. Stuart chuckled through the explanation, an introduction. "Jeremy, meet Yona, your new nanny. She'll live in the bedroom next to yours and make sure you have everything you need." Jeremy didn't respond, maintaining the surprised look.

"Nanny?" I said. "A live-in nanny?" Shocked, I stood frozen, then leaned against the van for support as my knees weakened. The Target bag I held met the driveway with a *plop.*

The twenty-something woman, black as a midnight sky, first nodded at me, then her mouth stretched to a cheeky, familiar smile. Her exposed gums, so pink and shiny, and her glowing white teeth both looked painted in contrast to the dark of her skin.

A live-in nanny? What the fuck? Wide-eyed, I stared at Stuart with an open mouth, my face a question mark. Then I spoke to the smiling Yona, minding my manners. "Uh, hi... uh, Yona," I said. "I'm not sure what–"

Stuart interrupted, answering the question I hadn't yet asked. "Of *course* we need a nanny, Lela! We have a *kid,* and a kid needs a *nanny.* Yona comes with excellent recommendations and was available immediately. She's perfect!"

"I have four years' experience, Mizz Lela, and six-year-olds are my favorite.

Jeremy will be happy because I'll make *sure* he is."

I relaxed in small increments, finally accepting the situation. She winked at me, then shifted her focus to Jeremy, kneeling to be equal in height with the child. Yona opened her arms; it took only a heartbeat for Jeremy to run to her.

The nervous, non-trusting, all-negative kid who arrived three minutes ago burst into a happy, transformed child and fell into Yona's arms as if she was a long-lost friend. She laughed and whispered something in his ear, prompting a cackle from Jeremy. Then, through her own chuckle, Yona said, "Our secret," teasing him.

Jeremy reacted to her sing-song voice, capping the instant bond with a "loco handshake," a term they knew but we didn't.

Though she was flat-chested like a preteen girl, her body was strong, sturdy, and in perfect proportion. She carried herself with pride and confidence as she stood to full height, stepping forward to shake my hand. Yona's pink-brown palm pressed against mine and her left hand covered the top of my right. Five strong shakes. All with a genuine smile... deep-brown eyes, glowing with kindness... it seemed impossible to *not* like Yona and her humble attitude.

Her face was flawless... not a pore in sight and as velvety as a baby's skin. She shifted her weight on well-worn huarache sandals and smoothed the wrinkles from a pair of bright madras shorts and a bright turquoise cotton tank.

At last, I found my voice. "Well, Yona, welcome. It's true I could use some help with Jeremy. I'm... uh, not used to having a little kid. Not for a long time."

"I will make the house run smoothly so you can relax, Mizz Lela. I like a spotless home, and for you, I cook all types of food: American, Cuban, Italian, and of course, Jamaican. Just not French cooking." A giggle, from deep within her belly, amused me. She was flat-out cute.

Her words continued; she was on a roll, it seemed, enjoying herself while sharing her capabilities. "And I know the best fishermen on the coast... we'll have the best seafood in Palm Beach County. I do the shopping, too, but all with your direction, of course."

I was speechless... silent, still wide-eyed with my mouth agape. *A live-in nanny is a live-in cook? And housekeeper? Wow!* Yona continued, "We will have fun, the two of us, and the five of us. And no worries... I have a teaching background, perfect for first-grade homework. I can do laundry with both eyes closed." Again, that cute little-girl giggle.

But the whole thing confused me; I felt like I'd been railroaded. Furrowing my brow, I asked, "If you do everything, then what do *I* do?"

"No worries!" She tinkled like a wind chime. "I will make life easy for you and Mr. Stuart, and make Jeremy's world as happy as I know. Now, let me help you with these bags." Still stunned, I watched her open the van's door and gather the large bags from Target. With what must have been her third hand, she took Jeremy's and said, "Show me your room, my friend!"

Jeremy hadn't seen his room yet... hadn't seen this house at all, but I unlocked the front door and let them go inside alone. "Jeremy's is second on the left. With the bunk beds, Yona. Yours will be the first on the left." I closed the door and collapsed onto the patio chair under the front-porch canopy. Stuart took the second chair, fidgeting as usual.

In a daze, I lit a cigarette and waited for Stuart to speak. Finally, he began. "We can't do this alone, Lela. You know that. And a nanny raised me, you know. Her name was Tonya... more of an influence than my mother. Yona seems wonderful and, look, Jeremy already likes her."

"But..." I couldn't finish the sentence, or the question, or whatever it was. Stuart found the Subway bag and put his hand on the small of my back. "Come on in. Let's eat."

Before I could understand what was happening, she'd washed and dried the new sheets and made Jeremy's bed. She scooped up the mess from our take-home dinner and straightened the kitchen. She worked like a machine set on full speed. And she whistled as she worked.

Stuart tried to educate me on how to "use" a nanny and a maid, what to say, what she would and wouldn't do. "The only problem is she doesn't have her license yet, so tomorrow, take her to the DMV. Then she'll take Jeremy to school, go to the grocery store, do all the errands. I'll buy her an old car."

"But..." I still couldn't finish the sentence.

"Here, baby, let me fix you a drink." The juicer made its lovely sound, and I decided I didn't have to understand, just... sit back and be. *I have a live-in maid, by God. Life is good!*

Yona sat on the sofa with me to confirm what Stuart had said. "My job is to keep the family happy, Mizz Lela, not just Jeremy. All you have to do is tell me what you want." She was well-spoken and the long phrase highlighted her melodic, sing-song accent.

"But will you be my friend, Yona? That's what I really need."

She smiled, put her fingers to her lips as if embarrassed. "Yes, I will be your friend, Mizz Lela. I will be whatever you want me to be."

<<<<<<<>>>>>>

After dark, with Jeremy finally asleep and every stitch of clothing washed, dried, and pressed, Yona retired to her bedroom. The woman amazed me, moving at the speed of a bullet and finding the needed "tools" for her work as if she'd been the one to arrange the house.

Jeremy followed her everywhere as Yona told him silly jokes and sang kid songs. I remember that specifically because I didn't get especially drunk that night, maybe wanting to protect my reputation in front of Yona.

Stuart went to the backyard pool for a dip just as I remembered to check my Visa statements to see why the card was declined. I found the folder in the cabinet I'd always used, and when Stuart took over the bills, he'd kept the system going.

Okay... no charges last month... or the month before... or the month before that. Then I saw the problem: a charge to Delta airlines for $1,860. Airline tickets for the wedding guests. My mind screamed: *He was supposed to put that on HIS card! He never told me anything about it! That SONOFABITCH!*

I flew outside to confront Stuart, who said the worst possible thing when speaking to an upset woman: "You're overreacting." Steam came from my ears I was so mad. At least he didn't laugh at my anger as he sometimes did. In the end, all I could do was take his assurance that he'd pay $1,000 next month and hold back some expenses in hopes to pay more toward the balance. "But with Jeremy here now... expenses will be higher. And don't forget Yona's pay. Nannies aren't cheap."

So frustrated and defeated, all I could do was cry. I put myself to bed, imaging a monster under Stuart's purple pool float, sending him flying. And I hoped he would land in Hell.

SALARY DESIRED
CHAPTER 46

Yona failed her driver's test twice, each time having to wait a week before the next trial. That put me in a bind because I couldn't begin a new job until she had a license and a car. I was manic as hell in those two weeks, and with nothing to do because I had a fucking maid. So I shopped, and I drank while writing cover letters and crafting resumes for potential employers.

Each day at 3:10, Yona and I drove to the elementary school; she went inside to retrieve Jeremy. Though the kid adored Yona and worked hard to please her, his ADHD and/or mood disorder, whatever it was, created a question about how he would act on any given day. It was a dice roll; sometimes Jeremy was calm and child-like for multiple days in a row. My nerves settled. Yona's and Stuart's did, too. Then, just as we all relaxed, he'd have two days of terrorizing behavior where he'd scream and fight every attempt to communicate with him.

The drama was exhausting.

That second Tuesday started as a good day; Jeremy proudly showed Yona his worksheets and coloring pages from the school day, prancing around the house like a normal, happy child. He even kissed me on the cheek. Again, I dared to think being a stepmother might be not so bad. I smiled watching Yona take charge of the afternoon snack and set him up at an impromptu desk for a sheet of math homework.

But the happy state of affairs didn't last long that day. His grilled cheese sandwich had too much brown on it, he deemed, and he threw a down-in-the-floor, kick-your-feet, end-of-the-world, two-year-old fit. Yona walked away (her solution: ignore him), but Jeremy chased her and bit her on the ankle so hard she bled.

Yona and I talked, but she seemed unfazed by his violent behavior. Her only concern, she said, was about driving Jeremy for the first time with her new license and in the "new" car Stuart bought for her. I purred assurances. "You'll be fine, Yona," I said, "And the timing is perfect, you know..."

"Right – your job interview."

"Tomorrow afternoon."

"I hope you get the job, Mizz Lela. I know you want to do good work." Furrowing my brow, I wondered how in the hell she would know what I wanted, or even if it was true. The truth: I'd been a basket case and didn't remember sharing my feelings with her, only repeating "You're my best friend ever in the whole world, Yona" over and over. Drunk love can be a beautiful thing.

The job possibility excited me. Smyth Software, in need of a technical writer. I had no technical writing experience, per se, but the ad explained the job was to "translate technical information into benefit-oriented instruction." I guessed that meant changing complicated stuff to "how-to" and "how wonderful" language. Right up my alley.

<<<<<<<>>>>>>

The building was a modern, five-story, glass-walled number, growing from a sizzling blacktop parking lot. I parked on the far right of the entrance, next to a bench with a closeup view of the railroad tracks. *Isn't that odd? A bench facing the railroad tracks?* As I exited the van, a train blew by. High-speed with no horn, just a rumble I could feel beneath my feet.

The contemporary, five-story lobby featured an oversized reception desk and three women who greeted me enthusiastically. One of them pressed a button and within a minute, a curly-headed man came to escort me into a door marked "Human Resources."

Though I had sent my résumé ahead of time and had another with me, "Curly" (I'd forgotten his name immediately after the introduction) asked me to complete a printed application.

On the top line, next to my name, the box label said: "Salary Desired." The subject of pay wasn't discussed in the phone interview, but I didn't want to leave a blank box, so I wrote "$500,000," a joke, and probably more than the CEO would have made at the time. Curly took the paper, looking at it quizzically. "Uh... salary desired?" His tone was scolding and his expression serious.

I grinned. "The box said *desired*, not *expected*." Curly didn't return the smile, looking at me with an expression of disdain. I explained, "It's a joke, sir."

Without changing his serious expression, he rolled his eyes and said, "Clever."

"Who's clever?" I surmised the voice belonged to my boss-to-be Dale, head of the tech-writing department. Standing at the doorway, Curly showed Dale the application, pointing to my entry in the Salary Desired box. Dale's eyebrows raised as he threw his head back to laugh. "Yes, very clever."

Good. He gets it. I relaxed, adding, "Of *course* that's my desire. Isn't it yours?" Dale repeated a laugh, then silenced it as if a steel curtain had dropped in front of his face.

"We will discuss salary at a later time." Serious as hell.

BOOM. He shut you down, Lela. And he's right... it's not the best day for clever jokes. I checked out the new boss with a sinking feeling about how I'd fit in. White socks showed under his too-short khakis, and with his shirt buttoned to the Adam's apple, Dale looked like the nerdiest nerd from my high school days.

"Right! Salary discussions later... first, you need to know why I'm worth that much!" I stared at two blank faces. *Oh, my God! How can they not understand that's a joke! You better cover your ass... or decide not to work for such dumbasses.* "Sorry, you two... I make jokes when I'm nervous." Still, no response.

Dale was younger than Curly, probably in his late thirties, about my age, pudgy in the middle but sturdy, strong... and well over six feet tall. Though nerdy, he put me at ease quickly, and when Curly closed the door, Dale began a soliloquy about Smyth Software and how I would fit into the overall framework.

Next came an intense drilling into my psyche, the most vigorous interview of my life. I sweat through questions that forced me to explain the gaps in my employment history and create lies on the spot. By the end, my heart beat like a bongo drum and I felt unqualified for any job forevermore, unworthy of consideration.

"Now for the practical test." Dale placed a stapler in the center of the desk. "Write step-by-step, A-to-Z instructions on how to use this stapler, for someone who's never seen a stapler." Shocked, I asked a few questions, but he offered no further info. I was on my own.

"You have fifteen minutes," he said. The door closed softly as he left the room.

I wrote furiously, three pages. It was a challenge; sweat beaded on my brow as time wound down. Dale returned in less than fifteen minutes and asked me to stop writing immediately. His face was unflinching as he scanned what I had written.

His bottom lip stuck out, and he nodded. Minutes passed. Finally, he spoke. "Nice, Lela. The best yet."

"It's a lot harder than a person would think."

His deep sigh, with an extra-long exhale, left me perplexed. He drew the word out for three syllables, "Welllll..." He cracked his knuckles and said, "The job is yours. When can you start?"

My eyes popped wide, and I squealed. "Thank you, thank you! You won't be sorry! I'll be your best employee!" I babbled until I saw Dale's pen impatiently tapping on his yellow notepad. "Um, oh! I can start immediately."

Dale enunciated carefully. "Hourly pay or a salary?"

"Oh. You mean... a choice? That's how I should've answered that question?"

"Right."

I reddened. A bad joke gone wrong in two ways! "Then... a salary I guess."

"And what amount of salary do you desire?"

"My answer was for a laugh! I wasn't asking for that mu–"

"Then give me a figure. What salary do you desire?" This wasn't the beginning of negotiations; it was harsh, a snappy and snippy request meant to put me in my place.

"But aren't *you* supposed to make an offer first?" Dale didn't answer, just impatiently tapped his pen on the notepad again. *Is my answer a test? This is too weird.* "So I go first? *I* start the bargaining?"

"Yes."

I smiled, ready for more joking about the money; I knew of no other way to deal with that touchy subject. "Then, I'll go down from my original 'desired salary.' How about $100,000 a year?" I didn't know how high a technical writer's salary would go, but this was almost as ridiculous as the original $500,000.

Dale's face was like stone, emotionless. Then he spoke matter-of-factly, looking at me so intensely I felt his eyes burning my skin... searing me like an attack. "The position pays an annual salary of $30,000. Do you still want the job?" His eyes never left mine.

I huffed, "If there's a set salary, then why are you messing with me?" *The sonofabitch is trying to trick you, Lela... or trip you up somehow. Stay calm and cool. Just accept and let it be.* His glare heightened, becoming a look full of hate and disdain. Ignoring the buzz of tension that built between my ears, I spoke softly. "I accept the position."

Dale stood, scoffed. "I would have offered $50,000 if you hadn't been such a smartass."

"But I wasn't being a smartass! It was a joke!" The final syllables of my comment were shouted at Dale's back. He stomped out of the room and slammed the door. I didn't even know if I had the job for sure or if he'd blown me off.

I found my way out of the building, despondent. With my head down, I counted the seconds it took to get to my vehicle, wondering if Dale or Curly would come to stop me. Tears rolled from the corners of my eyes; I felt like someone had punched me in the gut.

Once in the van, my focus changed to getting home ASAP; I needed the lift of a strong drink. I zig-zagged through traffic and squealed into the driveway. When I slammed through the front door, Yona asked in her too-damn-happy tone, "Mizz Lela! Did you get the job?"

I didn't bother to answer, stomping straight to the juicer. *Drinks desired: 500,00 of them.*

STARTING TOMORROW
CHAPTER 47

On the following Monday, my first day of work at Smyth Software, I joined forty new employees for a two-week training class. We learned the ins and outs of the company's very-capable software, trademarked SIMMY. Online sales were new and the computer program was a new approach to sales and inventory management. The owner's pictures splashed the covers of *TIME*, *Fortune*, and dozens of technical sales journals. SIMMY was hot.

Each trainee had a computer, and each station featured a copy of the existing User Manual, the very manual I would help write and revise. I flipped through, estimating the pages at maybe 650. I knew it was a lot to learn and organize, but I was damn-determined and up for the challenge.

Two days into it, I felt confident I'd made the right job choice; the "product" was solid and the staff members were sharp and motivated. Bi-Polar mania put me front-and-center in the class, pegged as a leader.

At work, I was rocking and rolling, able to jump tall buildings in a single bound.

At home, things were happening too fast, passing me by as I lived in a grapefruit-and-vodka stupor. In my mania, I'd forgotten about the upcoming court battle until the morning of Stuart's court date.

The process had started the first day Stuart got Jeremy from his mom. He hired a lawyer within the hour and demanded a drug test from Crazy Janey, a hair test, the next day. The test confirmed recent and continued use of cocaine and, of course, a shitload of alcohol in her system. Stuart had his lawyer file an emergency hearing for sole custody.

The court date was a Friday; Yona went with him. I got the quick version of the tale on a break in training but Stuart was full of details and giddiness when I got home. Jeremy didn't know how his life had just changed, so we talked while Yona and the boy played in the backyard.

Stuart said Janey had come to court still on crutches, full of drama and tears, and appealed to the judge with more accusations against Stuart... the same "he hangs out with prostitutes and drug dealers" bullshit. This time, she brought no doctored pictures or witnesses, just a pissy and desperate attitude. "Honestly, I think she was high," Stuart shared.

"But with the drug tests, where I passed with flying colors and she failed with multiple drugs in her system, the judge had no choice." Stuart said the judge seemed focused on the fact that Jeremy was in the car when she was drinking... "so that's something we can never do, Lela. No matter what! Another reason we need Yona so bad."

Stuart was talking nonstop, too excited to excuse me for a trip to the kitchen, so I got up to mix another drink, and he followed, still talking. "And you told me how awful Janey acted when you picked up Jeremy the first day, but the damn social worker was in court, too... the one who coordinated with us to get him, right?" I nodded. "I couldn't have written a better script... she detailed Janey's crazy behavior, quoted her on some things, including the fuck you's and fuck everything's. The judge didn't like that at all!" Stuart rubbed his hands together and shot an evil grin to the ceiling. "I *got* her, Lela! I got the bitch!"

His comment sent my stomach for a flip. *He doesn't want Jeremy; he just wants to screw Janey. Tell me it isn't true! What kind of shitty father does that?*

But Stuart hadn't stopped talking, summing the evidence he provided: enrollment in a five-star school beginning immediately (he took full credit for that, I noticed), six months of pay stubs to prove a higher income... and his lawyer's savvy to make Janey admit she was a phone psychic. Stuart said he'd seen the judge roll his eyes about that. "Bottom line," he said, "The judge was on her ass and I walked away the winner."

The gavel fell, and I became the full-time stepmother of a troubled, out-of-control first-grader. I didn't want to have Jeremy in our care, to be honest, but my upbringing told me to keep my mouth shut, support the wishes of my husband, and put Jeremy's needs first. So that's what I did.

That night, as with all previous nights, the problems began with the five-minute warning before Jeremy's bedtime. That's when Stuart escaped... supposedly to get cigarettes.

"Please don't leave right now, Stuart. You're leaving me with the drama... you should have to share."

"What good would that do? Besides, it's not your drama, it's Yona's. Go play on the computer with a nice drink. I'll be back soon."

My tone was matter-of-fact. I guess I'd realized that begging didn't work with Stuart anymore. "*You* are a sonofabitch. I hate it when you leave me to play the bad guy."

"It's not *you*... Yona is the bad guy. Quit your bitching." And in the snap of a finger, he was gone.

I couldn't just "let Yona handle it" without supporting her. I was no good at having a nanny, I guess. And that night was worse than the others, with Jeremy in the floor punching my shins with his bony fists. "I hate you!" he screamed, spouting obscenities. The one I remember the clearest: "I hope you die, you fucking bitch!"

Jeremy was so angry that saliva spewed on my feet as he punched. I ran from him; he chased me. Yona followed, trying to grab his arms from behind... the only way to calm him in these violent fits. But Jeremy continued to scream and punch and slap. Yona got the worst of it, a full black eye and dozens of scratches on her face and arms.

Finally, the physical struggle subsided just enough for Yona to push the wild child into his room and wedge a chair under the doorknob. Jeremy beat on the door, screaming "Fuck you" and "Go fuck yourself" repeatedly. The sadness of it all threatened to sober me up, so I mixed another drink even though the juicer was still too warm from the drink before.

Jeremy Tarzan-yelled and I heard a massive whoosh of air. Looking for verification, I asked Yona, "A sharp pencil into the inflatable chair, you think?" She nodded. More Tarzan yells, primal growls. Loud slams and bonks on the walls sounded like Legos and Matchbox cars taking chunks of sheetrock as they flew. The crashes against the door must have been the full set of hardback books we'd bought for him. And the screaming! Ear-piercing on the high end and hoarse honking on the other. He sounded unhuman. But wails became whines and slowly, all sound faded.

"He's worn himself out," I asked.

Yona answered, "I'll give him a minute... don't want to re-start his motor. Eventually, he will fall asleep."

"True so far."

During the wait, I dared to start the noisy juicer again, mixing yet-another drink in the "Big Gulp" cup I favored. I sat on the sofa with a watchful Yona, wondering why Stuart hadn't returned. "He's been gone a long time... too long for just getting cigarettes, right?"

Yona always seemed to have a handle on time and glanced at her oversized watch. "Mr. Stuart left 26 minutes ago."

"Yep, that's too long."

She ignored me. Deciding the time for a Jeremy-check had come, Yona crept into the child's room. I heard her whisper, "Jeremy? Are you sleeping?" before she disappeared into the dark of the room. Then it hit me: *Why is the room dark? Did he turn off the lights? What the hell is... Oh, my God!*

As my heart rate spiked with worry, Yona scrambled across the living room floor, aiming for her shoes. Her coal-black face seemed to pale. "Oh, Mother Mary! Jeremy has crawled out of the window!"

Yona moved fast, out the front door within seconds. I heard her calling Jeremy's name, no sing-song melody now, but her voice faded into the night quickly; she was running.

My stomach fell to my knees, and I didn't move, still sipping the Big Gulp and contemplating just how bad the situation could be in the worst-case scenario.

I shivered thinking of bad omens and cried with a double-dose of Guilt. *Please... I can't handle this child! I'm too selfish! Too distracted! I'm just not up for the job. And where in the hell is my husband? I hope Jeremy shows up before Stuart does!*

Maybe I was too drunk, too overwhelmed, or too numb... I don't know why I didn't join the hunt. I sat on the sofa with a reeling mind.

As I contemplated, I cried. In fact, I cried about the full gamut of my life's circumstances... not just the possibilities of losing Stuart's child. I cried about my inadequacies in being Stuart's wife and Jeremy's stepmother, and sobbed about my dependence on Yona.

Shame for my curious addiction reared its head, pounding me with the pain of knowing I was, indeed, an awful wife and a more-than-horrible stepmother. *You're no better than Crazy Janey, just substituting vodka for whiskey. The only bright spot: Stuart is clean. But he'll soon drop you, Lela, if you keep staying drunk all day and night, and keep doing shit like letting his kid run away. You irresponsible shithead... grow up!*

Stuart had quoted his sponsor many times, eloquently phrasing the importance of peace of mind, self-love, and spiritual growth... but I had none of that. I still questioned why he didn't go to meetings but he assured me that "cured" addicts didn't go after the first few months. Who was I to know any better?

I still bitched about the money he owed me, though he'd paid an ever-increasing amount of the Visa balance every month. But by then, the balance was so high the payments barely covered the minimum and interest amount. Nevertheless, the balance was decreasing, even if only a notch.

But now you're working and your first paycheck can go 100 percent to Visa. Hmm... 100 percent.

I turned up my drink to avoid thinking about what I knew was coming next... but I couldn't stop my reeling thoughts. *Lela, 100 percent of anything is too much for you. You're just a half-ass person doing a half-ass job as wife, mother, boss, and employee. And you're supposed to be an example for that child! SHAME ON YOU! What a piss-poor excuse of a person you are! And you know why... you know what you have to do.*

I came alive, realizing that I *did* know what I had to do. *But how can I stop drinking NOW? I just started a job, just became a parent... I'm too frail to start such a journey.* A tear dropped from my jaw and more burned in my eyes.

Scared.

Scared shitless.

But why not scared SOBER?

Will anything ever do that for me? If Jeremy's really gone, would that do it? Can I straighten up for the kid? Can I straighten up and look at the shitty way Stuart treats me? I mean LOOK at it instead of running from it? Lela Fox, can you get sober and live that way?

I sobbed into my hands, listening to the side of my brain that still had hope, the side that still thought I could have a normal life without alcohol. These thoughts scared me, but if I strained, I could hear them. The problem: the hopeless side of my brain had a higher volume. *I don't know HOW to be sober! And how can I possibly LEARN when I can't even take care of myself? I mean... your best friend is your nanny, Lela, and even SHE disapproves of you and your drinking.*

As I sobbed, the front door opened with a flourish. Stuart sauntered in, looking happy and carefree, carrying two bottles of champagne. When he saw my tears and splotchy face, his voice brimmed with concern. "Baby! What's wrong, Lela? What can I do?"

"You sonofabitch! Don't pretend to be all sweet and concerned when you've avoided all the bullshit that's just happened!"

"What? What's going on?"

"We need to talk. About Jeremy. About me. And you. We have to talk about everything."

Stuart chuckled. "Everything? That's a lot of stuff!" I knew that line was a quote from *Black Beauty*, his favorite old movie, but I didn't react to the reference... didn't laugh or roll my eyes or tell him it was corny. I kept my eyes straight ahead. "Damn, girl! Why are you so serious?"

Then I heard a song in a sweet voice coming from the porch... yep, it was *Row, Row, Row Your Boat*. Holding Yona's hand, Jeremy flashed a toothy smile and glowed in a regular six-year-old mood, it seemed. They were still singing when they walked in the door.

Jeremy customized the last line, holding an imaginary microphone and "performing" for Stuart and me as we sat on the sofa. "Merrily, merrily, merrily, life is a dream about butts!"

I cracked up laughing. "Very creative, Jeremy! I like it!"

Yona wiped the sweat from her brow, showing her anger with squinty eyes. "Mizz Lela... Mister Stuart... this is my two-week notice."

Stuart reacted immediately, "Yona, no! What happened!?"

I spoke to Yona. "I haven't had a chance to tell him yet."

The lack of information didn't affect Stuart; he was frantic... looking at Yona with pleading, desperate eyes. "Anything for you to stay! What in the hell happened? I'll fix it, whatever it is, I'll fix it."

Jeremy screamed at both of them, demanding to know what they were talking about. We all three ignored him.

I'd never heard Yona raise her voice, but she was livid. "I need hazard pay! Add fifty percent more or I have to give up. It's too much for me!" She was close to tears, even as Jeremy patted her leg and begged her to smile.

Stuart didn't flinch; he agreed to the raise with no hesitation. After a few minutes to catch her breath, Yona said, "I'll put him to bed. But if this happens again, I'm gone. I can't do the stress." Again, Yona's melodic voice was flat, depressed, exhausted.

Stuart asked me, "So that's what you mean.... 'it's about everything?'"

"Yep," I answered, staring at a stray Lego block in the corner of the room, "because I think it's my two-week notice, too."

"Whaaat?" Stuart's face paled, his brow knotted in confusion.

I chuckled, seeing such a frantic reaction. "No, babe. Not that. I'm not resigning from my job, or from marriage or motherhood either." Tears burned behind my eyes, realizing my next line would be the first step on a long road that led to an unknown place.

"Then you're 'resigning' from what?"

The tears flowed again. "Baby, I'm scared." Even though I knew he was probably faking this concern, it felt good when he reached to pat my shoulder. "I think I have to give up the Grey Goose." A long sigh escaped as I sat back against the sofa cushions.

Stuart's brow slowly relaxed in understanding. "You're going to stop drinking?" A slow, soft laugh began in his sinuses... grew to a belly chuckle... then to a loud guffaw. "You?" More laughing. "*You? You can't* stop drinking!"

I seethed. *How dare he assume I can't... how DARE he laugh at me!* With a sneer, the words spewed like a water hose on full-blast. "I *can't* you say? Why *not*, Asswipe? Why do you doubt me... when you know that won't help at all!"

"You don't understand about stopping drinking, Lela, but I know a few th –"

"SHUT UP!" I shouted, and he closed his mouth with an audible smack.

"You're telling me to shut up?"

"You heard me right." For two heartbeats, then three, the room vibrated with silence. My voice turned low in volume and shaky with fear. A buzz of terror vibrated between my ears... my stomach turned to acid instantly and a citrus burp brought the taste of fear to my mouth, along with the smell of failure.

Tears like bullets seemed to eject from my eyes but I was afraid to sob, afraid to make a noise, afraid to move. *It's not time yet, Lela. You've got to think this through, get used to the idea before just going cold turkey. I've heard that can be dangerous, anyway.* Those thoughts and a few deep breaths began to settle my stomach and ease the pounding of my head. *Yeah, you just need to go slow. Yes, you know you have to quit, but cut down first, just limit what you drink. No more doubles, maybe no more grapefruits. And you need to start when you're sober, not in the middle of a good buzz.*

"Yeah, Stuart. See, when I say 'shut up,' I mean shut up and open that champagne. We have a something to celebrate, after all. And I bet it's not the bottom-shelf bubbly either."

"Only the best for my baby." He cocked his head in thought. "Hell, only the best for *me*. I'm the one who pulled this off!"

He passed me the bottle and one of the monogrammed flutes we'd received as a wedding gift. "Cheers! Here's to being parents!"

I raised my glass. "And here's to being *sober* parents!"

Stuart froze. "I know you said 'change everything,' but there's one thing that can't change so easily... for either of us."

"Don't doubt me, Stuart Weinstein."

Stuart raised an eyebrow and sighed. "Who knows? You may be one of the lucky ones."

"We'll see... starting first thing in the morning."

~:~:~:~:~:~

The next morning, I awoke early. Usually one to roll out of bed immediately, I realized it was supposed to be a day when I did NOT run outside to get a grapefruit and churn the juicer. *Not even a single little drinkie-poo? Not even one? For the rest of my life? That's crazy shit!* I tried to play through the day without drinking, and each scenario I envisioned scared the hell out of me.

Three minutes later, after I'd devised a plan, I got up. While the house was quiet, I'd juice the grapefruit by hand instead of making the noise, and somehow that would make the one little drink okay. *Make it weak, Lela. Then you'll be okay.*

SNEAK PEEK AT BOOK 5
INSANITY: FAKE IT 'TIL YOU MAKE IT

Chapter 1: THE END BEGINS

I remember stealing the ashtray from the bar... an oversized, white ceramic one with purposely random splashes of bright-colored glazes. We'd been to a classic-rock bar on Highway A-1-A, arriving home about two AM. We were both drunk, and laughed at the vibrating hum of the air conditioner as it cooled the early June heat.

Happily obliterated, I sat on the sofa looking at the birthday card from my husband of five months. "Happy Number Forty," it said. He signed it: "Have a good one, old bitty." *What an ass.*

I smoked a cigarette and sang *Fly Like an Eagle* by the Steve Miller Band in my typical key of flat. Yona, our live-in Jamaican nanny, came out of her small bedroom to shush me. I supposed she thought I'd wake my stepson Jeremy, six years old and a light sleeper... and a trouble-maker.

Just to piss Yona off, I quit singing but hummed the same song as loud as I could, louder than the singing had been. She stood with her hand on her right hip and bounced. I thought it was hilarious and threw my head back for a long Tennessee laugh. Yona rolled her eyes within the sea of her coal-black face. We had become friends, or so I thought... but she kept her disapproval of me front and center.

I stood to dance on the tile floor of the rental house, still humming. Barefoot,

I wore a flower-print mini dress and no underwear. My golden-brown curls bounced to the beat in my head.

Stuart Weinstein, my husband number three, walked out of the bathroom zipping his fly. His beer belly was more prominent than usual in the profile view that night, it seemed, and his hair grayer in the shadowy light. In his curt New York accent, he said something smartass about how my "fat thighs" jiggled as I danced, and I yelled, "Shut the hell up." He yelled something back as he passed the French door to the patio.

The next thing I knew, the stolen ashtray was in the air, sailing toward Stuart's head. He ducked, and the ashtray crashed through the patio door.

The rest is a blackout.

<<<<<<<>>>>>>

Suddenly, though it must have been at least an hour later, I was in my driveway feeling overwrought and jittery. A pudgy hand held a Polaroid showing Stuart's scratched and bleeding face, pushing it toward me accusingly. With a smartass chuckle, the cop said, "I hear what you're saying, Ms. Fox, but *he* said you did it, and it sure *looks* like you did it, so the call is... you did it." Then he snapped handcuffs on my wrists. Tight.

On the way east, I wondered how the Palm Beach County jail would differ from the others I'd seen. Maybe the floor would be sandy? The inmates would be more ethnically diverse, with less East Tennessee rednecks, I knew. Those thoughts came before the big questions:

What have I done? And how am I going to get out of this?

The charge was domestic assault. After the fingerprints and mugshot downstairs, they threw me in the drunk tank. The cage brimmed with Haitian women, speaking their melodic language, laughing at nothing funny I could see. I sat with my head in my hands, miserable on the cold concrete bench, speaking to no one.

So who can I call? Who? I tried to ignore utter defeat, but I knew there was nobody to call; I had no friends except Yona. My work friends were just that: nine-to-five friends and I didn't like them worth a shit, anyway. Though I was groggy and still drunk, I was sober enough to know I was in big trouble.

An overweight female officer with a shock of frizzy black hair called my name. On our way to a cell downstairs, passing through four clanging cages of bars, her acrid body odor drilled my nostrils and my pride, adding to my apprehension. Facing the reality of what would come, I shivered.

The BANG of the cell door echoed in my head. I was in deep shit.

Hours passed with no communication from the female deputies who roamed the halls. Finally, when I asked for my phone call, I learned the bad news: there would be no easy-out tonight. Quick bail was for DUI arrests and minor things, not for domestic abusers like me, she said. Later in the morning, I'd see the judge, and he'd set my bail. He'd also determine if the charge would be a felony or misdemeanor; it could go both ways, she said.

Perhaps the worst news was that Stuart had filed for a restraining order and I wouldn't be released until they could verify a new home address. I couldn't go home, not even to get a pair of panties.

I racked my brain thinking of somebody who would post my bail, but my efforts were moot. There was no one to call. For the past six months, I had isolated myself with the high-tech fruit juicer and backyard grapefruit tree as my only friends. Oh, and of course the vodka, which was my main friend. The thought came: "my main squeeze" and I chuckled. *Who says a washed-up writer can't still make a good pun?*

The echo as we walked down the block of cells deafened me, the smell of urine and vomit grew as we walked further. Then the officer grunted and pushed me to the left, into the smallest cell I'd seen in my twenty-seven-year drinking career. Like any cell, it had an eerie sense of coldness and the austerity of sharp angles, but this one proudly emitted the distinctive smell of solid human waste.

The flip-flops they provided caught on the wide crack in the concrete floor, a diagonal crack that divided the tiny space into triangles. *Two Isosceles triangles*, I thought. Years beyond college, I still remembered a bit of the geometry. *See, Ms. Deputy... I'm too smart to be here.*

As the guard removed my cuffs, I saw the bare and dark-stained mattresses on the bunk beds. No blankets, no pillows. In the corner, the toilet leaned questionably to the left.

No cellmate. I sat on the bottom bunk and put my head in my hands. *That sonofabitch has thrown me under the bus on purpose! How can he treat me like this? His very own wife! Wouldn't love stop him from this kind of... cruelty? Yeah, that's what it is – cruelty!*

I peed, and not wanting to wake the dozens of sleeping women in the cell block, I didn't flush. A hoarse voice in the next cell shouted, "Flush your stinky pee!" I mumbled an apology and flushed, but the toilet gurgled a few seconds and stopped. *Great. A stopped-up toilet in a jail cell.* With a half-chuckle, half-belch, I blew a laugh at the irony of it all. *What the hell, Lela, you crazy drunk! You've really screwed yourself this time.* After a few sobs, which only hurt my head, I decided to sleep it off and try to avoid the biggest, grossest stains on the mattress. *Maybe you'll think of something in the morning.*

I woke with my contacts stuck to my eyeballs, as expected, and my head pounding, which surprised me. I wasn't usually one to have hangovers; Lela Fox was too adept at drinking for such kindergarten things. I closed my eyes after the lights came on and willed the headache away. It returned with the faceless delivery of a cold-egg, raw-bacon breakfast. With a sigh, I ate the toast and the bruised apple.

The germ of an idea formed in my mind.

Mid-morning, they led a chain of us to the courtroom, shackled together at the ankles and waist. *A damn chain-gang, as if I'm a common criminal!* The bailiff called my name first, and I stood, rattling the chains. The charges were now official: misdemeanor domestic assault. Bail was $5,000. In 1999, that was a lot of money.

Though I was antsy to set my new plan in motion, I had to wait for the other inmates' hearings before I could leave the courtroom. About an hour passed, and I needed to pee, bad. After the last in our group heard the judge's bullshit, the guards led us out in the same chain-gang. Complete humiliation, I thought, being treated like a criminal when I was innocent.

As I passed the District Attorney, I caught his eye and tried to garner a smile, but he looked straight through me. I wanted him to know I was somebody special within this chain-gang, somebody with sense, but his look of disdain burst my bubble of hope. This time, I realized, I was just a number in the system and my number was low, near the bottom. My stomach fell but I accepted the truth, swallowing hard. *Yep, you're in big trouble, bigger than ever before.*

My toilet was still stopped up, and I complained to the deputy who deposited us back in the cells. She said she'd "get right on it." *Yeah, right.* About an hour later, she took me upstairs to make my phone call. I asked if I could make two calls because I needed to call my boss, too. The fat jailer said no, as I expected, but it was worth a shot to ask.

He slid the phone book across the counter and my shaking hands found the number for the liquor store in Wellington, Florida, the one around the corner from our house in the upscale suburb of West Palm. Friendly Wine and Liquors, where they sold lottery tickets, too.

"Frank! It's Lela, your favorite customer."

"Hey, Lela! What can I do for you, hon?"

"Uh, Frank, I'm in trouble. Can I use your address as my home address so I can get out of jail? And I'll pay you back two-fold if you bail me out."

"What? Wait! Slow down! You're in *jail?*"

"Stuart said I beat him up and took out a restraining order on me. I can't go home and I can't leave jail until I give them an address where I'll supposedly be living."

There was a gasp from the other end of the phone. "Wait, no! I'm not asking to stay with you. I can stay at a hotel until I find a place. It's just... I need you to bail me out and give your address. Can you? Will you? Please?"

"Let me get this straight. You got arrested for beating Stuart up?"

"Right."

"But he was in here this morning and he didn't *look* beaten up! Bought his regular bottle of Crown and about a hundred scratch-off tickets. Honestly, I think he has a problem with the scratch-offs."

Not caring what the fidgety sonofabitch Stuart bought, I made sure I heard Frank right about the other. "No scratches on his face? No blood in his beard?"

"Nope."

"Just the same ol' donkey face?"

Frank spoke through his chuckle. "That's right."

"Dammit! I *knew* he set me up! The cops showed me pictures and stuff but I don't remember a thing except those accusing steel-gray eyes. He probably scratched himself!"

"Lela, I don't want to get in the middle of something like th–"

"No! It's not like that! There's no 'something' to get in the middle of!"

"But–"

"Just a favor, and we can go straight to the ATM, Frank. I'll pay you back, twice the amount. No shit."

"How much is your bail?"

"Five hundred. Any bondsman will work. Have you done this before?"

"No, and I'm not really interested in doing it now."

"Frank! Hey! It's *me!* Your favorite customer! Do you think I'm the kind of person who would jump bail?"

"Uh... Lela..." It was a scolding voice, and I panicked. I interrupted the objection before it came. "Frank, paying bail is easy. Just look in the phone book, the yellow pages, under bail bondsmen. They'll be dozens listed there. A simple phone call, a dude will meet you at the jail, you sign some bullshit papers and it's done. Then I'll need a ride to my van. Piece of cake. Surely I've given you enough business to pay for this favor. Come on!"

"Lela, damn..."

"Please, Frank. I'm desperate. This is my one phone call. I have nobody else."

"That's why Lela... I mean, your only friend is the liquor store owner?"

With a chuckle, I said, "Pretty funny, huh?" My eyebrows pushed together as it hit me. No, this was not funny at all. With more humility, I begged, "Frank, please. I'm in a tough spot. And I'll pay you back immediately! You can *count* on that! We'll go straight to the ATM!"

The officer glared at me and cleared his throat. His double chin creased as he nodded. "That's enough time, ma'am," he spat.

"Look, Frank, I gotta go but I'm depending on you, begging you. I'll write a good review for the Better Business Bureau about the store, write a good article for the *Wellington Shopper*, maybe produce a radio spot. Anything!"

Still twitching, I stopped, knowing there was nothing more to say. The pause was unnervingly long. Frank sighed. "Okay, Lela, dammit. I shouldn't, but I will. But I don't want to hear another word about it. Nothing! I don't want to be in the middle."

"Frankie-baby, you are a good friend."

"Well, I try. But this is really cra–"

"Thank you, man. I'll make it up to you somehow. Oh! Wait! One more thing..."

"What?" He sounded irritated now.

I squinted one eye and gritted my teeth, knowing I was pushing my luck.

"Can you call Stuart and ask him to put my purse in the van?" I said it fast, hoping to diminish it.

"Jeezus, Lela! This is beyond the scope of my–"

"But you won't have to talk to him, just leave a message." A *hmmph* exploded from Frank's end. "Please! I only get one phone call!"

"Okay, dammit! What's the number?" Thankfully, I had committed Stuart's work number to memory, even the foggy memory of the day after.

The officer took me back to the cell to wait for bail. *Would he come? Is my only shot at freedom going to come through?* Then I said aloud, "Frank, my dear Frank, please help me. And hurry!"

An hour later, a lunch tray slid through the bars. A bologna sandwich, I guessed. Just white bread and a warm chunk of fat-speckled meat of an unknown variety. The other tray compartments held warm applesauce, another bruised apple, and a warm pint of milk.

Another sigh as I ate the apple, which was as dry as a desert. As I gnawed on the core, a skinny black girl arrived in cuffs. My cellmate, nervous as a whore in church, or hopped up on something, maybe.

When the deputy removed the cuffs, she said, "Don't mess with me" and held a menacing glare. Then she curled her hands into fists and braced her feet as if ready to throw a punch. She repeated, "Don't mess with me, Curly Bitch."

I rolled over to face the wall, seeing a roadmap in the rubberized paint, a map I hoped Frank would soon follow. Would he show up with bail money?

Chapter 2: I NEED A NOTEPAD

My debit card was dead. According to the ATM, the account was "not found." With my head down and my lips quivering, I returned to Frank's car and slammed the door. Too numb to speak, I tasted bile. Frank had been a real champ throughout the drama of leaving the jail, and now he looked at me with grave concern. "What is it, Lela?" he whispered.

"The account is closed, Frank. Stuart stopped by the bank early, I guess. Damn, man, I'm so sorry. There's no way I can pay you back." A rack of sobs hiccupped against my ribs.

Silence.

303

Five seconds later, Frank banged his hand on the car wheel. "Dammit!" Then he mumbled to himself, saying versions of "I knew I shouldn't have done this! What a dumbass." Blah, blah, blah. I felt like a real ass, ashamed. *Some friend I am, huh?*

A thought struck. "Actually, Frank, Stuart will pay you back if you ask. He's only trying to screw *me*, not you. He wouldn't want you to be out the money. Underneath, he's a nice guy." Frank's answer was a sarcastic laugh, but I believed what I said. Despite all the red flags I had ignored over the past two years, I believed in Stuart, swooned for him with blind love and a desperate yearning for his approval. "Seriously, Frank. Ask him and he'll pay you."

"That's a bunch of bullshit, Lela. He tried to rip me off just this morning at the store. Like a sleight of hand thing, asking for change and scratch-offs at the same time. I still can't figure out if I got it right. He's a snake."

Again, I wondered why everybody was against Stuart; all my friends and family had warned me about something evil that just wasn't there. *So Frank is one of the non-believers... experience proves there's no way to change his mind.* So took an all-business stance. "Then, fuck it. Just take a left out of the parking lot... to Ashley Acres." The ride was silent, and I blew a sigh of relief when I saw my van in the driveway and Stuart's Lexus nowhere in sight. When I opened the van door, there it was... my purse on the driver's seat. *Thank you, Stuart! See, you're not a total asshole!*

I bid Frank a goodbye and used my key to open the front door. Yona stood in the living room holding a broom, eyes wide. "Mizz Lela! No! You're not supposed to be here!" Her normal sing-song voice had no song at all. "I'm supposed to call the po–"

"No! Don't call! Yona, I just need some things. I have no clothes, no underwear!" Though I knew I wouldn't be able to pay her back, I asked for money anyway. "Hey, Yona, sweetie, do you have any money I can borrow?" *This is bad, Lela, but you're too desperate to let morals interfere. And maybe Stuart will give her money or something.*

"Borrow money?"

"Yeah, girl! We can meet up for a payback, easy. I wanted to call you from jail but I don't know your number without my cell ph... Yona?" When I realized she wasn't listening, I stopped talking. Her eyes were far away, her hands gripping the broom handle like it might fly away. "Never mind. I'll be out of here in a flash. No worries."

Stuart's hiding place was stupid. I found five hundred-dollar-bills in his underwear drawer. Obviously, he had forgotten or he would have hidden them from me. I spent a max of three minutes collecting random clothes and shoes and stuffing them into a tote bag from the closet. *Hurry, hurry! You'll be in deep shit if Yona calls the cops.*

On the way out of the Master suite, I met Yona walking out of the kitchen. *The kitchen... where the phone is.* With a gasp, I asked, "Yona, did you call somebody?" She froze in place, her mouth open with no words coming out, just two feeble squeaks.

She snapped into motion, exaggerating her movements. "No, Mizz Lela. I'm just sweeping. See?" Still holding the broom, she brushed the tips of the straw against the floor, back and forth quickly while standing in one place, not at all like a normal person would sweep.

"Damn you, Yona!" I screamed over my shoulder, heading for the door. *I gotta get out of Wellington and fast!*

Two quick blocks later, I pulled into the small lot at Friendly Wine and Liquors and gave two of the bills to Frank. Deep in my purse, I found another treasure, a stack of winning scratch-off lottery tickets. Small potatoes, but the winnings totaled 32 bucks. I grabbed a bottle of Grey Goose and a bottle of tonic, cashed in the tickets, and took my change.

In the heat of the afternoon, I dashed toward the coast, toward last night's bar location. If I remembered right, there was a throwback motel just north of it, the Blue-something, something odd. I held up traffic as I looked for the motel on A-1-A, finally spotting it and turning left. The Blue Flamingo. "Well, that's stupid!" I said out loud. "I think they're mixed up with pelicans."

My room was on the far end of the last building, the size of a postage stamp and filled with a musty smell, the pungent odor of earth mixed with gasoline. I went in search of an ice machine and found none. *Oh, well. God knows I've had hot vodka before.* It was my first drink of the day and my hands shook as I filled the provided plastic-wrapped cup. The breeze blew through the open door and dried my sweaty brow.

Fear brought the need to get shit-faced, but I fought it. *Nope, don't go there, Lela. Be strong. Think, think, think. You need a plan. What are you going to do?* I stood outside the door on a crumbling sidewalk, then walked barefoot to the pool area. Oily globs and a green cast in the shallow end meant no swimming for me. With a sigh, I plopped down on a lounge chair and stared into space for a while, listening to the traffic noise.

Thinking of all the things I'd left behind... *uh, oh!* My medicine. Officially diagnosed Bi-Polar as Hell by multiple psychiatrists over the years, it was critical that I stay on the medicine, the five different prescriptions I took daily. Without my meds, I may drop into the depths of depression... or launch into a flying, manic voyage through the stratosphere. "Just hold it in the road, Lela," I said out loud. "Try to stay calm and don't drink too much."

A few minutes before five o'clock, I called my boss at Smyth Software, Dale the Nerd. The Dale who hated me... the Dale who had my number, the Dale who knew how fucked up I was and how much I was failing at work. But that day, he acted like a friend. "Lela! Where have you been? Are you okay?"

"Dale, uh... I have a few personal things going on. Trust me, you don't want to know. I'm sorry I didn't come in, but I wasn't in a place where I could call. But I'll be there bright-eyed in the morning, okay?"

He mumbled a few unintelligible words, and then said clearly, "You know this gets reported to HR, right? No show, no call. And strike one of three."

"Yes, I'm aware of that rule. I'm calling Kathy next. That's her name, right? The head of Human Resources?"

"Remember she's a friend of mine so don't be jerking her around."

"I'm not jerking anybody around, Dale. Mostly, I'm just sorry, truly sorry. But it couldn't be helped." Dale remained silent, so I kept babbling nervously. "And it won't happen again. You can trust me on that."

"*Trust* you?" Dale blew a sarcastic laugh. "Lela, don't be ridiculous." I felt the tension through the line.

All I could do was ignore his scolding and assure him again. "Bright and early tomorrow morning, Dale. I'll be there."

"Here's the deal... there was a program update today. You have a stack of projects, much to do, much to write."

"No problem. I'll handle it. As you know, you can always count on me."

"Sometimes I wonder. No, *oftentimes* I wonder."

I faked a laugh. "Good one, Dale! See you tomorrow."

With no intention of calling HR to report my absence, I poured another vodka-tonic, this time disgusted by the lack of ice. In a hurry, I left the drink on the pitted dresser and maneuvered through rush-hour traffic to get a bag of ice, a Styrofoam cooler, another bottle of tonic, a pack of cigs, and an insulated "Big Gulp" cup. As I paid the man, I realized my 300 bucks wouldn't last long.

Back to my cheap-as-hell room, I looked at the pathetic details as tears flowed, I lay back on the stained bedspread and screamed out loud. "This isn't real! This is not happening!"

After a few minutes of tears, I jumped from the bed. Determined to keep active and not fall into the dreariness of feeling sorry for myself, I washed the new insulated cup and fixed a proper drink. Then I drove to the public beach diagonally across from the motel. I took my purse to wade in the water, putting my sandals inside the bag. A long walk should've cleared my mind, but I felt wound tight. Tight as a banjo string, my Daddy would say.

I waded in the ankle-deep surf, thinking about my plight and trying to find the kernel of a plan. *So much to think about! I need a notepad to organize my thoughts!* With a sigh, I realized I'd have to buy a lot of things tonight, including a notepad. All the things easy to grab at home... the home I used to have, anyway. Thoughts bounced in my head like a ping-pong ball. More money to spend until I could gather these needed things at home.

I'd have to take a policeman to "supervise" when I went to the house for my things, they said. I guessed I'd just swing by the tiny Wellington station and get a Barney Fife. My head rattled with details of things I needed and where I'd keep them. Thoughts spun so fast I couldn't catch them.

The pain came when I thought about the man I considered my soulmate. *How can you do this to me, baby? I swear I didn't hurt you or do that to your face! Sweetie, I was just drunk, not dangerous! We were having fun, a nice birthday celebration, now this. What the hell?*

The more I thought about it, anger replaced the hurt. Still spinning in my head, I shook with fury. *You set me up, scratched your own face, you sonofabitch! You like calling the police on people – like you did to your poor ex-wife. So now, you've decided to screw me, too. Throw me under the bus. How could you? Don't do it! Please help me! I need you!*

I sat in the sand and cried. Sobbed. I wondered how it had come to this, what made him be so mean. I tried to keep the "sane side" of my brain at bay, but as I combed further into the past, I realized I should have seen it coming.

Even before we first moved to Florida last year, in 1998, Stuart drank too much, got mean when he was drunk. And getting custody of Jeremy was the last straw. How could a couple of drunks take care of a six-year-old, anyway?

Then came the "delusional side" of my brain, where I believed the problem was Stuart. I guessed maybe I drank a little too much, too. Sometimes. But that wasn't the point. At least I wasn't a former crack addict. At least I didn't like to hang out with prostitutes and those from the underworld, the lowest echelon of society. My mother had taught me manners; I had that, and people told me I was fun to be with most of the time. Lela Fox was doing just fine, I thought. *But now I'm screwed. How did it come to this?*

Convinced everything was 99 percent Stuart's fault, I walked back to the van. Along the shore, I had come to several conclusions. First, I was screwed. Second, I had to find a place to live. Third, I couldn't afford a place to live. That made me double-screwed. Mom couldn't get me out of this one like she had "fixed" things for me many times before. I was desperate.

From the beach, I drove back to the 7-Eleven for an *Apartment Guide*, and two other rags with "for rent" listings. The A/C had cooled the hotel room nicely. I mixed a drink and made calls to potential landlords, scribbling a budget in the margins while on hold.

It didn't take long to realize there was no way I could afford a proper apartment on my own paycheck. Dejected, I called a few places with rooms for rent and made a note of the address, planning an expedition to see the bad side of town where I'd be living.

Oh, shit! What am I thinking? He's closed the savings account, too! It doesn't matter that all the money started out as yours, Lela! You have no money for a security deposit. Mom warned you about making those accounts joint, you shithead! Why didn't you listen to her?

I mixed another drink and made it strong, then tried to find something to watch on the tiny TV. Within the half-hour, I poured another drink, knowing I was drinking too much but unable to stop. Another drink put me over the edge... sloppy, overwhelmed, tripping over my thoughts. I'd soon be bold enough to make the move that would clear my name and fix my financial situation.

It's a bit illegal... big-time risky, but I'm smart enough to get away with it.

END OF SAMPLE

MORE ABOUT ME

After my on-and-off career as an advertising writer, and twelve years as a certified picture framer, I retired and began writing for publication. My tidbits landed in AA's *Grapevine* magazine and several online journals, then a story about my dog was featured in *Chicken Soup for the Soul*.

An author-friend challenged me to write and publish a full book, with just one rule: "Write what you know." So I spent the next two years writing my life story, which became seven top-selling books.

I am beyond surprised by how many readers love the series. Gratitude to the max on that one, and thanks to you, too.

The best part is getting emails from readers who say my books have actually helped them in their quest for sobriety and self-confidence. What a joy those letters are! Helping others was the whole point, and it seems I *have* inspired readers let go of the past and stay open-minded for the future.

Hot-diggety-dog! And thank you, *thank you* for letting me share.

With the series complete, I'm now writing fiction under my pen name Patty Ayers. Look for my duo of mystery novels in the fall of 2020, titled *Box 13*. Updates to come. For now, sign up for the *Edge of My Seat* newsletter at lelafox.com.

I live in East Tennessee with a panoramic view of the Great Smoky Mountains from my window, and a sense of serenity in every corner of my little condo home. If I'm not writing, you'll find me tinkering in the workshop or playing tug-of-war with my distinguished editor, Stormin' Norman the Schnauzer.

Combining creativity with OCD, I also have a sideline called KID'S ART IN STITCHES where I embroider children's drawings in bright, bright colors. Suitable for framing, which I usually handle as a bonus service.

By the grace of God, I've been sober all day long.

OTHER BOOKS

Find out what happens!

See all books on my Amazon Author Page:

amazon.com/author/lelafox

Join my *Recovery Rollercoaster* for inside info
discounts, promos, and free recovery inspiration
Fun and inspiration at lelafox.com

Did you like the book? Tell me about it!
It's anonymous, helps others, and takes just a minute.
Go to the Amazon listing, scroll to the bottom,
and click the gray "Write a Review" button

Made in the USA
Coppell, TX
15 May 2020